Houghton
Mifflin
Harcourt

SCIENCE
FUSiON

fusion [FYOO • zhuhn] a combination of two
or more things that releases energy

This **Interactive Student Edition** belongs to

_____

Teacher/Room

_____

Consulting Authors

Michael A. DiSpezio

Global Educator
North Falmouth, Massachusetts

Michael DiSpezio is a renaissance educator who moved from the research laboratory of a Nobel Prize winner to the K–12 science classroom. He has authored or co-authored numerous textbooks and written more than 25 trade books. For nearly a decade he worked with the JASON Project, under the auspices of the National Geographic Society, where he designed curriculum, wrote lessons, and hosted dozens of studio and location broadcasts. Over the past two decades, he has developed supplementary material for organizations and shows that include PBS *Scientific American Frontiers, Discover* magazine, and the Discovery Channel. He has extended his reach outside the United States and into topics of crucial importance today. To all his projects, he brings his extensive background in science and his expertise in classroom teaching at the elementary, middle, and high school levels.

Marjorie Frank

*Science Writer and
Content-Area Reading Specialist*
Brooklyn, New York

An educator and linguist by training, a writer and poet by nature, Marjorie Frank has authored and designed a generation of instructional materials in all subject areas, including past HMH Science programs. Her other credits include authoring science issues of an award-winning children's magazine; writing game-based digital assessments in math, reading, and language arts; and serving as instructional designer and co-author of pioneering school-to-work software for Classroom Inc., a nonprofit organization dedicated to improving reading and math skills for middle and high school learners. She wrote lyrics and music for *SCIENCE SONGS,* which was an American Library Association nominee for notable recording. In addition, she has served on the adjunct faculty of Hunter, Manhattan, and Brooklyn Colleges, teaching courses in science methods, literacy, and writing.

Acknowledgments for Covers

Front cover: *W. M. Keck Observatory* (bg) © Alison Wright/Robert Harding World Imagery/Corbis

Printed in the U.S.A.

ISBN 978-0-544-77848-1

8 9 10 0928 24 23 22 21

4500821142   C D E F G

Michael R. Heithaus

Dean, College of Arts, Sciences & Education
Florida International University
North Miami, Florida

Mike Heithaus joined the Florida International University Biology Department in 2003. He is a professor in the Department of Biological Sciences and has served as Director of the Marine Sciences Program and Executive Director of the School of Environment and Society. His research focuses on predator-prey interactions and the ecological roles of large marine species including sharks, sea turtles, and marine mammals. His long-term studies include the Shark Bay Ecosystem Project in Western Australia. He also served as a Research Fellow with National Geographic, using remote imaging in his research and hosting a *Crittercam* television series on the National Geographic Channel.

Donna M. Ogle

Professor of Reading and Language
National-Louis University
Chicago, Illinois

Creator of the well-known KWL strategy, Donna Ogle has directed many staff development projects translating theory and research into school practice in middle and secondary schools throughout the United States. She is a past president of the International Reading Association and has served as a consultant on literacy projects worldwide. Her extensive international experience includes coordinating the Reading and Writing for Critical Thinking Project in Eastern Europe, developing an integrated curriculum for a USAID Afghan Education Project, and speaking and consulting on projects in several Latin American countries and in Asia. Her books include *Coming Together as Readers; Reading Comprehension: Strategies for Independent Learners; All Children Read;* and *Literacy for a Democratic Society.*

Program Reviewers

Content Reviewers

Paul D. Asimow, PhD
Professor of Geology and Geochemistry
Division of Geological and Planetary Sciences
California Institute of Technology
Pasadena, CA

Laura K. Baumgartner, PhD
Postdoctoral Researcher
Molecular, Cellular, and Developmental Biology
University of Colorado
Boulder, CO

Eileen Cashman, PhD
Professor
Department of Environmental Resources Engineering
Humboldt State University
Arcata, CA

Hilary Clement Olson, PhD
Research Scientist Associate V
Institute for Geophysics, Jackson School of Geosciences
The University of Texas at Austin
Austin, TX

Joe W. Crim, PhD
Professor Emeritus
Department of Cellular Biology
The University of Georgia
Athens, GA

Elizabeth A. De Stasio, PhD
Raymond H. Herzog Professor of Science
Professor of Biology
Department of Biology
Lawrence University
Appleton, WI

Dan Franck, PhD
Botany Education Consultant
Chatham, NY

Julia R. Greer, PhD
Assistant Professor of Materials Science and Mechanics
Division of Engineering and Applied Science
California Institute of Technology
Pasadena, CA

John E. Hoover, PhD
Professor
Department of Biology
Millersville University
Millersville, PA

William H. Ingham, PhD
Professor (Emeritus)
Department of Physics and Astronomy
James Madison University
Harrisonburg, VA

Charles W. Johnson, PhD
Chairman, Division of Natural Sciences, Mathematics, and Physical Education
Associate Professor of Physics
South Georgia College
Douglas, GA

Program Reviewers *(continued)*

Tatiana A. Krivosheev, PhD
Associate Professor of Physics
Department of Natural Sciences
Clayton State University
Morrow, GA

Joseph A. McClure, PhD
Associate Professor Emeritus
Department of Physics
Georgetown University
Washington, DC

Mark Moldwin, PhD
Professor of Space Sciences
Atmospheric, Oceanic, and
Space Sciences
University of Michigan
Ann Arbor, MI

Russell Patrick, PhD
Professor of Physics
Department of Biology,
Chemistry, and Physics
Southern Polytechnic State
University
Marietta, GA

Patricia M. Pauley, PhD
*Meteorologist, Data Assimilation
Group*
Naval Research Laboratory
Monterey, CA

Stephen F. Pavkovic, PhD
Professor Emeritus
Department of Chemistry
Loyola University of Chicago
Chicago, IL

L. Jeanne Perry, PhD
Director (Retired)
Protein Expression Technology
Center
Institute for Genomics and
Proteomics
University of California, Los
Angeles
Los Angeles, CA

Kenneth H. Rubin, PhD
Professor
Department of Geology and
Geophysics
University of Hawaii
Honolulu, HI

Brandon E. Schwab, PhD
Associate Professor
Department of Geology
Humboldt State University
Arcata, CA

Marllin L. Simon, Ph.D.
Associate Professor
Department of Physics
Auburn University
Auburn, AL

Larry Stookey, PE
Upper Iowa University
Wausau, WI

Kim Withers, PhD
Associate Research Scientist
Center for Coastal Studies
Texas A&M University-Corpus
Christi
Corpus Christi, TX

Matthew A. Wood, PhD
Professor
Department of Physics & Space
Sciences
Florida Institute of Technology
Melbourne, FL

Adam D. Woods, PhD
Associate Professor
Department of Geological
Sciences
California State University,
Fullerton
Fullerton, CA

Natalie Zayas, MS, EdD
Lecturer
Division of Science and
Environmental Policy
California State University,
Monterey Bay
Seaside, CA

Teacher Reviewers

Ann Barrette, MST
Whitman Middle School
Wauwatosa, WI

Barbara Brege
Crestwood Middle School
Kentwood, MI

**Katherine Eaton Campbell,
M Ed**
Chicago Public Schools-Area 2
Office
Chicago, IL

**Karen Cavalluzzi, M Ed,
NBCT**
Sunny Vale Middle School
Blue Springs, MO

Katie Demorest, MA Ed Tech
Marshall Middle School
Marshall, MI

Jennifer Eddy, M Ed
Lindale Middle School
Linthicum, MD

Tully Fenner
George Fox Middle School
Pasadena, MD

Dave Grabski, MS Ed
PJ Jacobs Junior High School
Stevens Point, WI

Amelia C. Holm, M Ed
McKinley Middle School
Kenosha, WI

Ben Hondorp
Creekside Middle School
Zeeland, MI

George E. Hunkele, M Ed
Harborside Middle School
Milford, CT

Jude Kesl
Science Teaching Specialist 6–8
Milwaukee Public Schools
Milwaukee, WI

Joe Kubasta, M Ed
Rockwood Valley Middle School
St. Louis, MO

Mary Larsen
Science Instructional Coach
Helena Public Schools
Helena, MT

Angie Larson
Bernard Campbell Middle School
Lee's Summit, MO

Christy Leier
Horizon Middle School
Moorhead, MN

Helen Mihm, NBCT
Crofton Middle School
Crofton, MD

Jeff Moravec, Sr., MS Ed
Teaching Specialist
Milwaukee Public Schools
Milwaukee, WI

**Nancy Kawecki Nega, MST,
NBCT, PAESMT**
Churchville Middle School
Elmhurst, IL

Mark E. Poggensee, MS Ed
Elkhorn Middle School
Elkhorn, WI

Sherry Rich
Bernard Campbell Middle School
Lee's Summit, MO

Mike Szydlowski, M Ed
Science Coordinator
Columbia Public Schools
Columbia, MO

Nichole Trzasko, M Ed
Clarkston Junior High School
Clarkston, MI

Heather Wares, M Ed
Traverse City West Middle School
Traverse City, MI

Contents in Brief

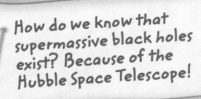

How do we know that supermassive black holes exist? Because of the Hubble Space Telescope!

In space, meteorites are a hazard for both astronauts and equipment.

Contents

Stars and solar systems are born out of clouds of gas and dust, like the one seen here.

Assignments:

_____

_____

_____

_____

_____

Earth orbits the sun in the "Goldilocks Zone," where it's not too hot and not too cold. It's just right for liquid water and life!

Contents *(continued)*

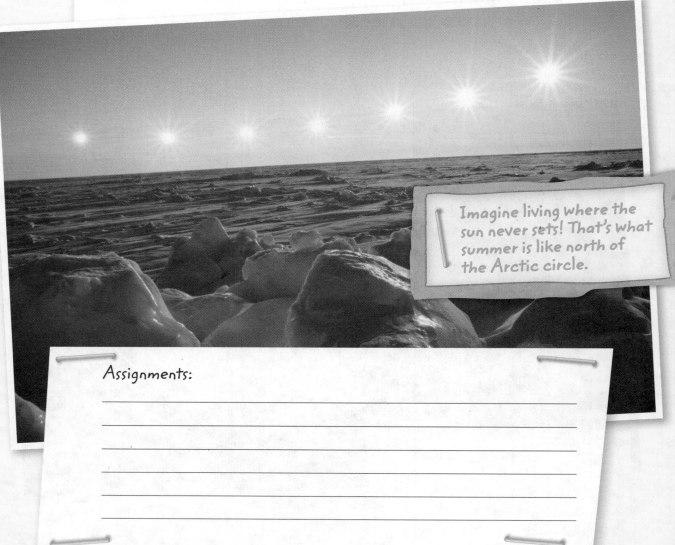

Imagine living where the sun never sets! That's what summer is like north of the Arctic circle.

Assignments:

_____

_____

_____

_____

_____

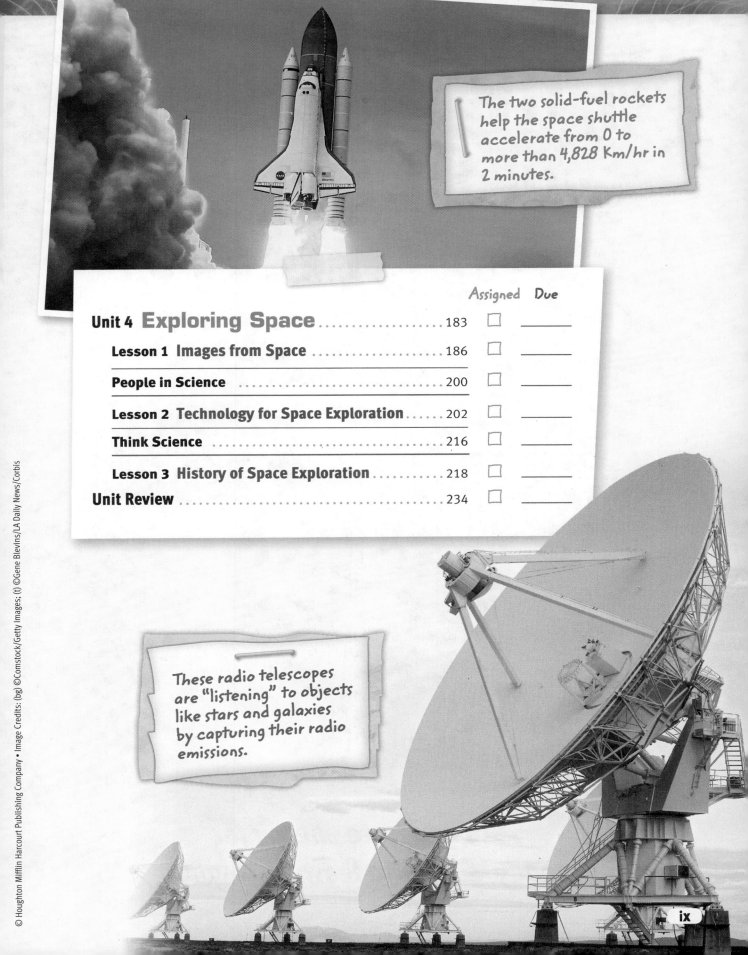

The two solid-fuel rockets help the space shuttle accelerate from 0 to more than 4,828 Km/hr in 2 minutes.

These radio telescopes are "listening" to objects like stars and galaxies by capturing their radio emissions.

Power up with Science Fusion!

Your program fuses...

e-Learning and Virtual Labs

Labs and Activities

Write-In Student Edition

... to generate energy for today's science learner — you.

Write-In Student Edition

Be an active reader and make this book your own!

You can answer questions, ask questions, create graphs, make notes, write your own ideas, and highlight information right in your book.

Learn science concepts and skills by interacting with every page.

Labs and Activities

ScienceFusion includes lots of exciting hands-on inquiry labs and activities, each one designed to bring science skills and concepts to life and get you involved.

QUICK LAB

...cting DNA

...you will use common household items to release, unravel, and ...ands of DNA. You will be extracting DNA from raw wheat ...ch is part of the seed of a wheat plant.

OBJECTIVES
- Extract and observe strands of DNA.
- Describe the function and location of DNA in living organisms.

MATERIALS
For each...
- balance
- beaker...
- dishw...
- deterg...
- gradu...
- cylind...

FIELD LAB

Investigating Parallax

In this lab, you will practice measuring the distances of faraway obj... on Earth.

ASK A QUESTION
1. In this lab, you will answer the following question: How can y... measure the distance to a star?

FORM A HYPOTHESIS
2. Write a hypothesis that might answer this question. Explain you... reasoning.

TEST THE HYPOTHESIS
3. Draw a line 4 cm away from the edge of one side of the piece of... poster board. Fold the poster board along this line.
4. Tape the protractor to the poster board, with its flat edge again... fold.
5. Use a pencil to carefully punch a hole through the poster board... along its folded edge at the center of the protractor.
6. Thread the string through the hole, and tape one end to the und... poster board. The other end should be long enough to hang off... poster board.
7. Carefully punch a second hole in the smaller area of the poster... between its short sides. The hole should be directly above the f... should be large enough for the pencil to fit through. This hole is the viewing hole of your new parallax device. This device will allow you to measure the distance of faraway objects.

ScienceFusion
Grade 8 Labs   3   Photosynthesis & Cell Respiration

EXPLORATION LAB

Beach Erosion

In this lab, you will demonstrate the effects of wave action and longshore currents on a beach, and describe ways to decrease the effects of wave action on beach sand.

ASK A QUESTION
1. This lab will help you answer the following question: How does wave action affect the amount of sand on a beach, and how can these effects be reduced?

FORM A HYPOTHESIS
2. Form a hypothesis that answers your question. Explain your reasoning.

TEST THE HYPOTHESIS
3. Make a model beach in a large, shallow **plastic container** by placing a mixture of **sand** and small **pebbles** at one end of the container. The beach should occupy about one-fourth of the length of the container.
4. In front of the sand, add **water** to a depth of 2–3 cm. Record what happens.

OBJECTIVES
- Create a model beach to explore the effects of wave action and longshore currents on shorelines.
- Design a breakwater to prevent beach erosion.

MATERIALS
For each group
- blocks, plaster (2)
- block, wooden, large
- container, plastic, large
- paper, blank
- pebbles
- ruler, metric
- sand (5–10 lb)
- water
For each student
- lab apron
- safety goggles

Benchmarks
SC.6.E.6.1
Describe and give examples of ways in which Earth's surface is built up and torn down by physical and chemical weathering, erosion, and deposition.
SC.6.E.6.2
Recognize that there are a variety of different landforms on Earth's surface such as coastlines, dunes, rivers, mountains, glaciers, deltas, and lakes and relate these landforms as they apply to Florida.

ScienceFusion
Grade 6 Labs   4   Weathering, Erosion, Deposition & Landforms

By asking questions, testing your ideas, organizing and analyzing data, drawing conclusions, and sharing what you learn…

You are the scientist!

e-Learning and Virtual Labs

Digital lessons and virtual labs provide e-learning options for every lesson of Science Fusion.

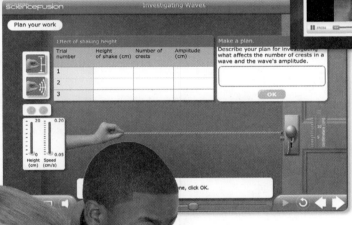

On your own or with a group, explore science concepts in a digital world.

360° of Inquiry

The Universe

Big Idea

The sun is one of billions of stars in one of billions of galaxies in the universe.

Viewing the night sky from an observatory

What do you think?

A telescope can be used to observe the night sky. What observations can you make about the universe from your own backyard?

Using high-powered binoculars

Galaxy Zoo

The human eye is far better at identifying characteristics of galaxies than any computer. So Galaxy Zoo has called for everyday citizens to help in a massive identification project. Well over a hundred thousand people have helped identify newly discovered galaxies. Now you can, too.

1 Think About It

The scientists using the Sloan Digital Sky Survey telescope can gather far more information than they can review quickly. Humans are better at galaxy identification than computers. Why might this be a difficult task for computers?

_____

_____

_____

Sloan Digital Sky Survey Camera

A galaxy seen edge-on

Spiral galaxy

② Ask A Question

How can people who aren't scientists help aid in galaxy identification?

With a partner, review the instructions on Galaxy Zoo's website and practice identifying galaxies. You will need to pay attention to the Galaxy Zoo classification system. Record your observations about the process.

_____

_____

_____

_____

_____

Things to Consider

Many different people review and classify each image of a galaxy at Galaxy Zoo. This way, scientists are able to control the mistakes that individuals may make.

✔ How can having many different people look at each galaxy help prevent errors?

③ Apply Your Knowledge

A List the characteristics you will be looking for when you examine a galaxy photo.

_____

_____

_____

_____

_____

_____

_____

B Review and classify galaxies on Galaxy Zoo's website.

C Create a classroom guide to the galaxies that you have identified.

Take It Home

What has the Citizen Science project known as Galaxy Zoo accomplished so far? Find out how many people have participated and compare that to the number of scientists working on the project. See _ScienceSaurus®_ for more information about galaxies.

Structure of the Universe

ESSENTIAL QUESTION

What makes up the universe?

By the end of this lesson, you should be able to describe the structure of the universe, including the scale of distances in the universe.

This image was taken from the Hubble Space Telescope. It shows just a small number of the galaxies that make up the universe.

Lesson Labs

Quick Labs
- Modeling the Expanding Universe
- Modeling Galaxies

Field Lab
- Schoolyard Solar System

Engage Your Brain

1 Predict Check T or F to show whether you think each statement is true or false.

T	F	
☐	☐	You live on Earth.
☐	☐	Earth orbits a star called the *moon*.
☐	☐	Earth and the sun have the same composition.
☐	☐	The sun is just one of many stars in the Milky Way galaxy.
☐	☐	Distances in the universe are extremely large.

2 Draw When you look into the night sky, you are seeing only a very small part of the universe. Use the space below to draw what you see in the night sky.

Active Reading

3 Synthesize Many English words have their roots in other languages. Use the Latin words below to make an educated guess about the meaning of the word *universe*.

Latin word	Meaning
unus	one
vertere	to turn

Example sentence
Earth is part of the universe.

universe:

_____

_____

_____

Vocabulary Terms

- solar system
- planet
- star
- galaxy
- light-year
- universe

4 Apply This list contains the key terms that you'll learn in this lesson. As you read, circle the definition of each term.

Our place in space

What makes up the universe?

You live on Earth, which is one of eight planets that orbit the sun. As you probably know, the sun is a star. A *star* is a large celestial body that is composed of gas and emits light. Stars are grouped together in structures known as galaxies. A *galaxy* is a large collection of stars, gas, and dust. Based on observations by the Hubble Space Telescope, there are an estimated 100 billion galaxies in the universe. *Universe* is the word that scientists use to describe space and all of the energy and matter in it.

Active Reading

5 Identify As you read the text, underline those characteristics of Earth that make it a special place.

Earth—Our Home Planet

Earth is a special place. Imagine Earth without water. There would be no vast, deep, blue oceans or broad, muddy rivers. If there was no water, there would be no evaporation. Therefore, no clouds would form in Earth's atmosphere, so there would be no rain or snow. Without water, there would be no plants to add oxygen to the atmosphere. And without oxygen, there would be no animal life on Earth.

Earth's atmosphere contains the combination of gases that animals need to breathe. The atmosphere also contains a thin layer of ozone gas. Ozone molecules in this layer absorb radiation from the sun that can be harmful to life. In addition, there are certain gases in the atmosphere that keep temperatures on Earth warm enough for life to exist.

From the moon, you can see Earth's continents, dark-blue oceans, and white clouds swirling in the atmosphere.

6 Analyze What is the relationship between the sizes of the planets and their distances from the sun?

Neptune Uranus Saturn Jupiter Earth Mercury sun

Mars Venus

Sizes are roughly to scale. Distances are not.

The Solar System

Active Reading **7 Identify** As you read the text, underline the different bodies that make up the solar system.

The **solar system** is the collection of large and small bodies that orbit our central star, the sun. The contents of the solar system are numerous and stretch across a large area of space. For example, the solar system is so big that the distance from the sun to Neptune is 4.5 billion kilometers.

If you crossed the solar system beginning at the sun, you would encounter eight large bodies called *planets*. A **planet** is a spherical body that orbits the sun. Planets are generally larger than the other bodies in the solar system. The four planets that orbit nearest to the sun are the terrestrial planets. They are Mercury, Venus, Earth, and Mars. The terrestrial planets are all rocky, dense, and relatively small. The four planets that orbit farthest from the sun are the gas giant planets. They are Jupiter, Saturn, Uranus, and Neptune. These large planets have thick, gaseous atmospheres; small, rocky cores; and ring systems of ice, rock, and dust.

Orbiting most of the planets are smaller bodies called *moons*. Earth has only one moon, but Jupiter has more than 60. The rest of the solar system is made up of other small bodies. These include dwarf planets, comets, asteroids, and meteoroids. Altogether, there are up to a trillion small bodies in the solar system.

Stars

A **star** is a large celestial body that is composed of gas and emits light. Like the sun, most stars are composed almost entirely of hydrogen and helium. Small percentages of other elements are also found in stars. Energy production takes place in the center, or core, of a star. Energy is produced by the process of nuclear fusion. In this process, stars fuse lighter elements, such as hydrogen, into heavier elements, such as helium. This energy leaves the core and eventually reaches the star's surface. There, energy escapes as visible light, other forms of radiation, heat, and even wind.

Stars vary greatly in size. Small stars, such as white dwarfs, may be about the size of Earth. Giant and supergiant stars may be from 10 to as much as 1,000 times as large as the sun.

Active Reading 9 **Compare** How does the composition of a star differ from the composition of a planet?

© Houghton Mifflin Harcourt Publishing Company • Image Credits: ©NASA,ESA,and the Hubble Heritage Team(STScI/AURA)-ESA/Hubble Collaboration

Galaxies

Our solar system is located in the Milky Way galaxy. A **galaxy** (GAL•eck•see) is a large collection of stars, gas, and dust that is held together by gravity. Small galaxies, called *dwarf galaxies,* may contain as few as 100 million stars. Giant galaxies, however, may contain hundreds of billions of stars.

The Milky Way is a spiral galaxy. Spiral galaxies are shaped like pinwheels. They have a central bulge from which two or more spiral arms extend. Stars form in or near the spiral arms. Elliptical galaxies and irregular galaxies are two other kinds of galaxies. Elliptical galaxies look like spheres or ovals, and they do not have spiral arms. Irregular galaxies appear as splotchy, irregularly shaped "blobs." Irregular galaxies are very active areas of star formation.

The Small Magellanic Cloud is an irregular dwarf galaxy that is located near the Milky Way. A few billion stars make up the Small Magellanic Cloud.

This image shows a star formation region within the Small Magellanic Cloud. The blue stars are very young and are still surrounded by the gas and dust from which they formed.

Visualize It!

10 Describe In the boxes below, write in your answers
to each of the questions.

You live on Earth. What is Earth's place in
the universe?

_____

_____

_____

Not to scale

Earth is part of the solar
system. What bodies make
up our solar system?

_____

_____

_____

_____

_____

The solar system is located
within a spiral arm of the
Milky Way galaxy. What is a
galaxy?

_____

_____

_____

_____

_____

_____

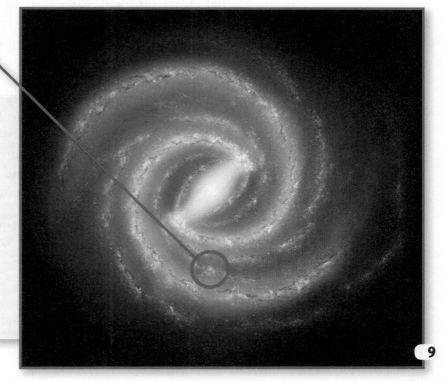

How big is

How are distances in the universe measured?

Distances between most objects in the universe are so large that astronomers do not use kilometers to measure distance. Instead, astronomers measure distance using the speed of light. This unit of measure is known as a light-year. A **light-year** is the distance that light travels through space in 1 year. Light travels through space at about 300,000 km/s, or about 9.5 trillion km in 1 year. The closest star to the sun and Earth is Proxima Centauri. It takes light about 4.3 years to travel from Proxima Centauri to us. Therefore, the distance from Proxima Centauri to Earth is around 4.3 light-years. Light from the sun travels to Earth in a little more than 8 minutes. Thus, the distance from the sun to Earth is around 8 light-minutes.

How do distances affect space travel? Our fastest interplanetary spacecraft travel through space at about 58,000 km/h. At this speed, it would take a spacecraft more than 75,000 years to reach Proxima Centauri.

11 **Explain** The Andromeda galaxy is located approximately 2.5 million light-years from Earth. Why is the light that reaches Earth 2.5 million years old?

_____

_____

_____

© Houghton Mifflin Harcourt Publishing Company • Image Credits: ©Stocktrek Images/Getty Images

big?

What is the structure of the universe?

The **universe** can be defined as space and all the matter and energy in it. However, this definition does not tell us about the structure of the universe. Astronomers now know that throughout the universe there are areas where galaxies are densely concentrated. These are areas where galaxies are found in what are called *clusters* and *superclusters*. Clusters contain as many as several thousand galaxies. Superclusters can be made up of ten or more clusters of galaxies. There are also areas throughout the universe where very little matter exists. These are huge, spherical areas called *voids*.

Astronomers have begun to think of the universe as having a structure similar to soap bubbles. Clusters and superclusters are located along the thin bubble walls. The interiors of the bubbles are voids. It takes light hundreds of millions of years to cross the largest voids.

The Voyager 2 spacecraft was launched in 1977. It explored Jupiter, Saturn, Uranus, and Neptune, and is now close to moving out of the solar system and into interstellar space.

Think Outside the Book Inquiry

12 Apply In the text, the universe is described as being composed of galaxies and voids. Design and build a model that shows the structure of the universe as you imagine it to be.

Active Reading **13 Describe** What is the general structure of the universe?

_____

_____

_____

_____

Visual Summary

To complete this summary, fill in the blanks with the correct word or phrase. Then use the key below to check your answers. You can use this page to review the main concepts of the lesson.

Structure
of the Universe

Earth is a planet.

14 What is Earth's place in the universe?
_____
_____

Bodies in our solar system orbit the sun.

15 What makes up our solar system?
_____
_____

The sun is a star.

16 What is a star?
_____
_____

The Milky Way is a galaxy.

17 What are galaxies made up of?
_____
_____

Answers: 14 a planet that orbits the sun; 15 the sun, planets, moons, dwarf planets, comets, asteroids, and meteoroids; 16 a large celestial body that is composed of gas and emits light; 17 stars, gas, and dust

18 Describe Beginning with Earth, summarize the structure of the universe.

Lesson Review

Vocabulary

Fill in the blank with the term that best completes the following sentences.

1 A _____ is a large collection of stars, gas, and dust that is held together by gravity.

2 Space and all matter and energy in it is called the _____.

3 A _____ consists of a star and all of the bodies in orbit around it.

Key Concepts

In the following table, write the name of the correct structure next to the definition.

Definition	Structure
4 Identify What is a large celestial body that is composed of gas and emits light?	
5 Identify What is a spherical body that orbits the sun?	

6 Explain Why can the structure of the universe be compared to soap bubbles?

_____

_____

_____

_____

7 Define Define light-year, and explain how and why light-years are used to measure distances in the universe.

_____

_____

_____

_____

Critical Thinking

Use the table to answer the following questions.

Object	Distance from Earth
sun (nearest star)	8.3 light-minutes
Proxima Centauri (nearest star to sun)	4.2 light-years
center of Milky Way galaxy	28,000 light-years
Andromeda galaxy (nearest large galaxy)	2.5 million light-years

8 Apply Given current spacecraft technology, which of the objects in the table do you think it would be possible for you to travel to in your lifetime?

_____

_____

9 Determine A planet in our solar system is located far from the sun. Describe the size and composition of this planet.

_____

_____

_____

_____

10 Deduce What do you think that astronomers mean when they use the term *observable universe*? (Hint: Think of the time it takes for light from very distant objects to reach Earth.)

_____

_____

_____

_____

_____

My Notes

Hakeem Oluseyi

ASTROPHYSICIST

Dr. Oluseyi's work has helped advance our understanding of the universe.

Dr. Hakeem Oluseyi always thought scientists were "supercool." Still, he didn't start right out of high school trying to become a scientist. He spent some time in the Navy before going to college. In college he studied physics and eventually earned a Ph.D. in astrophysics.

Dr. Oluseyi has worked on the manufacture of computer chips, developing ways to both make them smaller and make them operate more quickly. He has also assisted in the development of very sensitive detectors that go on spacecraft. These detectors measure different types of electromagnetic radiation that come from bodies in outer space. Dr. Oluseyi came up with ways to make these detectors more sensitive and stable. This made them better able to work in outer space.

Currently, Dr. Oluseyi is helping to develop the Large Synoptic Survey Telescope (LSST). This telescope will observe the entire sky every night for 10 years. (Other all-sky surveys typically take several years to complete!) Dr. Oluseyi plans to use the data to map out the galactic structure and to search for planets around pulsating stars. Pulsating stars are stars that show changes in brightness due to internal processes happening within the star.

Through work like Dr. Oluseyi's we are gaining a better understanding of the planets and stars. But Dr. Oluseyi would tell you, there is still plenty more he'd like to know.

Crab Nebula

Potentially hazardous near-Earth asteroids could be identified using the Large Synoptic Survey Telescope.

Social Studies Connection

The Crab Nebula is what remains of an exploding star. Research when the earliest observations of the Crab Nebula were made. Create a timeline of this discovery.

JOB BOARD

Public Education Space Specialist

What You'll Do: You will design, develop, and teach programs on different space topics for an organization. You will also give presentations and tours of space-related workplaces for teachers, students, and the media.

Where You Might Work: Observatories, museums, government buildings, NASA, and the National Science Foundation are places you might work.

Education: Specialists must have a bachelor's degree in astronomy, physical science, science education, or a related field. Experience in public speaking, teaching, and developing educational programs is a plus.

Other Job Requirements: You should be able to present information in a clear and interesting way to people of all ages.

Information Technology (IT) Technician

What You'll Do: Monitor computer systems and help other people use them.

Where You Might Work: Large organizations with mainframe computer systems, like multinational companies, government agencies, hospitals, or colleges.

Education: IT technicians usually have a college certificate in information systems, data processing, electronics technology, mainframe operations, or microcomputer systems.

Other Job Requirements: You need to be able to work on a team and have excellent problem-solving skills.

PEOPLE IN SCIENCE NEWS

Caroline Moore

Seeking Supernovae

Caroline Moore was only 14 years old when she discovered Supernova 2008ha, a new type of supernova, from her backyard observatory. Because the one she discovered is different from other supernovae, her discovery has encouraged scientists to reconsider how stars die. Moore continues to search for supernovae, and is now helping to teach and inspire other young people to take an interest in astronomy.

Stars

ESSENTIAL QUESTION

What are some properties of stars?

By the end of this lesson, you should be able to describe stars and their physical properties.

The Butterfly Cluster, part of which is seen here, is made up of mostly hot, blue stars. This star cluster is about 1,600 light-years away and is estimated to be 100 million years old.

© Houghton Mifflin Harcourt Publishing Company • Image Credits: ©Celestial Image Co./Photo Researchers, Inc.

👋 **Lesson Labs**

Quick Labs
• Modeling Star Magnitudes
• Using a Sky Map

Exploration Lab
• Star Colors and Temperatures

Engage Your Brain

1 Predict Check T or F to show whether you think each statement is true or false.

T   F

☐   ☐   The sun is a star.

☐   ☐   Stars are made mostly of nitrogen and oxygen.

☐   ☐   If two stars have the same apparent magnitude, they are the same distance from Earth.

☐   ☐   Red stars have higher surface temperatures than blue stars.

☐   ☐   Some stars are about as small as Earth.

2 Describe In the images below, the stars Betelgeuse (left) and Rigel (right) are shown. Both stars are located in the constellation Orion. Describe any differences between these two stars that you see in this pair of images.

_____

_____

_____

_____

Betelgeuse

Rigel

Active Reading

3 Synthesize Many English words have their roots in other languages. Use the Latin word below to make an educated guess about the meaning of the word *luminosity*.

Latin word	Meaning
lumen	light

Example sentence
The luminosity of stars is measured relative to the luminosity of the sun.

luminosity:

_____

_____

Vocabulary Terms

• star
• apparent magnitude
• luminosity
• absolute magnitude

4 Apply As you read, place a question mark next to any words that you don't understand. When you finish reading the lesson, go back and review the text that you marked. If the information is still confusing, consult a classmate or a teacher.

Reach for the Stars!

What is a star?

A **star** is a large celestial body that is composed of gas and emits light. The sun is a star. Stars are made mostly of hydrogen and helium. But stars also contain other elements in small amounts. Stars vary in brightness. Although the sun may appear bright from Earth, the sun is not a bright star in comparison to many other stars. The temperatures of stars also vary. These differences in temperature result in differences in color. Stars may range in color from red, which indicates a cool star, to blue, which indicates a very hot star. The sun is a relatively cool yellow star. Stars have different sizes. Stars may be 1/100 as large as the sun or as much as 1,000 times as large as the sun. In addition, two or more stars may be bound together by gravity, which causes those stars to orbit each other. Three or more stars that are bound by gravity are called *multiple stars* or *multiple star systems*.

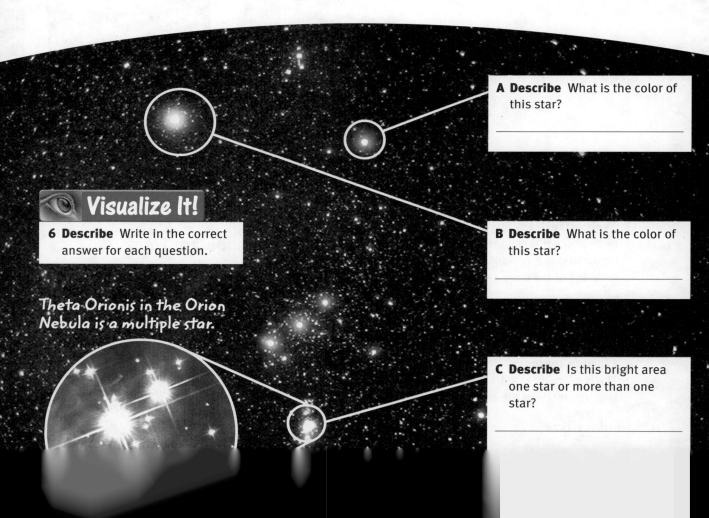

Visualize It!

6 Describe Write in the correct answer for each question.

Theta Orionis in the Orion Nebula is a multiple star.

A Describe What is the color of this star?

_____

B Describe What is the color of this star?

_____

C Describe Is this bright area one star or more than one star?

_____

t Publishing Company• Image Credits: ©Matthew Spinelli

The Sun Is a Star

To see a star, you need look no farther than the sun. The sun, like other stars, is composed mostly of hydrogen and helium. The sun also contains oxygen, carbon, neon, and iron.

At the center of the sun lies the core. In the sun's core, gases are compressed and heated, and temperatures reach 15,000,000 °C. The core is where matter is converted into energy.

The sun's surface, the photosphere, is the layer of the sun's atmosphere that we see from Earth. The photosphere has an average temperature of 5,527 °C. From the core, energy is continuously transferred to the photosphere. There, energy escapes into space as visible light, other forms of radiation, heat, and wind. The sun's atmosphere extends millions of kilometers into space. Temperatures in the sun's middle atmosphere, the chromosphere, are 4,225 °C to 6,000 °C. In the sun's outer atmosphere, or corona, temperatures may reach 2,000,000 °C.

This extreme ultraviolet image of the sun shows areas of different temperature that are found in the sun's atmosphere.

7 Compare Fill in the Venn diagram to compare and contrast the physical properties of the sun with the physical properties of other stars.

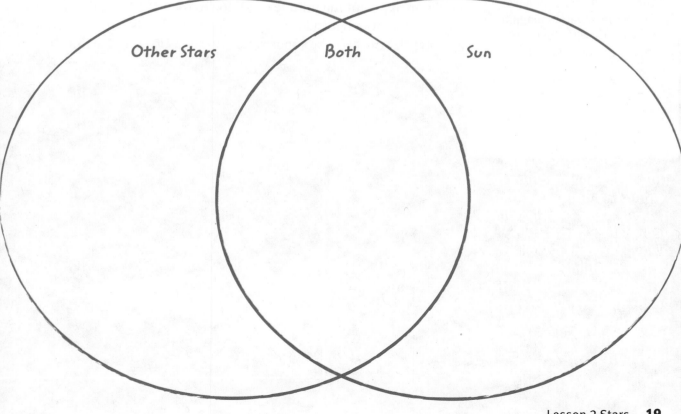

Other Stars   Both   Sun

You're a Shining Star

How is star brightness measured?

When you look at stars in the night sky, you see that stars vary in brightness. Some stars are bright, and other stars are dim. In reality, one star can appear brighter than another star simply because it is located closer to Earth.

By Apparent Magnitude

Apparent magnitude is the measure of a star's brightness as seen from Earth. Some stars are actually more luminous, or brighter, than the sun is. If these stars are located far from Earth, they may not appear bright to us.

Using only their eyes, ancient astronomers described star brightness by magnitude. They called the brightest stars they could see *first magnitude* and the faintest stars they could see *sixth magnitude*. Astronomers using telescopes see many stars that are too dim to see with the naked eye. Rather than replacing the magnitude system, astronomers added to it. Today, the brightest stars have a magnitude of about –2. The faintest stars that we can see with a telescope have a magnitude of +30.

The magnitude scale may seem backward. Faint stars have positive (larger) numbers; bright stars have negative (smaller) numbers. Sirius (SIR•ee•uhz), the brightest star in the night sky, has an apparent magnitude of –1.46. To the naked eye, the sun has an apparent magnitude of –26.8, even though it is not as luminous a star as Sirius is. The sun is simply located closer to Earth.

This girl is approaching her tent in the dark. The tent is dimly lit by the flashlight beam when she is 20 m away. The tent is well lit by the flashlight beam when she is 5 m away. The beam appears dimmer at 20 m than at 5 m, but the flashlight is equally bright in both cases.

Mifflin Harcourt Publishing Company

How is star luminosity measured?

When astronomers use the word **luminosity**, they mean the *actual* brightness of a star. To measure a star's luminosity, astronomers use an absolute brightness scale called *absolute magnitude*.

By Absolute Magnitude

Absolute magnitude is a measure of how bright a star would be if the star were located at a standard distance. In other words, absolute magnitude is a measure of the brightness of a star whose distance from Earth is known. Just like apparent magnitude, absolute magnitude uses the magnitude scale.

To understand the difference between apparent magnitude and absolute magnitude, let's use the sun as an example. The apparent magnitude of the sun is −26.8. However, the absolute magnitude of the sun is +4.8, which is typical of many stars. Now compare the sun, which is located 8.3 light-minutes from Earth, to Sirius, which is located 8.6 light-years from Earth. Sirius has an apparent magnitude of −1.46 and an absolute magnitude of +1.4. Therefore, Sirius is much more luminous than the sun is.

Magnitudes of Selected Stars			
Star	Distance from Earth	Apparent Magnitude	Absolute Magnitude
sun	8.3 light-minutes	−26.8	+4.8
Sirius	8.6 light-years	−1.46	+1.4
Betelgeuse	640 light-years	+0.45	−5.6

10 Explain Why does a star such as Betelgeuse, which is located far from Earth, have a much greater absolute magnitude than apparent magnitude?

_____

_____

_____

_____

_____

_____

_____

Too Hot to Handle

How are the surface temperatures of stars measured?

If you look into the night sky, you may be able to see that stars have different colors. Why do the colors of stars vary? The answer is that differences in the colors of stars are due to differences in their surface temperatures. The same is true of all objects that glow.

By Color

You can see how temperature affects color in heated metal. As shown in the illustrations below, a steel bar glows different colors as it is heated to higher and higher temperatures. If an object's color depends only on temperature, the object is called a *blackbody*. As the temperature of a blackbody rises, it glows brighter and brighter red. As it gets hotter, its color changes to orange, yellow, white, and blue-white. It also glows more brightly.

The table shows the way in which the surface temperatures of stars are related to color. Stars that have the lowest surface temperatures (below 3,500 °C) are red. Stars that have the highest surface temperatures (above 25,000 °C) are blue.

Color and Surface Temperatures of Stars	
Color	Surface Temperature (°C)
blue	Above 25,000
blue-white	10,000–25,000
white	7,500–10,000
yellow-white	6,000–7,500
yellow	5,000–6,000
orange	3,500–5,000
red	Below 3,500

A steel bar glows red when heated to about 600 °C.

At about 1,200 °C, the metal glows yellow.

When heated to about 1,500 °C, a steel bar gives off a brilliant white light.

11 Explain Explain how the colors of stars that have different surface temperatures are similar to the colors of a steel bar that is heated to different temperatures.

_____

_____

_____

© Houghton Mifflin Harcourt Publishing Company • (all) ©Dave King/Dorling Kindersley/Getty Images

Think Outside the Book

12 Formulate Come up with a creative way to remember the colors of stars, from coolest to hottest.

The size of the sun is compared to the blue supergiant star Rigel and the red supergiant star Antares.

sun = 1 solar radius (yellow)

Rigel = 78 solar radii (blue)

Antares = 776 solar radii (red)

Visualize It!

13 Apply From Earth, the sun appears to be a very large star. In reality, the sun is quite small when compared to stars such as Rigel and Antares. At the scale shown on this page, why would it be impossible to illustrate stars that are smaller than the sun?

_____

_____

_____

_____

_____

How are the sizes of stars measured?

Like the colors of stars, the sizes of stars differ greatly. Stars may be about the same size as Earth or larger than the size of Earth's orbit around the sun. So what do astronomers use to measure star size? It is always easiest to start with an object that is familiar. That is why astronomers use the size of the sun to describe the size of other stars.

Using Solar Radii

Astronomers have indirectly measured the dimensions of the sun. The sun's radius is approximately 695,000 km, or about 109 times the radius of Earth. Astronomers use this measure, the radius of the sun, to measure the size of other stars. Very small stars, which are called *white dwarfs,* are about the same size as Earth. The size of a white dwarf can be expressed as approximately 0.01 solar radius. Very large stars, which are called *giant stars,* typically have sizes of between 10 and 100 times the radius of the sun. There are also rare, extremely large stars that have sizes of up to 1,000 solar radii. These stars are called *supergiants.* Supergiants are often red or blue stars.

Visual Summary

To complete this summary, fill in the blanks with the correct word or phrase. Then use the key below to check your answers. You can use this page to review the main concepts of the lesson.

The brightness and luminosity of stars can be measured.

14 _____ is the measure of a star's brightness as seen from Earth.

15 _____ is the measure of how bright a star would be if it were located at a standard distance from Earth.

Properties
of Stars

The color of stars is related to their surface temperature.

17 What is the color and surface temperature of the star in the illustration below?

_____

_____

_____

Stars have different sizes.

16 What is the standard unit that astronomers use to measure the size of stars?

_____

_____

18 What is the color and surface temperature of the star in the illustration below?

_____

_____

_____

Answers: 14 Apparent magnitude; 15 Absolute magnitude; 16 solar radius; 17 blue, >25,000 °C; 18 yellow, 5,000 °C to 6,000 °C.

19 Contrast How does the sun compare to other stars in terms of surface temperature, apparent magnitude, absolute magnitude, and size?

Lesson Review

Vocabulary

In your own words, define the following terms.

1 star

_____

_____

2 luminosity

_____

_____

3 apparent magnitude

_____

_____

Key Concepts

4 List What are some of the physical properties of stars?

_____

_____

_____

_____

5 Analyze Why is the absolute magnitude of some stars greater than their apparent magnitude?

_____

_____

_____

_____

_____

6 Compare How does the size of the sun compare to the sizes of other stars?

_____

_____

_____

7 Apply Mizar is a star system that is composed of two pairs of stars, Mizar A and Mizar B, or four stars in total. What do astronomers call a system that is composed of more than two stars?

_____

_____

_____

Critical Thinking

Use the table to answer the following questions.

Color and Surface Temperature of Stars	
Color	Surface Temperature (K)
blue	Above 25,000
blue-white	10,000–25,000
white	7,500–10,000
yellow-white	6,000–7,500
yellow	5,000–6,000
orange	3,500–5,000
red	Below 3,500

8 Apply Which stars have the highest surface temperatures, red stars or blue stars?

_____

_____

9 Apply The sun has a surface temperature of 5800 K. What is the color of the sun?

_____

_____

10 Calculate A star has a size of 0.1 solar radius. How many times larger is the sun than this star?

_____

_____

My Notes

The Life Cycle of Stars

ESSENTIAL QUESTION

How do stars change over time?

By the end of this lesson, you should be able to describe the stages of the life cycles of stars.

Massive stars really go out with a bang. The remains of a supernova called **Cassiopeia** are still glowing with energy long after the star exploded.

© Houghton Mifflin Harcourt Publishing Company • Image Credits: (bg) ©NASA/ESA/Hubble Heritage (STScI/AURA)

Engage Your Brain

1 Predict Check T or F to show whether you think each statement is true or false.

T F

☐ ☐ Our sun is among the most massive stars in our galaxy.

☐ ☐ A neutron star is an extremely dense ball of neutrons.

☐ ☐ Astronomers use the H-R diagram to predict when comets will travel close to Earth.

☐ ☐ Stars develop from white dwarfs.

2 Explain Humans pass through a series of stages called a *life cycle*. Stars go through a series of stages, too. What stage of the human life cycle are you currently in? What stage of the star life cycle do you think the sun is in?

_____

_____

_____

_____

Active Reading

3 Synthesize You can often define an unknown word if you know the meaning of its word parts. Use the words and sentence below to make an educated guess about the meaning of the word *supernova*.

Word part	Meaning
super	large, extreme
novus	fresh, new

Example sentence:
As a part of its normal life cycle, a massive star becomes a <u>supernova</u>.

supernova:

_____

_____

Vocabulary Terms

- **nebula**
- **white dwarf**
- **supernova**
- **neutron star**
- **H-R diagram**
- **main sequence**

4 Identify As you read, create a reference card for each vocabulary term. On one side of the card, write the term and its meaning. On the other side, draw an image that illustrates or makes a connection to the term. These cards can be used as bookmarks in the text so that you can refer to them while studying.

© Houghton Mifflin Harcourt Publishing Company • Image Credits: (bg) ©NASA/ESA/Hubble Heritage (STScI/AURA; (t) ©Chris Williams/Alamy

A Star Is Born

What is the life cycle of a star?

The sky is full of stars that are at different stages in their life cycles. A star begins life within a cloud of gas and dust. Gravity pulls parts of this cloud into dense regions. Stars begin life in the cores of these regions when the process of nuclear fusion begins. When stars age, much of their material returns to space to form new stars.

Stars Form in Nebulae

Stars form in nebulae [NEB•yuh•lee]. A **nebula** [NEB•yuh•luh] is a large cloud of gas and dust. Like stars, nebulae are composed of mostly hydrogen and helium. They also contain small amounts of heavier elements. A nebula may be compressed by an outside force, such as the explosion of a nearby star. This causes the nebula to contract and cool. Gravity causes parts of the nebula to collapse.

According to Newton's law of universal gravitation, all objects in the universe attract one another. The force of gravity increases with increasing mass and decreasing distance between objects. As particles within the nebula are pulled closer together, gravitational attraction increases. As a result, dense regions of gas and dust form within the nebula. The densest regions, which are called *dense cores*, form new stars.

Visualize It!

5 Identify What is happening in the circled part of this nebula?

_____

_____

_____

The bright regions within this nebula are areas of greater density.

Stars Emit Energy by the Process of Nuclear Fusion

The temperature within dense cores increases. At about 10 million °C, the process of nuclear fusion begins. This process releases enormous amounts of energy. Nuclear fusion takes place when high temperature and pressure cause two or more low-mass atomic nuclei to form a heavier nucleus. A nucleus is an atom's central region, which is made up of neutrons and protons.

The start of hydrogen fusion marks the birth of a star. The active fusion stage is the longest stage in the life cycle of a star. This stage can last for billions of years. The active fusion stage ends when a star runs out of hydrogen.

Active Reading

6 Identify What process begins when a star is born?

Visualize It!

For most of its life, a star fuses hydrogen nuclei in a multistep process that releases energy.

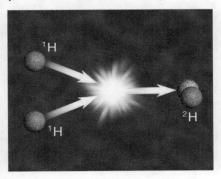

Hydrogen nuclei are fused together under great heat and pressure to form helium nuclei.

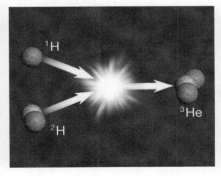

Some of the energy and nuclei released at the end of the process cause fusion to continue.

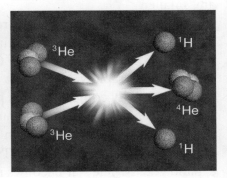

7 Examine Look at the start of the first reaction. Compare this to the end of the last reaction. What type of nuclei are found at both ends of the reaction?

Nuclear Fusion in Stars Stops

A star enters the next stage of its life cycle when nearly all of the hydrogen in its core has fused into helium. The core of the star contracts under its own gravity. This contraction increases the temperature of the core. Energy is transferred to a thin shell of hydrogen that surrounds the core. Hydrogen fusion continues in this outer shell. The ongoing fusion radiates large amounts of energy outward. The outer shell of the star expands, which makes the star grow much larger.

When fusion ends completely, stars begin to eject matter. Stars rapidly lose mass until only the core remains. The final stages in a star's life cycle depend on the mass of the star.

What is the life cycle of a low-mass star?

The mass of a star determines the different stages that it will pass through during its life cycle. Low-mass stars, including our sun, grow larger and become giants. Then, they end their lives as objects called *white dwarfs*.

The Low-Mass Star Becomes a Giant

During the active fusion stage, energy generated by fusion reactions causes an outward pressure. At the same time, gravity pulls inward toward the star's center. These outward and inward forces balance each other, and the star does not get any larger or any smaller.

After a star fuses all the hydrogen in its core into helium, fusion no longer takes place within the core. So, the outward forces are smaller than the inward force of gravity. This causes the star's core to shrink rapidly. However, a shell of fresh hydrogen surrounds the core. Gravity compresses this hydrogen shell until temperatures within the shell become high enough for hydrogen fusion to take place. The outward pressure from the energy of fusion in the shell is now able to overcome gravity. This causes the hydrogen shell to expand greatly. The star becomes much larger and brighter, and is now called a *giant*. Giants are red because the surface temperature of the star becomes cooler as the outer shell expands.

Active Reading **8 Identify** When does a low-mass star become a giant?

_____

_____

_____

Think Outside the Book Inquiry

9 Research If our sun grows to 10 times its current size at the end of its life cycle, how big will it be? Will Mercury be engulfed? Venus? Earth? What if our sun grows to 100 times its current size?

Giants are large because gases that surround the core have expanded. The red color is associated with lower surface temperatures than when stars were yellow or orange.

Our sun is an example of a low-mass star. Near the end of its life cycle it will swell into a red giant.

The Giant Loses Material, Leaving a White Dwarf

Over time, a giant's outer gases drift away from the core. The gases appear as a cloud around a dying, sunlike star. Some clouds form a simple sphere or ring around the star. Many form more complex shapes.

As the clouds disperse, gravity causes the remaining matter in the star's core to collapse inward. The core of the star becomes denser and very hot. At this stage, the star is known as a white dwarf. A **white dwarf** is the hot, dense core of matter that remains from the collapse of a low-mass star. White dwarfs are very small. A white dwarf is about the size of Earth.

White dwarfs shine for billions of years before they cool completely. As white dwarfs cool, they become fainter. This is the final stage in the life cycle of low-mass stars.

 **Visualize It!**

10 Describe Using the image below, describe the process by which a giant becomes a white dwarf.

_____

_____

Gravity causes the star's core to contract and form a white dwarf.

White dwarf

White dwarfs are hot but dim. Their energy radiates away into space over billions of years. Thus, white dwarfs become fainter as they cool.

The Heavyweights

What is the life cycle of a high-mass star?

High-mass stars follow a different life cycle than low-mass stars do. High-mass stars become supergiants rather than giants. Following the supergiant stage, the collapse of the star's core at the end of the fusion process causes the formation of very strange objects. These objects include supernovae, neutron stars, and black holes.

The High-Mass Star Becomes a Supergiant

When hydrogen fusion in a high-mass star ends, other types of fusion begin that involve the fusion of nuclei into elements heavier than carbon. The star expands to become a supergiant. The hydrogen fusion stage in high-mass stars ends much sooner than it does in low-mass stars. A star with 10 times the mass of our sun will become a supergiant in just 20 million years. By comparison, it takes 10 billion years for low-mass stars such as the sun to become giants.

The Supergiant Collapses, Triggering a Supernova

In the supergiant stage, the high-mass star fuses larger and larger nuclei until all its nuclear fuel is used up. The supergiant no longer generates the energy needed to keep its core from collapsing. The core rapidly collapses, and a tremendous amount of energy is released. This causes the collapse to halt and the supergiant to become a supernova. A **supernova** is a gigantic explosion in which a high-mass star throws its outer layers into space. But its core remains.

11 Explain What causes a supernova?

_____

_____

Supergiants are fantastically large and bright. This makes supergiants easy to identify, even though they are rare and distant.

High-mass stars, though larger than the sun, are much smaller than supergiants. The blue color indicates that this is a very hot, active star.

Our sun looks very small when compared to a high-mass blue star. But, it is absolutely tiny when compared to a supergiant.

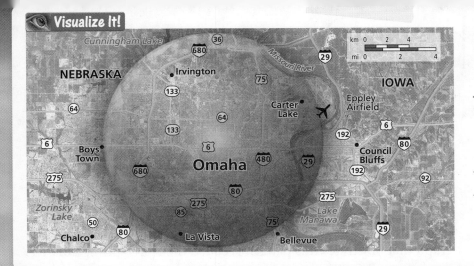

A neutron star is a tiny star, but contains 1.4 to 2 times the mass of our sun!

12 Relate Use the scale to find the diameter of this neutron star in miles.

_____

_____

The Collapsed Supergiant Becomes a Neutron Star

The core of a supernova continues to collapse under the force of gravity. Its protons and electrons smash together to form neutrons. The resulting **neutron star** is a small, incredibly dense ball of closely packed neutrons. A neutron star may have a diameter of only 20 km, yet it may emit the energy of 100,000 suns.

Neutron stars rotate very rapidly. Some emit a beam of electromagnetic radiation that can be detected every time the beam sweeps by Earth. These stars are called *pulsars*.

Active Reading **13 Explain** What is a pulsar?

_____

_____

_____

The Most Massive Supergiants Collapse to Form Black Holes

There are stars that are so massive that their cores continue to collapse under the force of gravity. As their cores collapse, the mass of the star is compressed into a single point. This point is called a *black hole*. A black hole is an invisible object with gravity so great that nothing, not even light, can escape it.

Though black holes are invisible, they can be observed by the gravitational effect they have on their surroundings. Matter is pulled into a black hole. It swirls around the black hole just before being pulled in. The matter becomes so hot that it emits x-rays. Astronomers use x-rays and other means to locate black holes—even within our own galaxy!

Gases that swirl in toward a black hole are heated to high temperatures.

Black holes cannot be seen directly. Instead, black holes are "observed" by the effect that they have on their surroundings.

A Graphic Display

How are stars plotted on the H-R diagram?

Astronomers refer to brightness as *luminosity*. Luminosity is actually a measure of the total amount of energy a star gives off each second. When the surface temperatures of stars are plotted against their luminosity, a consistent pattern is revealed. The graph that illustrates this pattern is called the Hertzsprung-Russell diagram, or **H-R diagram**.

The hottest stars are located on the left side of the H-R diagram and are blue. Stars become progressively cooler the farther to the right they are located on the diagram. The coolest stars are located on the right side of the diagram and are red. The brightest stars are located at the top of the diagram, and the dimmest stars are located at the bottom.

© Houghton Mifflin Harcourt Publishing Company

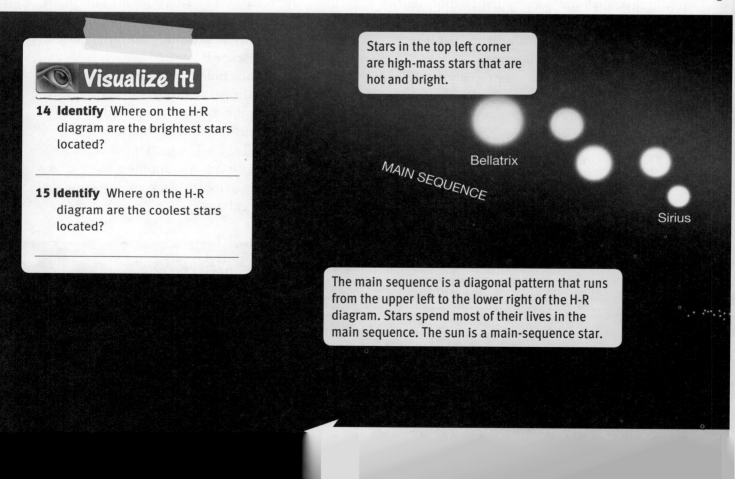

Visualize It!

14 Identify Where on the H-R diagram are the brightest stars located?

15 Identify Where on the H-R diagram are the coolest stars located?

Stars in the top left corner are high-mass stars that are hot and bright.

Bellatrix

MAIN SEQUENCE

Sirius

The main sequence is a diagonal pattern that runs from the upper left to the lower right of the H-R diagram. Stars spend most of their lives in the main sequence. The sun is a main-sequence star.

How does the H-R diagram show different life cycle stages?

Most stars fall within a band that runs diagonally through the middle of the H-R diagram. This band extends from hot, bright blue stars at the upper left to cool, dim red stars at the lower right. It is called the main sequence. The **main sequence** is the region of the diagram where stars spend most of their lives. Stars within this band are actively fusing hydrogen and are called *main-sequence stars*.

The sun is a main-sequence star. When nuclear fusion ends in the sun, it will become a giant and will move to the upper right corner of the H-R diagram. When the outer layers of the giant are lost to space, the sun will become a white dwarf and move to the bottom of the diagram.

Active Reading **16 Identify** What is the region of the H-R diagram where stars spend most of their lives called?

_____

Visualize It!

17 Explain The sun is now at position A. How will the sun change in terms of temperature and brightness as it moves from position A to B and then to C on the H-R diagram?

_____

_____

_____

_____

_____

Giants are plotted in the upper right corner. Although large, these stars are relatively cool and have a red glow.

GIANTS

Polaris

B

Procyon

Arcturus

Betelgeuse

SUPERGIANTS

BRIGHTER

MAIN SEQUENCE

Sun

A

WHITE DWARFS

Proxima Centauri

C

RED DWARFS

At the end of their life cycles, most low-mass stars become white dwarfs. White dwarfs are the small, hot cores of giant stars.

Visual Summary

To complete the summary cards, check the box that indicates true or false. Then, use the key below to check your answers. You can use this page to review the main concepts of the lesson.

The Life Cycle of Stars

Low-mass stars end their lives as white dwarfs.

T F

18 ☐ ☐ Carbon and helium combine during nuclear fusion to form hydrogen.

The H-R diagram plots the temperature and brightness of stars.

T F

19 ☐ ☐ The relative brightness and temperature of a star change over time.

High-mass stars end their lives as neutron stars or black holes.

T F

20 ☐ ☐ High-mass stars spend more time in the main sequence than do low-mass stars.

Answers: 18 F; 19 T; 20 F

21 Synthesize Relate the life stages of a star to the process of nuclear fusion.

Lesson Review

Vocabulary

Draw a line to connect the following terms to their definitions.

1 nebula   **A** a large cloud of gas and dust in space

2 main sequence   **B** an explosion in which the outer layers of a star are thrown off

3 neutron star   **C** a life-cycle stage of stars

4 supernova   **D** a small, very dense star that has formed from the collapsed core of a star

Key Concepts

5 Identify What force causes a star to form from a nebula?

6 Explain What triggers nuclear fusion in stars?

7 Contrast Describe how the life cycle of a low-mass star differs from the life cycle of a high-mass star.

8 Explain Why is the H-R diagram useful in plotting the life cycles of stars?

Critical Thinking

Use this drawing to answer the following questions.

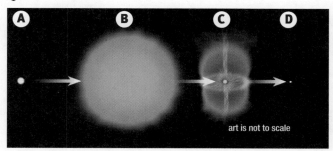

art is not to scale

9 Analyze What changes within the star (A) lead to the red giant (B)?

10 Explain Why will the color of the sun change from yellow to red when it becomes a giant?

11 Relate Black holes cannot be seen. However, scientists think that black holes exist because of their effect on surrounding matter. Describe another force or phenomenon that cannot be seen directly. Give examples of the effects of this force on everyday objects.

My Notes

Unit 1 ◀ Big Idea ◀ The sun is one of billions of stars in one of billions of galaxies in the universe.

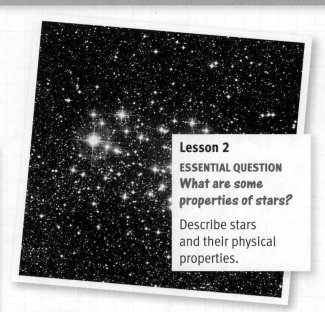

Lesson 1

ESSENTIAL QUESTION
What makes up the universe?

Describe the structure of the universe, including the scale of distances in the universe.

Lesson 2

ESSENTIAL QUESTION
What are some properties of stars?

Describe stars and their physical properties.

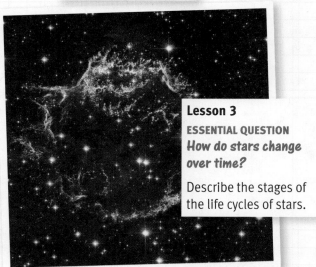

Lesson 3

ESSENTIAL QUESTION
How do stars change over time?

Describe the stages of the life cycles of stars.

Connect ESSENTIAL QUESTIONS
Lessons 2 and 3

1 Synthesize Explain why a cool, yellow star of average size and luminosity, such as the sun, spends a longer time in the main sequence than a hot, blue star of large size and high luminosity.

_____

_____

_____

_____

Think Outside the Book

2 Synthesize Choose one of these activities to help synthesize what you have learned in this unit.

☐ Using what you learned in lessons 2 and 3, write a short essay describing how a low-mass star like the sun changes in luminosity, color, and size over its lifetime.

☐ Using what you learned in lessons 1, 2, and 3, create a poster presentation that explains how matter is converted into energy in the core of a star.

Name _____

Vocabulary

Fill in each blank with the term that best completes the following sentences.

1 A large celestial body that is composed of gas and that emits light is a(n)

_____.

2 A(n) _____ consists of one star or more than one star and all the objects in orbit around the central star.

3 A(n) _____ is a large group of stars, gas, and dust bound together by gravity.

4 A large, cold cloud of gas and dust in interstellar space is called

a(n) _____.

5 The distance that light can travel in one year, also known as

a(n) _____, is about 9.5 trillion km.

Key Concepts

Read each question below, and circle the best answer.

6 While planets are smaller than stars, planets are generally larger than which of the following?

A the stars they orbit around

B the solar system

C the galaxy they are contained within

D the other bodies in a solar system

7 Where do stars form?

A in a planet's core

B in nebulae

C on asteroids

D in sun spots on the surface of the sun

8 What causes a supernova?

  A the collision of several small stars that forms a new giant star

  B the collapse of a giant cloud of gas and dust in a nebula

  C the expansion of a shell of gas around a star that creates a giant star

  D the collapse of the core of a high-mass star

9 The following table displays the average distance from Earth for four objects.

Object	Average Distance from Earth
Barnard's Star	6 light years
Andromeda Galaxy	2.5 million light years
Triangulum Galaxy	2.6 million light years
Planet Neptune	4.3 billion km

Which object is farthest away from Earth?

A Barnard's Star

B Planet Neptune

C Andromeda Galaxy

D Triangulum Galaxy

10 How do galaxies range in size?

  A from dwarf galaxies with approximately 100 million stars to giant galaxies with more than 1 trillion stars

  B as large as the distance from Earth to the sun and back

  C from the smallest speck of dust to infinity

  D from as small as the Milky Way to as large as the universe

11 How do astronomers measure the brightness of a star?

  A by describing how large it is

  B by explaining how old the star is

  C by measuring the amount of energy it emits

  D by using apparent magnitude, a measure of the brightness of stars as they appear to an observer on Earth

12 The table below relates color and surface temperature for different stars.

Color	Surface Temperature (K)
blue	Above 25,000
blue-white	10,000–25,000
white	7,500–10,000
yellow-white	6,000–7,500
yellow	5,000–6,000
orange	3,500–5,000
red	Below 3,500

The color of the surface of a star can be used to determine temperature. Which color in the table is the coolest star?

A blue

C yellow-white

B red

D yellow

Critical Thinking

Answer the following questions in the space provided.

13 Below is a drawing of a galaxy that is similar to the Milky Way Galaxy.

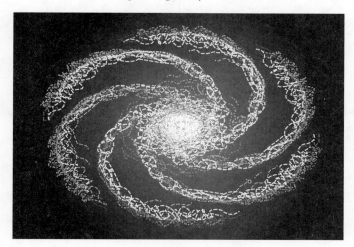

Describe the shape and composition of the Milky Way Galaxy.

_____

_____

_____

_____

_____

14 Summarize the process by which a low-mass star becomes a giant.

_____

_____

_____

_____

Connect **ESSENTIAL QUESTIONS**
Lessons 1, 2, and 3

Answer the following question in the space provided.

15 Study the diagram below.

Star

Planet

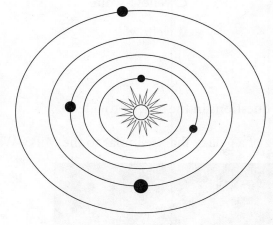

What are characteristics of planets and stars and what is their relationship within solar systems, galaxies, and the universe? Use the drawing as a reference.

_____

_____

_____

_____

_____

_____

_____

_____

The Solar System

A brass orrery shows the rotation of planets around the sun.

Big Idea

Planets and a variety of other bodies form a system of objects orbiting the sun.

What do you think?

For thousands of years, scientists have created models to help us understand the solar system. What are some different ways in which scientists have modeled the solar system?

The Human Orrery models the solar system.

45

Unit 2
The Solar System

Solar System Discoveries

Today's knowledge of the solar system is the result of discoveries that have been made over the centuries. Discoveries will continue to change our view of the solar system.

Moons of Jupiter, 1610
On January 7, 1610, Galileo used a telescope he had improved and discovered the four largest moons of Jupiter. The moons are some of the largest objects in our solar system!

Ganymede is the largest of Jupiter's moons.

William Herschel

Comet Hyakutake

Comet Hyakutake, 1996
Amateur astronomer Yuji Hyakutake discovered Comet Hyakutake on January 31, 1996, using a pair of powerful binoculars. This comet will approach Earth only once every 100,000 years.

Neptune, 1846
Mathematics helped scientists discover the planet Neptune. Astronomers predicted Neptune's existence based on irregularities in Uranus's orbit. On September 23, 1846, Neptune was discovered by telescope almost exactly where it was mathematically predicted to be.

Neptune

Uranus, 1781
British astronomer Sir William Herschel discovered Uranus on March 13, 1781. It was the first planet discovered with a telescope. Our knowledge of the solar system expanded in ways people had not expected.

Take It Home → Future Explorations
See **ScienceSaurus**® for more information about solar system objects.

(1) Think About It

What are some recent discoveries that have been made about the solar system?

_____

_____

_____

_____

B Will crewed missions to distant places in the solar system ever be possible? Justify your answer.

_____

_____

_____

_____

_____

(2) Ask Some Questions

Research efforts such as NASA's Stardust spacecraft to learn more about how space is being explored now.

A How is information being transmitted back to Earth?

_____

_____

(3) Make A Plan

Design a poster to explain why humans are exploring the solar system. Be sure to include the following information:

- How we are using technology for exploration
- Why it benefits all of us to learn about the solar system

Historical Models
of the Solar System

ESSENTIAL QUESTION

How have people modeled the solar system?

By the end of this lesson, you should be able to compare various historical models of the solar system.

The Earth-centered model of the solar system was accepted for almost 1,400 years. It was replaced by the sun-centered model of the solar system, which is shown in this 17th-century illustration.

Lesson Labs

Quick Labs
• The Geocentric Model of the Solar System
• The Heliocentric Model of the Solar System
• Orbital Ellipses

Field Lab
• Investigating Parallax

Engage Your Brain

1 Predict Check T or F to show whether you think each statement is true or false.

T	F	
☐	☐	The sun and planets circle Earth.
☐	☐	Most early astronomers placed the sun at the center of the solar system.
☐	☐	The planets orbit the sun in ellipses.
☐	☐	The telescope helped to improve our understanding of the solar system.

2 Evaluate What, if anything, is wrong with the model of the solar system shown below?

_____

_____

_____

Active Reading

3 Synthesis You can often define an unknown word if you know the meaning of its word parts. Use the word parts and sentence below to make an educated guess about the meaning of the word *heliocentric*.

Word part	Meaning
helio-	sun
-centric	centered

Example sentence
The <u>heliocentric</u> model of the solar system was first proposed by Aristarchus.

heliocentric:

_____

_____

_____

Vocabulary Terms

• solar system   • geocentric
• heliocentric   • parallax

4 Apply As you learn the definition of each vocabulary term in this lesson, create your own definition or sketch to help you remember the meaning of the term.

What is the solar system?

The **solar system** is the sun and all of the bodies that orbit the sun. Our current model of the solar system is the *sun-centered* or *heliocentric* (hee•lee•oh•SEN•trik) model. In the **heliocentric** model, Earth and the other planets orbit the sun. The earliest models for the solar system assumed that the Earth was at the center of the solar system, with the sun, moon, and planets circling it. These models, which used Earth as the center, are called *Earth-centered* or **geocentric** (jee•oh•SEN•trik) models. The heliocentric model was not generally accepted until the work of Copernicus and Kepler in the late 16th to early 17th centuries.

Active Reading

5 Identify As you read the text, underline the definitions of geocentric and heliocentric.

Who proposed some early models of the solar system?

Until Galileo improved on the telescope in 1609, people observed the heavens with the naked eye. To observers, it appeared that the sun, the moon, the planets, and the stars moved around Earth each day. This caused them to conclude that Earth was not moving. If Earth was not moving, then Earth must be the center of the solar system and all other bodies revolved around it.

This geocentric model of the solar system became part of ancient Greek thought beginning in the 6th century BCE. Aristotle was among the first thinkers to propose this model.

Think Outside the Book

6 Research Use different sources to research a geocentric model of the solar system from either ancient Greece, ancient China, or Babylon. Write a short description of the model you choose.

Aristotle (384–322 BCE)

Aristotle

Aristotle (AIR•ih•staht'l) was a Greek philosopher. Aristotle thought Earth was the center of all things. His model placed the moon, sun, planets, and stars on a series of circles that surrounded Earth. He thought that if Earth went around the sun, then the relative positions of the stars would change as Earth moves. This apparent shift in the position of an object when viewed from different locations is known as **parallax** (PAIR•uh•laks). In fact, the stars are so far away that parallax cannot be seen with the naked eye.

of the Solar System?

Aristarchus

Aristarchus (air•i•STAHR•kuhs) was a Greek astronomer and mathematician. Aristarchus is reported to have proposed a heliocentric model of the solar system. His model, however, was not widely accepted at the time. Aristarchus attempted to measure the relative distances to the moon and sun. This was a major contribution to science. Aristarchus's ratio of distances was much too small but was important in the use of observation and geometry to solve a scientific problem.

Aristarchus (about 310–230 BCE)

Aristotle thought that if Earth were moving, the positions of the stars should change as Earth moved. In fact, stars are so far away that shifts in their positions can only be observed by telescope.

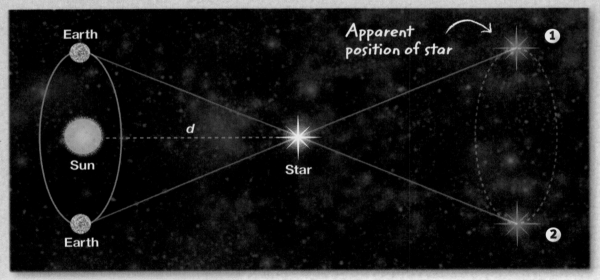

Diagram showing the shift in apparent position of a star at two different times of year seen from a telescope on Earth. A star first seen at point 1 will be seen at point 2 six months later.

 **Visualize It!**

7 Predict If a star appears at position 1 during the summer, during which season will it appear at position 2?

_____

_____

_____

Ptolemy (about 100–170 CE)

Ptolemy

Ptolemy (TOHL•uh•mee) was an astronomer, geographer, and mathematician who lived in Alexandria, Egypt, which was part of ancient Rome. His book, the *Almagest*, is one of the few books that we have from these early times. It was based on observations of the planets going back as much as 800 years. Ptolemy developed a detailed geocentric model that was used by astronomers for the next 14 centuries. He believed that a celestial body traveled at a constant speed in a perfect circle. In Ptolemy's model, the planets moved on small circles that in turn moved on larger circles. This "wheels-on-wheels" system fit observations better than any model that had come before. It allowed prediction of the motion of planets years into the future.

Visualize It!

8 Describe Use the diagram at the right to describe Ptolemy's geocentric model of the solar system.

_____

_____

_____

_____

_____

Think Outside the Book (Inquiry)

9 Defend As a class activity, defend Ptolemy's geocentric model of the solar system. Remember that during Ptolemy's time people were limited to what they could see with the naked eye.

Ptolemaic Model

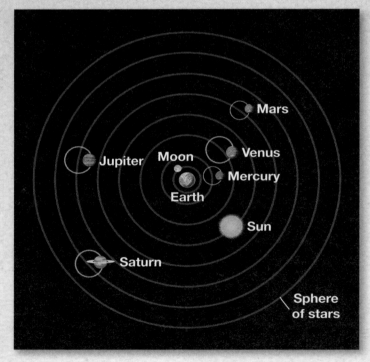

Mars

Jupiter   Moon   Venus

Mercury

Earth

Sun

Saturn

Sphere of stars

Copernicus

The Polish astronomer Nicolaus Copernicus (nik•uh•LAY•uhs koh•PER•nuh•kuhs) felt that Ptolemy's model of the solar system was too complicated. He was aware of the heliocentric idea of Aristarchus when he developed the first detailed heliocentric model of the solar system. In Copernicus's time, data was still based on observations with the naked eye. Because data had changed little since the time of Ptolemy, Copernicus adopted Ptolemy's idea that planetary paths should be perfect circles. Like Ptolemy, he used a "wheels-on-wheels" system. Copernicus's model fit observations a little better than the geocentric model of Ptolemy. The heliocentric model of Copernicus is generally seen as the first step in the development of modern models of the solar system.

Nicolaus Copernicus (1473—1543)

Copernican Model

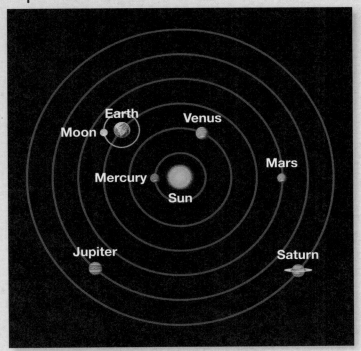

10 Compare How does Copernicus's model of the solar system differ from Ptolemy's model of the solar system?

Ptolemaic model	Copernican model

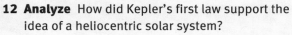
11 Identify Underline text that summarizes Kepler's three laws.

Kepler

Johannes Kepler (yoh•HAH•nuhs KEP•luhr) was a German mathematician and astronomer. After carefully analyzing observations of the planets, he realized that requiring planetary motions to be exactly circular did not fit the observations perfectly. Kepler then tried other types of paths and found that ellipses fit best.

Kepler formulated three principles, which today are known as Kepler's laws. The first law states that planetary orbits are ellipses with the sun at one focus. The second law states that planets move faster in their orbits when closer to the sun. The third law relates the distance of a planet from the sun to the time it takes to go once around its orbit.

Johannes Kepler (1571–1630)

12 Analyze How did Kepler's first law support the idea of a heliocentric solar system?

_____

_____

_____

_____

Kepler's First Law

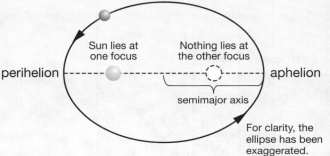

perihelion

Sun lies at one focus

Nothing lies at the other focus

semimajor axis

aphelion

For clarity, the ellipse has been exaggerated.

Galileo

Galileo Galilei (gahl•uh•LAY•oh gahl•uh•LAY) was a scientist who approached questions in the fashion that today we call *scientific methods*. Galileo made significant improvements to the newly invented telescope. He then used his more powerful telescope to view celestial objects. Galileo observed the moons Io, Europa, Callisto, and Ganymede orbiting Jupiter. Today, these moons are known as the Galilean satellites. His observations showed that Earth was not the only object that could be orbited. This gave support to the heliocentric model. He also observed that Venus went through phases similar to the phases of Earth's moon. These phases result from changes in the direction that sunlight strikes Venus as Venus orbits the sun.

Galileo Galilei (1564–1642)

Why It Matters

Galileo

Galileo Galilei was an Italian mathematician, physicist, and astronomer who lived during the 16th and 17th centuries. Galileo demonstrated that all bodies, regardless of their mass, fall at the same rate. He also argued that moving objects retain their velocity unless an unbalanced force acts upon them. Galileo made improvements to telescope technology. He used his telescopes to observe sunspots, the phases of Venus, Earth's moon, the four Galilean moons of Jupiter, and a supernova.

Galileo's Telescopes
This reconstruction of one of Galileo's telescopes is on exhibit in Florence, Italy. Galileo's first telescopes magnified objects at 3 and then 20 times.

The *Galileo* Spacecraft
The *Galileo* spacecraft was launched from the space shuttle *Atlantis* in 1989. *Galileo* was the first spacecraft to orbit Jupiter. It studied the planet and its moons.

Inquiry

Extend

13 Identify What were Galileo's most important contributions to astronomy?

14 Research Galileo invented or improved upon many instruments and technologies, such as the compound microscope, the thermometer, and the geometric compass. Research one of Galileo's technological contributions.

15 Create Describe one of Galileo's experiments concerning the motion of bodies by doing one of the following:

- make a poster
- recreate the experiment
- draw a graphic novel of Galileo conducting an experiment

Visual Summary

To complete this summary, fill in the blanks with the correct word or phrase. Then use the key below to check your answers. You can use this page to review the main concepts of the lesson.

Models of the Solar System

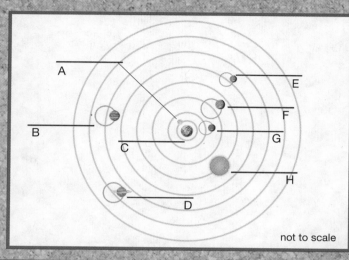

not to scale

Early astronomers proposed a geocentric solar system.

16 Label the solar system bodies as they appear in the geocentric model.

17 Which astronomers are associated with this model of the solar system?

_____

_____

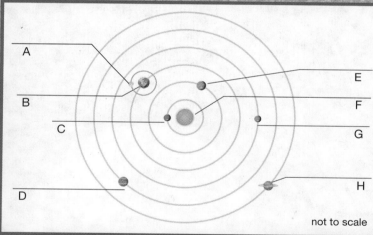

not to scale

The heliocentric solar system is the current model.

18 Label the solar system bodies as they appear in the heliocentric model.

19 Which astronomers are associated with this model of the solar system?

_____

_____

_____

_____

20 Compare How does the geocentric model of the solar system differ from the heliocentric model of the solar system?

Lesson Review

Vocabulary

Fill in the blank with the term that best completes the following sentences.

1 The _____ is the sun and all of the planets and other bodies that travel around it.

2 Until the time of Copernicus, most scientists thought the _____ model of the solar system was correct.

3 An apparent shift in the position of an object when viewed from different locations is called _____.

Key Concepts

In the following table, write the name of the correct astronomer next to that astronomer's contribution.

Contribution	Astronomer
4 Identify Who first observed the phases of Venus?	
5 Identify Who attempted to measure the relative distances to the moon and the sun?	
6 Identify Who replaced circles with ellipses in a heliocentric model of the universe?	
7 Identify Whose geocentric model of the solar system was accepted for 1,400 years?	
8 Identify Whose heliocentric model is seen as the first step in the development of modern models of the solar system?	

Critical Thinking

Use the illustration to answer the following question.

9 Appraise How did data gathered using Galileo's early telescope support the heliocentric model?

_____

_____

_____

_____

10 Explain How did Aristotle's inability to detect parallax lead him to propose a geocentric model of the solar system?

_____

_____

_____

_____

_____

_____

My Notes

Mean, Median, Mode, and Range

You can analyze both the measures of central tendency and the variability of data using mean, median, mode, and range.

Tutorial

Orbit eccentricity measures how oval-shaped the elliptical orbit is. The closer a value is to 0, the closer the orbit is to a circle. Examine the eccentricity values below.

Orbit Eccentricities of Planets in the Solar System			
Mercury	0.205	Jupiter	0.049
Venus	0.007	Saturn	0.057
Earth	0.017	Uranus	0.046
Mars	0.094	Neptune	0.011

Mean The mean is the sum of all of the values in a data set divided by the total number of values in the data set. The mean is also called the *average*.	$$\frac{0.007 + 0.011 + 0.017 + 0.046 + 0.049 + 0.057 + 0.094 + 0.205}{8}$$ **1** Add up all of the values. **2** Divide the sum by the number of values. **mean = 0.061**
Median The median is the value of the middle item when data are arranged in numerical order. If there is an odd number of values, the median is the middle value. If there is an even number of values, the median is the mean of the two middle values.	0.007 0.011 0.017 0.046 0.049 0.057 0.094 0.205 **1** Order the values. **2** The median is the middle value if there is an odd number of values. If there is an even number of values, calculate the mean of the two middle values. **median = 0.0475**
Mode The mode is the value or values that occur most frequently in a data set. Order the values to find the mode. If all values occur with the same frequency, the data set is said to have no mode.	0.007 0.011 0.017 0.046 0.049 0.057 0.094 0.205 **1** Order the values. **2** Find the value or values that occur most frequently. **mode = none**
Range The range is the difference between the greatest value and the least value of a data set.	0.205 − 0.007 **1** Subtract the least value from the greatest value. **range = 0.198**

You Try It!

The data table below shows the masses and densities of the planets.

Mass and Density of the Planets		
	Mass (× 10²⁴ kg)	Density (g/cm³)
Mercury	0.33	5.43
Venus	4.87	5.24
Earth	5.97	5.52
Mars	0.64	3.34
Jupiter	1,899	1.33
Saturn	568	0.69
Uranus	87	1.27
Neptune	102	1.64

Using Formulas Find the mean, median, mode, and range for the density of the planets.

Using Formulas Find the mean, median, mode, and range for the mass of the planets.

③

Analyzing Data Find the mean density of the inner planets (Mercury through Mars). Find the mean density of the outer planets (Jupiter through Neptune). Compare these values.

Mean density of the inner planets: _____

Mean density of the outer planets: _____

Comparison:

_____

④

Evaluating Data The mean mass of the outer planets is 225 times greater than the mean mass of the inner planets. How does this comparison and the comparison of mean densities support the use of the term *gas giants* to describe the outer planets? Explain your reasoning.

_____

_____

Gravity and the Solar System

ESSENTIAL QUESTION

Why is gravity important in the solar system?

By the end of this lesson, you should be able to explain the role that gravity played in the formation of the solar system and in determining the motion of the planets.

Gravity keeps objects, such as these satellites, in orbit around Earth. Gravity also affects the way in which planets move and how they are formed.

Lesson Labs

Quick Labs
• Gravity's Effect
• Gravity and the Orbit of a Planet

Exploration Lab
• Weights on Different Celestial Bodies

Engage Your Brain

1 Predict Check T or F to show whether you think each statement is true or false.

T	F	
☐	☐	Gravity keeps the planets in orbit around the sun.
☐	☐	The planets follow circular paths around the sun.
☐	☐	Sir Isaac Newton was the first scientist to describe how the force of gravity behaved.
☐	☐	The sun formed in the center of the solar system.
☐	☐	The terrestrial planets and the gas giant planets formed from the same material.

2 Draw In the space below, draw what you think the solar system looked like before the planets formed.

Active Reading

3 Synthesize You can often define an unknown word if you know the meaning of its word parts. Use the word parts and sentence below to make an educated guess about the meaning of the word *protostellar*.

Word part	Meaning
proto-	first
-stellar	of or having to do with a star or stars

Example sentence
The <u>protostellar</u> disk formed after the collapse of the solar nebula.

protostellar:

_____

_____

Vocabulary Terms

• gravity
• orbit
• aphelion
• perihelion
• centripetal force
• solar nebula
• planetesimal

4 Apply This list contains the key terms you'll learn in this section. As you read, circle the definition of each term.

Gravity

What is gravity?

Active Reading **5 Identify** Underline the definition of and the effects of gravity.

Gravity is a force of attraction between objects that is due to their masses and the distances between them. Every object in the universe pulls on every other object. Objects with greater masses have a greater force of attraction than objects with lesser masses have. Objects that are close together have a greater force of attraction than objects that are far apart have.

Gravity is the weakest force in nature. A toy magnet can overcome the gravitational force acting on a paperclip by the entire mass of Earth. Yet, gravity is one of the most important forces in the universe. It accounts for the formation of planets, stars, and galaxies. It also keeps smaller bodies in orbit around larger bodies. An **orbit** is the path that a body follows as it travels around another body in space. For example, the moon orbits Earth, and Earth orbits the sun.

When astronauts are in orbit, Earth's gravity still pulls them downward toward the planet. However, they appear to be weightless and floating. They "float" because everything around them is falling at the same speed.

What are Kepler's laws?

The 16th-century Polish astronomer Nicolaus Copernicus (nik•uh•LAY•uhs koh•PER•nuh•kuhs) (1473–1543) changed our view of the solar system. He discovered that the motions of the planets could be best explained if the planets orbited the sun. But, like astronomers who came before him, Copernicus thought the planets followed circular paths around the sun.

Danish astronomer Tycho Brahe (TY•koh BRAH) (1546–1601) built what was at the time the world's largest observatory. Tycho used special instruments to measure the motions of the planets. His measurements were made over a period of 20 years and were very accurate. Using Tycho's data, Johannes Kepler (yoh•HAH•nuhs KEP•luhr) (1571–1630) made discoveries about the motions of the planets. We call these *Kepler's laws of planetary motion*.

Kepler found that objects that orbit the sun follow elliptical orbits. When an object follows an elliptical orbit around the sun, there is one point, called **aphelion** (uh•FEE•lee•uhn), where the object is farthest from the sun. There is also a point, called **perihelion** (perh•uh•HEE•lee•uhn), where the object is closest to the sun. Today, we know that the orbits of the planets are only slightly elliptical. However, the orbits of objects such as Pluto and comets are highly elliptical.

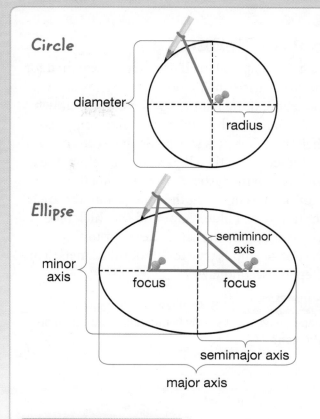

Circle

Ellipse

6 Compare How is a circle different from an ellipse?

_____

_____

_____

_____

Kepler's First Law

Kepler's careful plotting of the orbit of Mars kept showing Mars's orbit to be a deformed circle. It took Kepler eight years to realize that this shape was an ellipse. This clue led Kepler to propose elliptical orbits for the planets. Kepler placed the sun at one of the foci of the ellipse. This is Kepler's first law.

Active Reading **7 Contrast** What is the difference between Copernicus's and Kepler's description of planetary orbits?

_____

_____

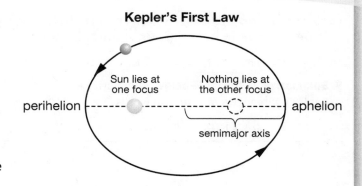

Kepler's First Law

Sun lies at one focus

Nothing lies at the other focus

perihelion

aphelion

semimajor axis

Each planet orbits the sun in an ellipse with the sun at one focus. (For clarity, the ellipse is exaggerated here.)

Kepler's Second Law

Using the shape of an ellipse, Kepler searched for other regularities in Tycho's data. He found that an amazing thing happens when a line is drawn from a planet to the sun's focus on the ellipse. At aphelion, its speed is slower. So, it sweeps out a narrow sector on the ellipse. At perihelion, the planet is moving faster. It sweeps out a thick sector on the ellipse. In the illustration, the areas of both the thin blue sector and the thick blue sector are exactly the same. Kepler found that this relationship is true for all of the planets. This is Kepler's second law.

Active Reading **8 Analyze** At which point does a planet move most slowly in its orbit, at aphelion or perihelion?

As a planet moves around its orbit, it sweeps out equal areas in equal times.

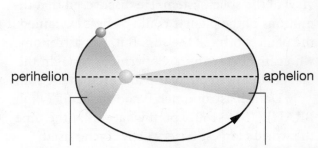

Kepler's Second Law

Near perihelion, a planet sweeps out an area that is short but wide.

Near aphelion, in an equal amount of time, a planet sweeps out an area that is long but narrow.

Kepler's Third Law

When Kepler looked at how long it took for the planets to orbit the sun and at the sizes of their orbits, he found another relationship. Kepler calculated the orbital period and the distance from the sun for the planets using Tycho's data. He discovered that the square of the orbital period was proportional to the cube of the planet's average distance from the sun. This law is true for each planet. This principle is Kepler's third law. When the units are years for the period and AU for the distance, the law can be written:

(orbital period in years)² = (average distance from the sun in astronomical units [AU])³

The square of the orbital period is proportional to the cube of the planet's average distance from the sun.

Kepler's Third Law
$$p^2 \text{ yrs} = a^3 \text{ AU}$$

perihelion ← - - - a - - - → aphelion

9 Summarize In the table below, summarize each of Kepler's three laws in your own words.

First law	Second law	Third law

What is the law of universal gravitation?

Using Kepler's laws, Sir Isaac Newton (EYE•zuhk NOOT'n) became the first scientist to mathematically describe how the force of gravity behaved. How could Newton do this in the 1600s before the force could be measured in a laboratory? He reasoned that gravity was the same force that accounted for both the fall of an apple from a tree and the movement of the moon around Earth.

In 1687, Newton formulated the *law of universal gravitation*. The law of universal gravitation states that all objects in the universe attract each other through gravitational force. The strength of this force depends on the product of the masses of the objects. Therefore, the gravity between objects increases as the masses of the objects increase. Gravitational force is also inversely proportional to the square of the distance between the objects. Stated another way this means that as the distance between two objects increases, the force of gravity decreases.

Sir Isaac Newton
(1642–1727)

Do the Math

Newton's law of universal gravitation says that the force of gravity:
- increases as the masses of the objects increase and
- decreases as the distance between the objects increases

In these examples, M = mass, d = distance, and F = the force of gravity exerted by two bodies.

Sample Problems

A. In the example below, when two balls have masses of M and the distance between them is d, then the force of gravity is F. If the mass of each ball is increased to 2M (to the right) and the distance stays the same, then the force of gravity increases to 4F.

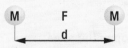

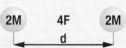

B. In this example, we start out again with a distance of d and masses of M, and the force of gravity is F. If the distance is decreased to ½ d, then the force of gravity increases to 4F.

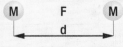

You Try It

Recall that M = mass, d = distance, and F = the force of gravity exerted by two bodies.

10 Calculate Compare the example below to the sample problems. What would the force of gravity be in the example below? Explain your answer.

2M ————— 2d ————— 2M

_____

_____

_____

_____

_____

How does gravity affect planetary motion?

The illustrations on this page will help you understand planetary motion. In the illustration at the right, a girl is swinging a ball around her head. The ball is attached to a string. The girl is exerting a force on the string that causes the ball to move in a circular path. The inward force that causes an object to move in a circular path is called **centripetal** (sehn•TRIP•ih•tuhl) **force**.

In the illustration at center, we see that if the string breaks, the ball will move off in a straight line. This fact indicates that when the string is intact, a force is pulling the ball inward. This force keeps the ball from flying off and moving in a straight line. This force is centripetal force.

In the illustration below, you see that the planets orbit the sun. A force must be preventing the planets from moving out of their orbits and into a straight line. The sun's gravity is the force that keeps the planets moving in orbit around the sun.

As the girl swings the ball, she is exerting a force on the string that causes the ball to move in a circular path.

Centripetal force pulls the ball inward, which causes the ball to move in a curved path.

direction centripetal force pulls the ball

direction ball would move if string broke

Center of rotation

String

path ball takes when moving around the center of rotation

Just as the string is pulling the ball inward, gravity is keeping the planets in orbit around the sun.

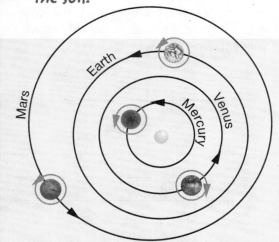

Mars

Earth

Venus

Mercury

11 Explain In the illustration at the top of the page, what does the hand represent, the ball represent, and the string represent? (Hint: Think of the sun, a planet, and the force of gravity.)

_____

_____

_____

_____

Collapse

How did the solar system form?

The formation of the solar system is thought to have begun 4.6 billion years ago when a cloud of dust and gas collapsed. This cloud, from which the solar system formed, is called the **solar nebula** (SOH•ler NEB•yuh•luh). In a nebula, the inward pull of gravity is balanced by the outward push of gas pressure in the cloud. Scientists think that an outside force, perhaps the explosion of a nearby star, caused the solar nebula to compress and then to contract under its own gravity. It was in a single region of the nebula, which was perhaps several light-years across, that the solar system formed. The sun probably formed from a region that had a mass that was slightly greater than today's mass of the sun and planets.

Active Reading 12 **Define** What is the solar nebula?

_____

_____

A cloud of dust and gas collapsed 4.6 billion years ago, then began to spin. It may have spun around its axis of rotation once every million years.

A Protostellar Disk Formed from the Collapsed Solar Nebula

As a region of the solar nebula collapsed, gravity pulled most of the mass toward the center of the nebula. As the nebula contracted, it began to rotate. As the rotation grew faster, the nebula flattened out into a disk. This disk, which is called a *protostellar disk* (PROH•toh•stehl•er DISK), is where the central star, our sun, formed.

As a region of the solar nebula collapsed, it formed a slowly rotating protostellar disk.

The Sun Formed at the Center of the Protostellar Disk

As the protostellar disk continued to contract, most of the matter ended up in the center of the disk. Friction from matter that fell into the disk heated up its center to millions of degrees, eventually reaching its current temperature of 15,000,000 °C. This intense heat in a densely packed space caused the fusion of hydrogen atoms into helium atoms. The process of fusion released large amounts of energy. This release of energy caused outward pressure that again balanced the inward pull of gravity. As the gas and dust stopped collapsing, a star was born. In the case of the solar system, this star was the sun.

Active Reading **13 Identify** How did the sun form?

_____
_____
_____
_____
_____

This is an artist's conception of what the protoplanetary disk in which the planets formed might have looked like.

 Visualize It!

14 Describe Use the terms *planetesimal* and *protoplanetary disk* to describe the illustration above.

_____
_____
_____
_____
_____
_____

Planetesimals Formed in the Protoplanetary Disk

As the sun was forming, dust grains collided and stuck together. The resulting *dust granules* grew in size and increased in number. Over time, dust granules increased in size until they became roughly meter-sized bodies. Trillions of these bodies occurred in the protostellar disk. Collisions between these bodies formed larger bodies that were kilometers across. These larger bodies, from which planets formed, are called **planetesimals** (plan•ih•TES•ih•muhls). The protostellar disk had become the *protoplanetary disk*. The protoplanetary disk was the disk in which the planets formed.

Dust grains collided and stuck together.

Over time, dust granules grew to become meter-sized bodies.

Planetesimals formed from the collisions of meter-sized bodies.

Visualize It! Inquiry

15 Explain How can objects as small as dust grains become the building blocks of planets?

_____

_____

_____

_____

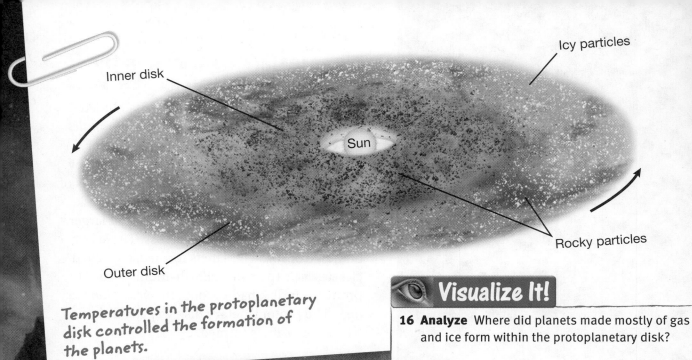

Inner disk

Icy particles

Sun

Outer disk

Rocky particles

Temperatures in the protoplanetary disk controlled the formation of the planets.

Visualize It!

16 Analyze Where did planets made mostly of gas and ice form within the protoplanetary disk?

_____

_____

_____

Terrestrial planets formed when rocky planetesimals collided.

The Planets Formed from Planetesimals

The inner part of the protoplanetary disk was so hot that only rocks and metals were in solid form. Therefore, rocky, metallic planets formed in the inner disk. These planets formed from the collisions and mergers of rocky planetesimals. We call these inner planets the *terrestrial planets*.

In the cold outer disk, ices, gases, rocks, and metals were all found. At first, massive planets made of icy and rocky planetesimals may have formed. The gravity of these planets was so strong that they captured gas and other matter as they grew. Therefore, planets that formed in the outer disk have rocky or metallic cores and deep atmospheres of gas and ice. We call these outer planets the *gas giant planets*.

Gas giant planets captured gas and other matter in the area of their orbits.

Visualize It!

17 Describe In the spaces on the left, describe Steps 2 and 4 in the formation of the solar system. In the spaces on the right, draw the last two steps in the formation of the solar system.

Steps in the Formation of the Solar System

Step 1 The Solar Nebula Collapses

A cloud of dust and gas collapses. The balance between the inward pull of gravity and the outward push of pressure in the cloud is upset. The collapsing cloud forms a rotating protostellar disk.

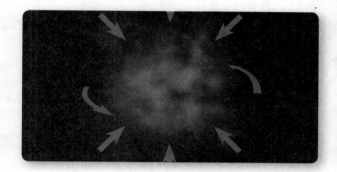

Step 2 The Sun Forms

_____
_____
_____
_____
_____

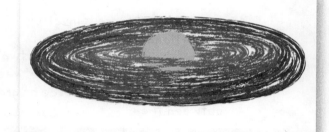

Step 3 Planetesimals Form

Dust grains stick together and form dust granules. Dust granules slowly increase in size until they become meter-sized objects. These meter-sized objects collide to form kilometer-sized objects called *planetesimals*.

Step 4 Planets Form

_____
_____
_____
_____
_____

Visual Summary

To complete this summary, fill in the blank with the correct word or phrase. Then use the key below to check your answers. You can use this page to review the main concepts of the lesson.

The Law of Universal Gravitation

Mass affects the force of gravity.

18 The strength of the force of gravity depends on the product of the _____ of two objects. Therefore, as the masses of two objects increase, the force that the objects exert on one another _____.

Distance affects the force of gravity.

19 Gravitational force is inversely proportional to the square of the _____ between two objects. Therefore, as the distance between two objects increases, the force of gravity between them _____.

Gravity affects planetary motion.

20 The sun exerts a _____, indicated by line B, on a planet so that at point C it is moving around the sun in orbit instead of moving off in a _____ as shown at line A.

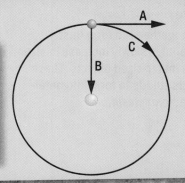

Answers: **18** masses, increases; **19** distance, decreases; **20** gravitational force or centripetal force, straight line

21 Explain In your own words, explain Newton's law of universal gravitation.

Lesson Review

Vocabulary

Fill in the blank with the term that best completes the following sentences.

1 Small bodies from which the planets formed are called _____

2 The path that a body follows as it travels around another body in space is its _____

3 The _____ is the cloud of gas and dust from which our solar system formed.

Key Concepts

4 Define In your own words, define the word *gravity*.

_____

_____

5 Describe How did the sun form?

_____

_____

_____

_____

_____

_____

_____

6 Describe How did planetesimals form?

_____

_____

_____

_____

_____

_____

Critical Thinking

Use the illustration below to answer the following question.

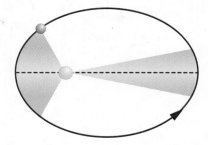

7 Identify What law is illustrated in this diagram?

_____

8 Analyze How does gravity keep the planets in orbit around the sun?

_____

_____

_____

_____

_____

_____

9 Explain How do temperature differences in the protoplanetary disk explain the arrangement of the planets in the solar system?

_____

_____

_____

_____

_____

_____

_____

_____

My Notes

The Sun

ESSENTIAL QUESTION

What are the properties of the sun?

By the end of this lesson, you should be able to describe the structure and rotation of the sun, energy production and energy transport in the sun, and solar activity on the sun.

prominence

Different types of activity occur on the sun's surface. This loop of gas that extends outward from the sun's surface is a prominence.

Engage Your Brain

1 Predict Check T or F to show whether you think each statement is true or false.

T	F	
☐	☐	The sun is composed mostly of hydrogen and helium.
☐	☐	Energy is produced in the sun's core.
☐	☐	The process by which energy is produced in the sun is known as *nuclear fission*.
☐	☐	Energy is transferred to the surface of the sun by the processes of radiation and conduction.
☐	☐	A dark area of the sun's surface that is cooler than the surrounding areas is called a *sunspot*.

2 Explain In your own words, explain the meaning of the word *sunlight*.

_____
_____
_____
_____
_____
_____
_____
_____
_____

Active Reading

3 Synthesize You can often define an unknown word if you know the meaning of its word parts. Use the word parts and sentence below to make an educated guess about the meaning of the word *photosphere*.

Word Part	Meaning
photo-	light
-sphere	ball

Example sentence
Energy is transferred to the sun's photosphere by convection cells.

photosphere:

_____
_____
_____

Vocabulary Terms

• nuclear fusion
• sunspot
• solar flare
• prominence

4 Apply This list contains the key terms you'll learn in this section. As you read, circle the definition of each term.

Here Comes the Sun

What do we know about the sun?

Since early in human history, people have marveled at the sun. Civilizations have referred to the sun by different names. Gods and goddesses who represented the sun were worshipped in different cultures. In addition, early astronomical observatories were established to track the sun's motion across the sky.

By the mid-19th century, astronomers had discovered that the sun was actually a hot ball of gas that is composed mostly of the elements hydrogen and helium. Scientists now know that the sun was born about 4.6 billion years ago. Every second, 4 million tons of solar matter is converted into energy. Of the light emitted from the sun, 41% is visible light, another 9% is ultraviolet light, and 50% is infrared radiation. And, perhaps most important of all, without the sun, there would be no life on Earth.

Active Reading

5 Identify As you read the text, underline different discoveries that scientists have made about the sun.

Sun Statistics

Avg. dist. from Earth	149.6 million km
Diameter	1,390,000 km
Average density	1.41 g/cm^3
Period of rotation	25 days (equator); 35 days (poles)
Avg. surface temp.	5,527 °C
Core temp.	15,000,000 °C
Composition	74% hydrogen, 25% helium, 1% other elements

Do the Math You Try It

6 Calculate The diameter of Earth is 12,756 km. How many times greater is the sun's diameter than the diameter of Earth?

_____

_____

_____

A solar flare, which is shown in this image, is a sudden explosive release of energy in the sun's atmosphere.

What is the structure of the sun?

The composition of the sun and Earth are different. However, the two bodies are similar in structure. Both are spheres. And both have a layered atmosphere and an interior composed of layers.

In the middle of the sun is the core. This is where energy is produced. From the core, energy is transported to the sun's surface through the radiative zone and the convective zone.

The sun's atmosphere has three layers—the photosphere, the chromosphere, and the corona. The sun's surface is the photosphere. Energy escapes the sun from this layer. The chromosphere is the middle layer of the sun's atmosphere. The temperature of the chromosphere rises with distance from the photosphere. The sun's outer atmosphere is the corona. The corona extends millions of kilometers into space.

7 Analyze Why is the structure of the sun different from the structure of Earth?

_____
_____
_____
_____
_____
_____

Corona The corona is the outer atmosphere of the sun. Temperatures in the corona may reach 2,000,000 °C.

Chromosphere The chromosphere is the middle layer of the sun's atmosphere. Temperatures in the chromosphere increase outward and reach a maximum of about 6,000 °C.

Photosphere The photosphere is the visible surface of the sun. It is the layer from which energy escapes into space. The photosphere has an average temperature of 5,527 °C.

Convective Zone The convective zone is the layer of the sun through which energy travels by convection from the radiative zone to the photosphere.

Radiative Zone The radiative zone is the layer of the sun through which energy is transferred away from the core by radiation.

Core The core is the very dense center of the sun. The core has a temperature of 15,000,000 °C, which is hot enough to cause the nuclear reactions that produce energy in the sun.

Let's Get Together

How does the sun produce energy?

Early in the 20th century, physicist Albert Einstein proposed that matter and energy are interchangeable. Matter can change into energy according to his famous equation $E = mc^2$. E is energy, m is mass, and c is the speed of light. Because c is such a large number, tiny amounts of matter can produce huge amounts of energy. Using Einstein's formula, scientists were able to explain the huge quantities of energy produced by the sun.

By Nuclear Fusion

Scientists know that the sun generates energy through the process of *nuclear fusion*. **Nuclear fusion** is the process by which two or more low-mass atomic nuclei fuse to form another, heavier nucleus. Nuclear fusion takes place in the core of stars. In stars that have core temperatures similar to the sun's, the fusion process that fuels the star starts with the fusion of two hydrogen nuclei. In older stars in which core temperatures are hotter than the sun's, the fusion process involves the fusion of helium into carbon.

Think Outside the Book

8 Discussion Einstein's equation $E = mc^2$ is probably the most famous equation in the world. With your classmates, discuss the kinds of technologies that rely on the conversion of matter to energy.

 **Visualize It!**

9 Identify Fill in the circles to label the particles in the diagrams.

P	Proton
N	Neutron

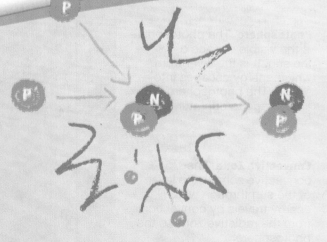

Three Steps of Nuclear Fusion in the Sun

Step 1: Deuterium Two hydrogen nuclei (protons) collide. One proton emits particles and energy and then becomes a neutron. The proton and neutron combine to produce a heavy form of hydrogen called *deuterium*.

© Houghton Mifflin Harcourt Publishing Company • Image Credits: ©Bettmann/Corbis

By the Fusion of Hydrogen into Helium

The most common elements in the sun are hydrogen and helium. Under the crushing force of gravity, these gases are compressed and heated in the sun's core, where temperatures reach 15,000,000 °C. In the sun's core, hydrogen nuclei sometimes fuse to form a helium nucleus. This process takes three steps to complete. This three-step process is illustrated below.

Most of the time, when protons are on a collision course with other protons, their positive charges instantly repel them. The protons do not collide. But sometimes one proton will encounter another proton and, at that exact moment, turn into a neutron and eject an electron. This collision forms a nucleus that contains one proton and one neutron. This nucleus is an isotope of hydrogen called *deuterium*. The deuterium nucleus collides with another proton and forms a variety of helium called *helium-3*. Then, two helium-3 nuclei collide and form a helium-4 nucleus that has two protons and two neutrons. The remaining two protons are released back into the sun's core.

The entire chain of fusion reactions requires six hydrogen nuclei and results in one helium nucleus and two hydrogen nuclei. There are approximately 10^{38} collisions between hydrogen nuclei taking place in the sun's core every second, which keeps the sun shining.

Active Reading

10 Identify As you read the text, underline the steps in the nuclear fusion process in the sun.

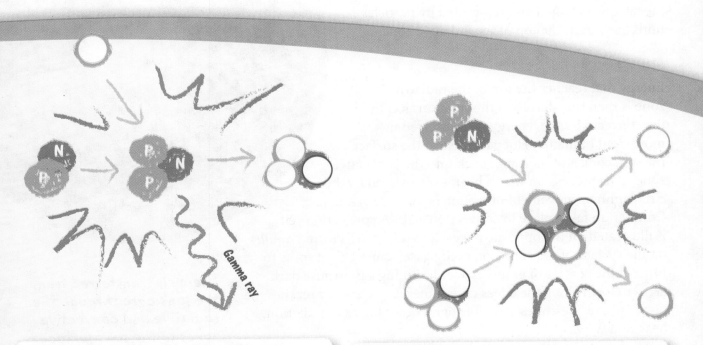

Step 2: Helium-3 Deuterium combines with another hydrogen nucleus to form a variety of helium called **helium-3**. More energy, including gamma rays, is released.

Step 3: Helium-4 Two helium-3 nuclei combine to form helium-4, which releases more energy and a pair of hydrogen nuclei (protons).

Mixing It Up

How is energy transferred to the sun's surface?

Energy is transferred to the surface of the sun by two different processes. Energy that is transferred from the sun's core through the radiative zone is transferred by the process of radiation. Energy that is transferred from the top of the radiative zone through the convective zone to the photosphere is transferred by the process of convection. Energy flow from the sun's core outward to the sun's surface by radiation and convection happens continuously.

By Radiation

When energy leaves the sun's core, it moves into the radiative zone. Energy travels through the radiative zone in the form of electromagnetic waves. The process by which energy is transferred as electromagnetic waves is called *radiation*. The radiative zone is densely packed with particles such as hydrogen, helium, and free electrons. Therefore, electromagnetic waves cannot travel directly through the radiative zone. Instead, they are repeatedly absorbed and re-emitted by particles until they reach the top of the radiative zone.

By Convection

Energy that reaches the top of the radiative zone is then transferred to the sun's surface. In the convective zone, energy is transferred by the movement of matter. Hot gases rise to the surface of the sun, cool, and then sink back into the convective zone. This process, in which heat is transferred by the circulation or movement of matter, is called *convection*. Convection takes place in convection cells. A convection cell is illustrated on the opposite page. Convection cells form *granules* on the surface of the sun. Hot, rising gases cause bright spots to form in the centers of granules. Cold, sinking gases cause dark areas to form along the edges of granules. Once energy reaches the photosphere, it escapes as visible light, other forms of radiation, heat, and wind.

Energy is transferred from the sun's core through the radiative and convective zones to the sun's surface.

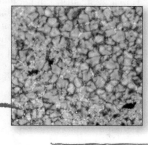

The tops of convection cells form granules on the sun's surface.

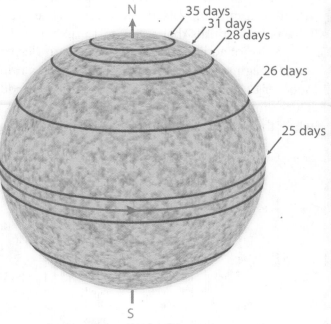

Hot, rising gases and colder, sinking gases form convection cells in the convective zone.

11 Compare How is energy transferred from the sun's core to the sun's surface in the radiative zone and in the convective zone?

Radiative zone	Convective zone

The sun's period of rotation varies with latitude.

35 days
31 days
28 days
26 days
25 days

N

S

How does the sun rotate?

The sun rotates on its axis like other large bodies in the solar system. However, because the sun is a giant ball of gas, it does not rotate in the same way as a solid body like Earth does. Instead, the sun rotates faster at its equator than it does at higher latitudes. This kind of rotation is known as differential rotation. *Differential rotation* is the rotation of a body in which different parts of a body have different periods of rotation. Near the equator, the sun rotates once in about 25 days. However, at the poles, the sun rotates once in about 35 days.

Even stranger is the fact that the sun's interior does not rotate in the same way as the sun's surface does. Scientists think that the sun's core and radiative zone rotate together, at the same speed. Therefore, the sun's radiative zone and core rotate like Earth.

12 Define In your own words, define the term *differential rotation*.

_____

_____

_____

_____

© Houghton Mifflin Harcourt Publishing Company • Image Credits: ©National Optical Astronomy Observatories/SPL/Photo Researchers, Inc.

The Ring of Fire

What is solar activity?

Solar activity refers to variations in the appearance or energy output of the sun. Solar activity includes dark areas that occur on the sun's surface known as *sunspots*. Solar activity also includes sudden explosive events on the sun's surface, which are called *solar flares*. Prominences are another form of solar activity. *Prominences* are vast loops of gases that extend into the sun's outer atmosphere.

Sunspots

Dark areas that form on the surface of the sun are called **sunspots**. They are about 1,500 °C cooler than the areas that surround them. Sunspots are places where hot, convecting gases are prevented from reaching the sun's surface.

Sunspots can appear for periods of a few hours or a few months. Some sunspots are only a few hundred kilometers across. Others have widths that are 10 to 15 times the diameter of Earth.

Sunspot activity occurs on average in 11-year cycles. When a cycle begins, the number of sunspots is at a minimum. The number of sunspots then increases until it reaches a maximum. The number then begins to decrease. A new sunspot cycle begins when the sunspot number reaches a minimum again.

Sunspots, solar flares, and prominences are three kinds of solar activity that occur on the sun's surface.

sunspot

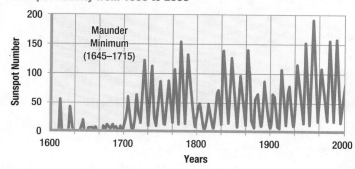

Sunspot Activity from 1600 to 2000

Maunder Minimum (1645–1715)

(graph: Sunspot Number from 0 to 200 on vertical axis; Years from 1600 to 2000 on horizontal axis)

Do the Math You Try It

13 Analyze The sunspot range is the difference between the maximum number of sunspots and the minimum number of sunspots for a certain period of time. To find this range, subtract the minimum number of sunspots from the maximum number of sunspots. What is the range of sunspot activity between 1700 and 1800?

_____

_____

_____

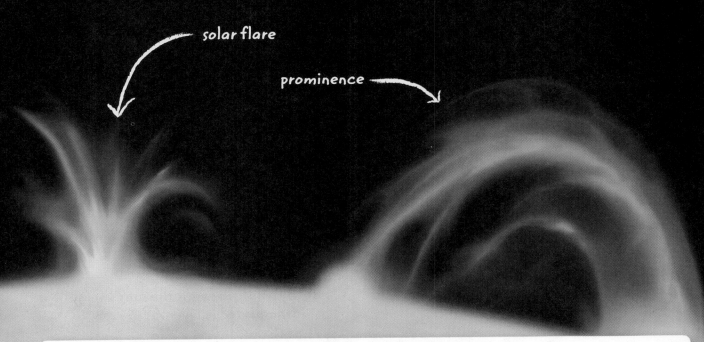

solar flare

prominence

Solar Flares

Solar flares appear as very bright spots on the sun's photosphere. A **solar flare** is an explosive release of energy that can extend outward as far as the sun's outer atmosphere. During a solar flare, enormous numbers of high-energy particles are ejected at near the speed of light. Radiation is released across the entire electromagnetic spectrum, from radio waves to x-rays and gamma rays. Temperatures within solar flares reach millions of degrees Celsius.

Prominences

Huge loops of relatively cool gas that extend outward from the photosphere thousands of kilometers into the outer atmosphere are called **prominences**. Several objects the size of Earth could fit inside a loop of a prominence. The gases in prominences are cooler than the surrounding atmosphere.

Prominences generally last from several hours to a day. However, some prominences can last for as long as several months.

14 Compare Use the Venn diagram below to compare solar flares and prominences.

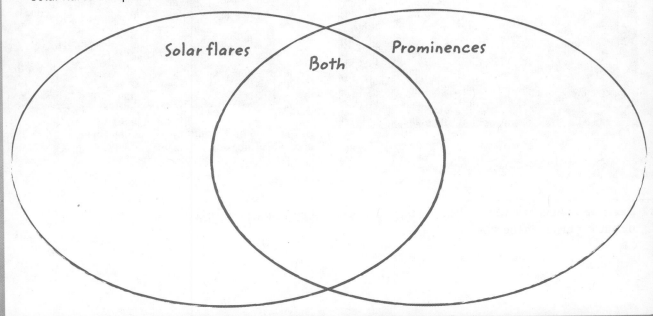

Solar flares   Both   Prominences

Visual Summary

To complete this summary, fill in the blanks with the correct word or phrase. Then use the key below to check your answers. You can use this page to review the main concepts of the lesson.

Properties of the Sun

The sun is composed of layers.

15 Identify the six layers of the sun, beginning with the innermost layer.

_____

_____

_____

_____

Energy is transferred from the sun's core to the photosphere.

16 By what process is the sun's energy transported in layer A?

_____

By what process is the sun's energy transported in layer B?

_____

Answers: 15 the core, the radiative zone, the convective zone, the photosphere, the chromosphere, and the corona; 16 Layer A: radiation, Layer B: convection

17 **Describe** In your own words, describe the process of energy production by nuclear fusion in the sun.

_____

_____

Lesson Review

Vocabulary

Fill in the blank with the term that best completes the following sentences.

1 The process by which two or more low-mass atomic nuclei fuse to form another, heavier nucleus is called _____.

2 A _____ is a dark area on the surface of the sun that is cooler than the surrounding areas.

3 A _____ is a loop of relatively cool gas that extends above the photosphere.

Key Concepts

In the following table, write the name of the correct layer next to the definition.

Definition	Layer
4 Identify What is the layer of the sun from which energy escapes into space?	
5 Identify What is the layer of the sun in which energy is produced?	
6 Identify What is the layer of the sun through which energy is transferred away from the core by radiation?	

7 Identify What is the composition of the sun?

_____

_____

8 Explain What is the sunspot cycle?

_____

_____

_____

Critical Thinking

Use the illustration to answer the following questions.

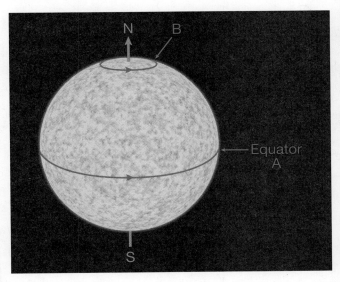

9 Determine How many days does it take for the sun to spin once on its axis at location A? How many days does it take for the sun to spin once on its axis at location B?

_____

_____

10 Compare How is the rotation of the sun different from the rotation of Earth?

_____

_____

_____

11 Explain In your own words, explain how energy is transported from the core to the surface of the sun by radiation and by convection.

_____

_____

_____

_____

_____

My Notes

The Terrestrial Planets

ESSENTIAL QUESTION

What is known about the terrestrial planets?

By the end of this lesson, you should be able to describe some of the properties of the terrestrial planets and how the properties of Mercury, Venus, and Mars differ from the properties of Earth.

Mars

Earth

Venus

Mercury

The terrestrial planets are the four planets that are closest to the sun. Distances between the planets shown here are not to scale.

sun

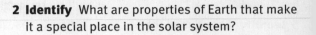
🧠 Engage Your Brain

1 Define Circle the term that best completes the following sentences.

Venus/Earth/Mars is the largest terrestrial planet.

Mercury/Venus/Mars has clouds that rain sulfuric acid on the planet.

Huge dust storms sweep across the surface of *Mercury/Venus/Mars*.

Venus/Earth/Mars is the most geologically active of the terrestrial planets.

Mercury/Venus/Earth has the thinnest atmosphere of the terrestrial planets.

2 Identify What are properties of Earth that make it a special place in the solar system?

_____

_____

_____

_____

✏️ Active Reading

3 Synthesize Many English words have their roots in other languages. Use the Latin words below to make an educated guess about the meaning of the word *astronomy*.

Latin word	Meaning
astrón	star
nomos	law

Example sentence
Some students who are interested in the night sky enter college to study <u>astronomy</u>.

 astronomy:

_____

_____

Vocabulary Terms

• terrestrial planet
• astronomical unit

4 Apply As you learn the definition of each vocabulary term in this lesson, create your own definition or sketch to help you remember the meaning of the term.

Extreme
to the Core

Active Reading

5 Identify As you read the text, underline important characteristics of the planet Mercury.

What are the terrestrial planets?

The **terrestrial planets** are the four small, dense, rocky planets that orbit closest to the sun. In order by distance from the sun, these planets are Mercury, Venus, Earth, and Mars. The terrestrial planets have similar compositions and consist of an outer crust, a central core, and a mantle that lies between the crust and core.

What is known about Mercury?

Mercury (MUR•kyuh•ree) is the planet about which we know the least. Until NASA's *Mariner 10* spacecraft flew by Mercury in 1974, the planet was seen as a blotchy, dark ball of rock. Today, scientists know that the planet's heavily cratered, moon-like surface is composed largely of volcanic rock and hides a massive iron core.

Mercury orbits only 0.39 AU from the sun. The letters *AU* stand for *astronomical unit*, which is the term astronomers use to measure distances in the solar system. One **astronomical unit** equals the average distance between the sun and Earth, or approximately 150 million km. Therefore, Mercury lies nearly halfway between the sun and Earth.

Statistics Table for Mercury	
Distance from the sun	0.39 AU
Period of rotation (length of Mercury day)	58 days 15.5 h
Period of revolution (length of Mercury year)	88 days
Tilt of axis	0°
Diameter	4,879 km
Density	5.44 g/cm³
Surface temperature	-184 °C to 427 °C
Surface gravity	38% of Earth's gravity
Number of satellites	0

Although this may look like the moon, it is actually the heavily cratered surface of the planet Mercury.

Mercury Has the Most Extreme Temperature Range in the Solar System

On Earth, a day lasts 24 h. On Mercury, a day lasts almost 59 Earth days. What does this fact have to do with temperatures on Mercury? It means that temperatures on that part of Mercury's surface that is receiving sunlight can build for more than 29 days. When it is day on Mercury, temperatures can rise to 427 °C, a temperature that is hot enough to melt certain metals. It also means that temperatures on the part of Mercury's surface that is in darkness can fall for more than 29 days. When it is night on Mercury, temperatures can drop to −184 °C. This means that surface temperatures on Mercury can change by as much as 600 °C between day and night. This is the greatest difference between high and low temperatures in the solar system.

Mercury Has a Large Iron Core

Mercury is the smallest planet in the solar system. It has a diameter of only 4,879 km at its equator. Amazingly, Mercury's central core is thought to be around 3,600 km in diameter, which accounts for most of the planet's interior. Scientists originally thought that Mercury had a core of solid iron. However, by observing changes in Mercury's spin as it orbits the sun, astronomers now think that the core is at least partially molten. Why is the core so large? Some scientists think that Mercury may have been struck by another object in the distant past and lost most of the rock that surrounded the core. Other scientists think that long ago the sun vaporized the planet's surface and blasted it away into space.

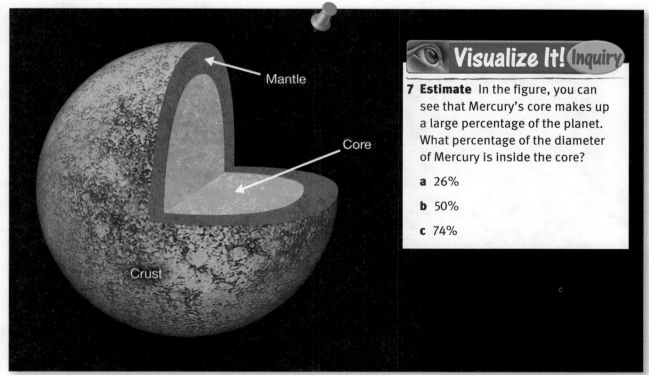

Mantle

Core

Crust

Visualize It! Inquiry

7 Estimate In the figure, you can see that Mercury's core makes up a large percentage of the planet. What percentage of the diameter of Mercury is inside the core?

a 26%

b 50%

c 74%

Harsh Planet

What is known about Venus?

Science-fiction writers once imagined Venus (VEE•nuhs) to be a humid planet with lush, tropical forests. Nothing could be further from the truth. On Venus, sulfuric acid rain falls on a surface that is not much different from the inside of an active volcano.

Venus Is Similar to Earth in Size and Mass

Venus has often been called "Earth's twin." At 12,104 km, the diameter of Venus is 95% the diameter of Earth. Venus's mass is around 80% of Earth's. And the gravity that you would experience on Venus is 89% of the gravity on Earth.

The rotation of Venus is different from the rotation of Earth. Earth has prograde rotation. *Prograde rotation* is the counterclockwise spin of a planet about its axis as seen from above the planet's north pole. Venus, however, has retrograde rotation. *Retrograde rotation* is the clockwise spin of a planet about its axis as seen from above its north pole.

Venus differs from Earth not only in the direction in which it spins on its axis. It takes more time for Venus to rotate once about its axis than it takes for the planet to revolve once around the sun. Venus has the slowest period of rotation in the solar system.

![Active Reading]

8 Identify Underline the definitions of the terms *prograde rotation* and *retrograde rotation* that appear in the text.

Venus has landforms such as highlands and plains, volcanoes, and impact craters.

Statistics Table for Venus	
Distance from the sun	0.72 AU
Period of rotation	243 days (retrograde rotation)
Period of revolution	225 days
Tilt of axis	177.4°
Diameter	12,104 km
Density	5.20 g/cm³
Average surface temperature	465 °C
Surface gravity	89% of Earth's gravity
Number of satellites	0

© Houghton Mifflin Harcourt Publishing Company • Image Credits: ©NASA/Science Source/Photo Researchers Inc.

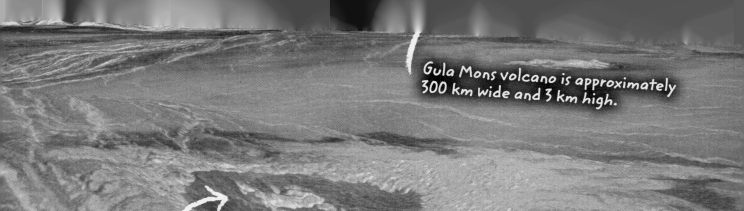

Gula Mons volcano is approximately 300 km wide and 3 km high.

Impact crater Cunitz, which is 48.5 km wide, was named after Maria Cunitz, a 17th-century European astronomer and mathematician.

Venus Has Craters and Volcanoes

In 1990, the powerful radar beams of NASA's *Magellan* spacecraft pierced the dense atmosphere of Venus. This gave us our most detailed look ever at the planet's surface. There are 168 volcanoes on Venus that are larger than 100 km in diameter. Thousands of volcanoes have smaller diameters. Venus's surface is also cratered. These craters are as much as 280 km in diameter. The sizes and locations of the craters on Venus suggest that around 500 million years ago something happened to erase all of the planet's older craters. Scientists are still puzzled about how this occurred. But volcanic activity could have covered the surface of the planet in one huge outpouring of magma.

The Atmosphere of Venus Is Toxic

Venus may have started out like Earth, with oceans and water running across its surface. However, after billions of years of solar heating, Venus has become a harsh world. Surface temperatures on Venus are hotter than those on Mercury. Temperatures average around 465 °C. Over time, carbon dioxide gas has built up in the atmosphere. Sunlight that strikes Venus's surface warms the ground. However, carbon dioxide in the atmosphere traps this energy, which causes temperatures near the surface to remain high.

Sulfuric acid rains down onto Venus's surface, and the pressure of the atmosphere is at least 90 times that of Earth's atmosphere. No human—or machine—could survive for long under these conditions. Venus is a world that is off limits to human explorers and perhaps all but the hardiest robotic probes.

9 Contrast How is the landscape of Venus different from the landscape of Earth?

_____

_____

_____

_____

_____

_____

Active Reading

10 Identify As you read the text, underline those factors that make Venus an unlikely place for life to exist.

© Houghton Mifflin Harcourt Publishing Company • Image Credits: ©Corbis

No Place Like Home

What is special about Earth?

As far as scientists know, Earth is the only planet in the solar system that has the combination of factors needed to support life. Life as we know it requires liquid water and an energy source. Earth has both. Earth's atmosphere contains the oxygen that animals need to breathe. Matter is continuously cycled between the environment and living things. And a number of ecosystems exist on Earth that different organisms can inhabit.

Earth Has Abundant Water and Life

Earth's vast liquid-water oceans and moderate temperatures provided the ideal conditions for life to emerge and flourish. Around 3.5 billion years ago, organisms that produced food by photosynthesis appeared in Earth's oceans. During the process of making food, these organisms produced oxygen. By 560 million years ago, more complex life forms arose that could use oxygen to release energy from food. Today, the total number of species of organisms that inhabit Earth is thought to be anywhere between 5 million and 30 million.

Active Reading

11 Identify As you read the text, underline characteristics that make Earth special.

Statistics Table for Earth

Distance from the sun	1.0 AU
Period of rotation	23 h 56 min
Period of revolution	365.3 days
Tilt of axis	23.45°
Diameter	12,756 km
Density	5.52 g/cm³
Temperature	-89 °C to 58 °C
Surface gravity	100% of Earth's gravity
Number of satellites	1

From space, Earth presents an entirely different scene from that of the other terrestrial planets. Clouds in the atmosphere, blue bodies of water, and green landmasses are all clues to the fact that Earth is a special place.

Earth Is Geologically Active

Earth is the only terrestrial planet whose surface is divided into tectonic plates. These plates move around Earth's surface, which causes the continents to change positions over long periods of time. Tectonic plate motion, together with weathering and erosion, has erased most surface features older than 500 million years.

Humans Have Set Foot on the Moon

Between 1969 and 1972, 12 astronauts landed on the moon. They are the only humans to have set foot on another body in the solar system. They encountered a surface gravity that is only about one-sixth that of Earth. Because of the moon's lower gravity, astronauts could not walk normally. If they did, they would fly up in the air and fall over.

Like Mercury, the moon's surface is heavily cratered. It is estimated that about 500,000 craters larger than 1 km dot the moon. There are large dark areas on the moon's surface. These are plains of solidified lava. There are also light-colored areas. These are the lunar highlands.

The moon rotates about its axis in the same time it orbits Earth. Therefore, it keeps the same side facing Earth. During a lunar day, which is a little more than 27 Earth days, the daytime surface temperature can reach 127 °C. The nighttime surface temperature can fall to −173 °C.

The moon is the only other body in the solar system where humans have been.

Statistics Table for the Moon

Distance from Earth	384,400 km (0.0026 AU)
Period of rotation	27.3 days
Period of revolution	27.3 days
Axial tilt	1.5°
Diameter	3,476 km
Density	3.34 g/cm³
Temperature	−173°C to 127°C
Surface gravity	16.5% of Earth's gravity

12 Identify In the image, circle any signs of life that you see.

Is It Alive?

What is known about Mars?

A fleet of spacecraft is now in orbit around Mars (MARZ) studying the planet. Space rovers have also investigated the surface of Mars. These remote explorers have discovered a planet with an atmosphere that is 100 times thinner than Earth's and temperatures that are little different from the inside of a freezer. They have seen landforms on Mars that are larger than any found on Earth. And these unmanned voyagers have photographed surface features on Mars that are characteristic of erosion and deposition by water.

Mars Is a Rocky, Red Planet

The surface of Mars is better known than that of any other planet in the solar system except Earth. It is composed largely of dark volcanic rock. Rocks and boulders litter the surface of Mars. Some boulders can be as large as a house. A powdery dust covers Martian rocks and boulders. This dust is the product of the chemical breakdown of rocks rich in iron minerals. This is what gives the Martian soil its orange-red color.

© Houghton Mifflin Harcourt Publishing Company • Image Credits: ©U.S. Geological Survey/Science Source/Photo Researchers, Inc

Think Outside the Book

13 **Debate** Research the surface features of the northern and southern hemispheres of Mars. Decide which hemisphere you would rather explore. With your class, debate the merits of exploring one hemisphere versus the other.

Statistics Table for Mars

Distance from the sun	1.52 AU
Period of rotation	24 h 37 min
Period of revolution	1.88 y
Tilt of axis	25.3°
Diameter	6,792 km
Density	3.93 g/cm³
Temperature	-140°C to 20°C
Surface gravity	37% of Earth's gravity
Number of satellites	2

Mars's northern polar ice cap is composed of carbon dioxide ice and water ice. Its size varies with the seasons.

Mars Has Interesting Surface Features

The surface of Mars varies from hemisphere to hemisphere. The northern hemisphere appears to have been covered by lava flows. The southern hemisphere is heavily cratered.

Large volcanoes are found on Mars. At 27 km high and 600 km across, Olympus Mons (uh•LIM•puhs MAHNZ) is the largest volcano and mountain in the solar system. Mars also has very deep valleys and canyons. The canyon system Valles Marineris (VAL•less mar•uh•NAIR•iss) runs from west to east along the Martian equator. It is about 4,000 km long, 500 km wide, and up to 10 km deep. It is the largest canyon in the solar system.

Olympus Mons is the largest volcano in the solar system.

Mars Has a Thin Atmosphere

Mars has a very thin atmosphere that is thought to have been thicker in the past. Mars may have gradually lost its atmosphere to the solar wind. Or a body or bodies that collided with Mars may have caused much of the atmosphere to have been blown away.

Unlike Earth, Mars's atmosphere is composed mostly of carbon dioxide. During the Martian winter, temperatures at the planet's poles grow cold enough for carbon dioxide to freeze into a thin coating. During the summer, when temperatures grow warmer, this coating vanishes.

Winds on Mars can blow with enough force to pick up dust particles from the planet's surface. When this happens, giant dust storms can form. At times, these storms cover the entire planet.

Active Reading **14 Explain** What are two possible reasons why the atmosphere on Mars is so thin?

_____

_____

_____

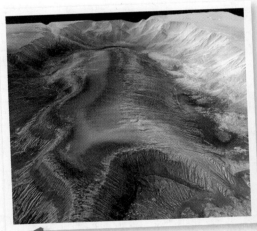

Hebes Chasma is a 6,000 m–deep depression that is located in the Valles Marineris region.

15 Compare Compare and contrast the physical properties of Mars to the physical properties of Earth.

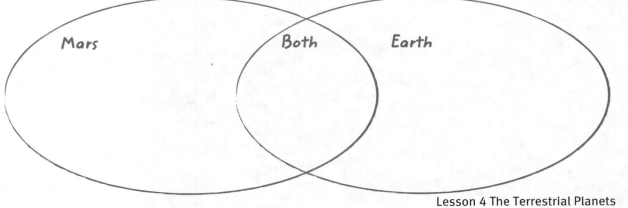

Mars   Both   Earth

Liquid Water Once Flowed on Mars

A number of features on Mars provide evidence that liquid water once flowed on the planet's surface. Many of these features have been struck by asteroids. These asteroid impacts have left behind craters that scientists can use to find the approximate dates of these features. Scientists estimate that many of these features, such as empty river basins, existed on Mars more than 3 billion years ago. Since then, little erosion has taken place that would cause these features to disappear.

In 2000, the *Mars Global Surveyor* took before-and-after images of a valley wall on Mars. Scientists observed the unmistakable trace of a liquid substance that had flowed out of the valley wall and into the valley. Since 2000, many similar features have been seen. The best explanation of these observations is that water is found beneath Mars's surface. At times, this water leaks out onto the Martian surface like spring water on Earth.

This image shows gullies on the wall of a Martian crater. Water that may be stored close to the Martian surface has run downhill into the crater.

Visualize It!

16 Describe How do the features in the image at the right indicate that liquid water once flowed on Mars?

_____

_____

_____

_____

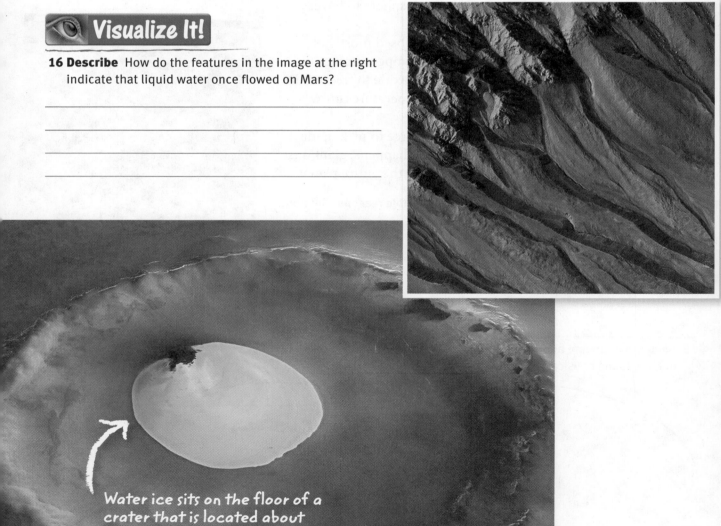

Water ice sits on the floor of a crater that is located about 20 degrees below Mars's north pole.

© Houghton Mifflin Harcourt Publishing Company • Image Credits: (l) ©European Space Agency/DLR/FU Berlin/G. Neukum/Photo Researchers, Inc.; (r) ©NASA/JPL/University of Arizona

Roving Mars

The Mars Exploration Rovers *Spirit* and *Opportunity* landed safely on Mars in January 2004. These robotic geologists were sent to find out if Mars ever had water. They found landforms shaped by past water activity as well as evidence of past groundwater. The last communication from *Spirit* was received in 2010. *Opportunity* was still exploring Mars in 2015.

Curiosity

Curiosity landed on Mars in 2012 to find out if Mars could have once supported life. It has been exploring ever since then and has found the ingredients needed to support life in some of Mars' rocks.

Testing the Rovers on Earth
Before leaving Earth, the rovers were tested under conditions that were similar to those that they would encounter on the Martian surface.

Collecting Data on Mars
The Mars rover *Spirit* took this picture of itself collecting data from the Martian surface.

Extend

Inquiry

17 Infer What advantages would a robotic explorer have over a manned mission to Mars?

18 Hypothesize What kind of evidence would the Mars Exploration Rovers be looking for that indicated that water once flowed on Mars?

Visual Summary

To complete this summary, write the answers to the questions on the lines. Then use the key below to check your answers. You can use this page to review the main concepts of the lesson.

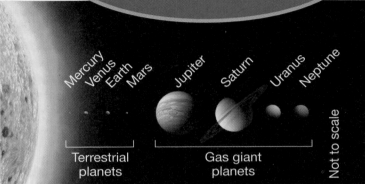

Properties
of Terrestrial Planets

Mercury Venus Earth Mars Jupiter Saturn Uranus Neptune

Terrestrial planets Gas giant planets Not to scale

Mercury orbits near the sun.

19 Why do temperatures on Mercury vary so much?

_____
_____
_____

Venus is covered with clouds.

20 Why is Venus's surface temperature so high?

_____
_____
_____

Earth has abundant life.

21 What factors support life on Earth?

_____
_____
_____

Mars is a rocky planet.

22 What makes up the surface of Mars?

_____
_____
_____

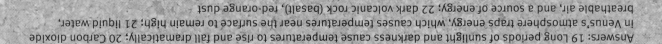

Answers: 19 Long periods of sunlight and darkness cause temperatures to rise and fall dramatically; 20 Carbon dioxide in Venus's atmosphere traps energy, which causes temperatures near the surface to remain high; 21 liquid water, breathable air, and a source of energy; 22 dark volcanic rock (basalt), red-orange dust

---

23 Compare How are important properties of Mercury, Venus, and Mars different from important properties of Earth?

Lesson Review

Vocabulary

Fill in the blanks with the terms that best complete the following sentences.

1 The _____ are the dense planets nearest the sun.

2 An _____ is equal to the distance between the sun and Earth.

Key Concepts

In the following table, write the name of the correct planet next to the property of that planet.

Properties	Planet
3 Identify Which planet has the highest surface temperature in the solar system?	
4 Identify Which planet has very large dust storms?	
5 Identify Which planet is the most heavily cratered of the terrestrial planets?	
6 Identify Which planet has the highest surface gravity of the terrestrial planets?	

7 Explain What is the difference between prograde rotation and retrograde rotation?

_____

_____

_____

8 Describe What characteristics of Venus's atmosphere make the planet so harsh?

_____

_____

_____

_____

Critical Thinking

Use this table to answer the following questions.

Planet	Period of rotation	Period of revolution
Mercury	58 days 15.5 h	88 days
Venus	243 days (retrograde rotation)	225 days
Earth	23 h 56 min	365.3 days
Mars	24 h 37 min	1.88 y

9 Analyze Which planet rotates most slowly about its axis?

_____

10 Analyze Which planet revolves around the sun in less time than it rotates around its axis?

_____

11 Analyze Which planet revolves around the sun in the shortest amount of time?

_____

12 Explain Why are the temperatures on each of the other terrestrial planets more extreme than the temperatures on Earth?

_____

_____

_____

_____

_____

_____

_____

_____

_____

_____

My Notes

A. Wesley Ward
GEOLOGIST

Geologist Dr. Wesley Ward lives in a desert region of the western United States. The living conditions are sometimes harsh, but the region offers some fascinating places to study. For a geologist like Dr. Ward, who tries to understand the geologic processes on another planet, the desert may be the only place to be.

Dr. Ward was a leading scientist on the Mars Pathfinder mission. The surface of Mars is a lot like the western desert. Dr. Ward helped scientists map the surface of Mars and plan for the Pathfinder's landing. Using data from the Pathfinder, Dr. Ward studied how Martian winds have shaped the planet's landscape. This information will help scientists better understand what conditions are like on the surface of Mars. More importantly, the information will guide scientists in choosing future landings sites. Dr. Ward's work may determine whether human beings can safely land on Mars.

You could say that Dr. Ward's scientific career has hit the big-time. He helped in the making of the Discovery Channel's documentary *Planet Storm*. The program features scientists describing weather conditions on other planets. Dr. Ward and the scientists worked with special effects artists to simulate what these conditions might feel like to astronauts.

The Mars Pathfinder rover **Sojourner** was designed to withstand the fierce Martian dust storms, such as the one shown.

Social Studies Connection

The Pathfinder is not the first attempt scientists have made to explore the surface of Mars. In fact, scientists in different countries have been exploring Mars for over 50 years. Research other missions to Mars and attempts to send rovers to Mars, and present your research in a timeline. Remember to identify where the mission started, what its goals were, and whether it achieved them.

JOB BOARD

Science Writer

What You'll Do: Research and write articles, press releases, reports, and sometimes books about scientific discoveries and issues for a wide range of readers. Science writers who write for a broad audience must work to find the stories behind the science in order to keep readers interested.

Where You Might Work: For a magazine, a newspaper, or a museum, or independently as a freelance writer specializing in science. Some science writers may work for universities, research foundations, government agencies, or non-profit science and health organizations.

Education: A bachelor's degree in a scientific field, with courses in English or writing.

Other Job Requirements: Strong communications skills. Science writers must not only understand science, but must also be able to interview scientists and to write clear, interesting stories.

Telescope Mechanic

What You'll Do: Keep telescopes at large observatories working, climbing heights of up to 30 meters to make sure the telescope's supports are in good shape, which includes welding new components, cleaning, and sweeping.

Where You Might Work: A large observatory or research institution with large telescopes, possibly in the desert.

Education: A high-school diploma with some experience performing maintenance on delicate equipment.

Other Job Requirements. Strong communications skills to consult with other mechanics and the scientists who use the telescopes. Mechanics must be able to weld and to use tools. Mechanics must also have good vision (or wear glasses to correct their vision), and be able to climb up high and carry heavy equipment.

PEOPLE IN SCIENCE NEWS

Anthony Wesley

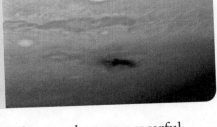

Witnessing Impact

Anthony Wesley was sitting in his backyard in Australia on July 19, 2009, gazing at Jupiter through his custom-built telescope, when he saw a dark spot or "scar" on the planet (shown). Wesley sent his tip to the National Aeronautics and Space Administration (NASA).

NASA has much more powerful telescopes than a citizen scientist usually does. Scientists at NASA confirmed that a comet had crashed into the planet, leaving a scar. Coincidentally, this crash happened almost exactly 15 years after another comet crashed into Jupiter.

Lesson 5

The Gas Giant Planets

ESSENTIAL QUESTION

What is known about the gas giant planets?

By the end of this lesson, you should be able to describe some of the properties of the gas giant planets and how these properties differ from the physical properties of Earth.

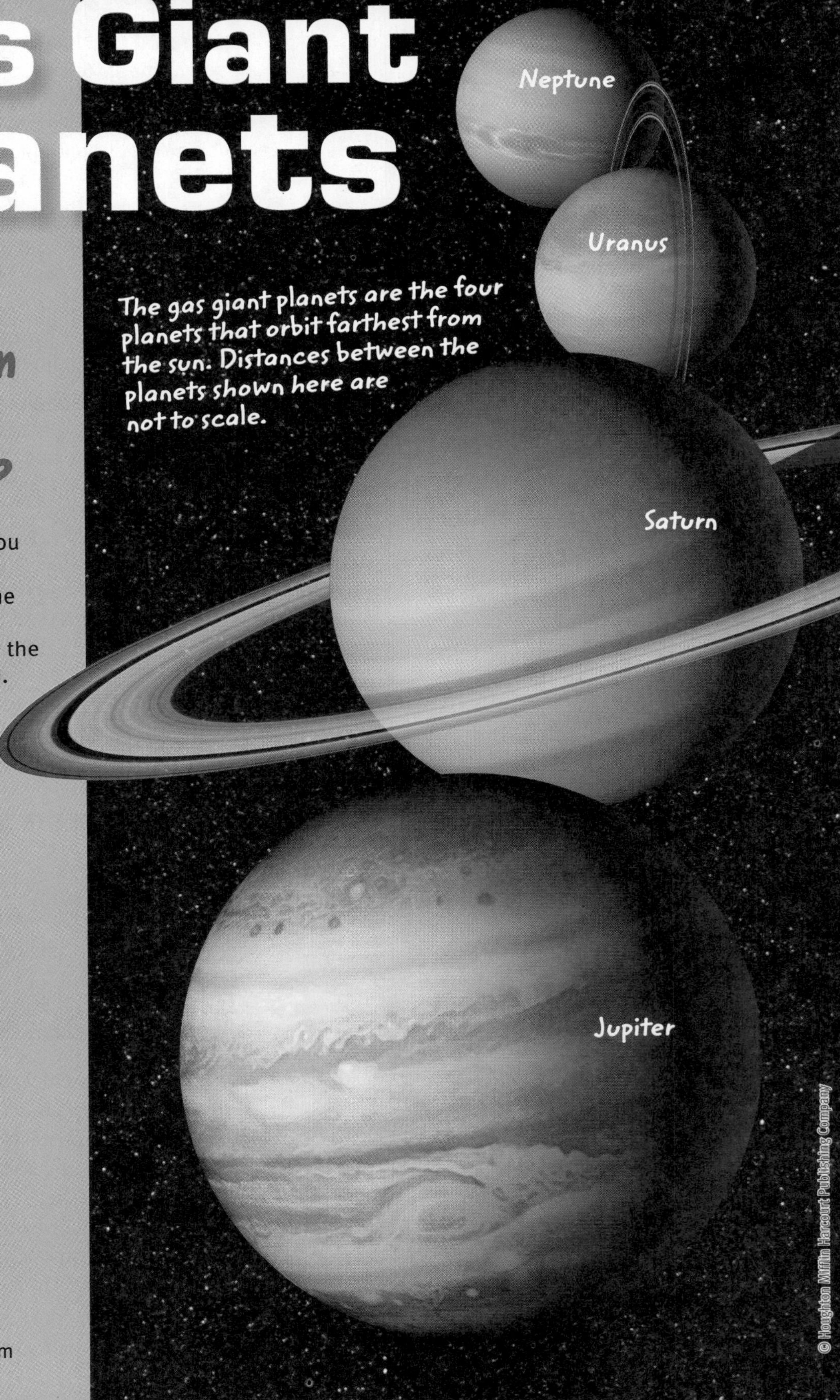
Neptune
Uranus
Saturn
Jupiter

The gas giant planets are the four planets that orbit farthest from the sun. Distances between the planets shown here are not to scale.

Engage Your Brain

1 Predict Circle the term that best completes the following sentences.

Jupiter/Saturn/Uranus is the largest planet in the solar system.

Jupiter/Uranus/Neptune has the strongest winds in the solar system.

Saturn/Uranus/Neptune has the largest ring system of the gas giant planets.

Jupiter/Saturn/Neptune has more moons than any other planet in the solar system.

Jupiter/Uranus/Neptune is tilted on its side as it orbits the Sun.

2 Identify What are the objects that circle Saturn? What do you think they are made of?

_____

_____

_____

Active Reading

3 Apply Many scientific words, such as *gas*, also have everyday meanings. Use context clues to write your own definition for each meaning of the word *gas*.

Example sentence
Vehicles, such as cars, trucks, and buses, use <u>gas</u> as a fuel.

_____

_____

Example sentence
<u>Gas</u> is one of the three common states of matter.

gas:

_____

_____

_____

Vocabulary Terms

- **gas giant**
- **planetary ring**

4 Apply This list contains the key terms you'll learn in this section. As you read, circle the definition of each term.

A Giant Among

Jupiter's high winds circle the planet and cause cloud bands to form. Storms, such as the Great Red Spot shown here, form between the cloud bands.

Ganymede

Callisto

Statistics Table for Jupiter

Distance from the sun	5.20 AU
Period of rotation	9 h 55 min
Period of revolution	11.86 y
Tilt of axis	3.13°
Diameter	142,984 km
Density	1.33 g/cm³
Mean surface temperature	−145 °C
Surface gravity	253% of Earth's gravity
Number of known satellites	62

Active Reading

5 Identify As you read the text, underline important physical properties of the planet Jupiter.

What is a gas giant planet?

Jupiter, Saturn, Uranus, and Neptune are the gas giant planets. They orbit far from the sun. **Gas giants** have deep, massive gas atmospheres, which are made up mostly of hydrogen and helium. These gases become denser the deeper you travel inside. All of the gas giants are large. Neptune, the smallest gas giant planet, is big enough to hold 60 Earths within its volume. The gas giant planets are cold. Mean surface temperatures range from −145 °C on Jupiter to −220 °C on Neptune.

What is known about Jupiter?

Jupiter (JOO•pih•ter) is the largest planet in the solar system. Its volume can contain more than 900 Earths. Jupiter is also the most massive planet. Its mass is twice that of the other seven planets combined. Jupiter has the highest surface gravity in the solar system at 253% that of Earth. And, although all of the gas giant planets rotate rapidly, Jupiter rotates the fastest of all. Its period of rotation is just under 10 h. Wind speeds on Jupiter are high. They can reach 540 km/h. By contrast, Earth's wind speed record is 372 km/h.

Giants!

Europa

Io

Io, Europa, Callisto, and Ganymede are Jupiter's largest moons. All four moons were named for figures in Greek mythology.

Huge Storms Travel Across Jupiter's Surface

Jupiter has some of the strangest weather conditions in the solar system. The winds on Jupiter circle the planet. Clouds are stretched into bands that run from east to west. Storms appear as white or red spots between cloud bands. The best known of these storms is the Great Red Spot. The east–west width of this storm is three times the diameter of Earth. Incredibly, this storm has been observed by astronomers on Earth for the past 350 years.

Jupiter Has the Most Moons

More than 60 moons have been discovered orbiting Jupiter. This is the greatest number of moons to orbit any planet. Jupiter's moons Io (EYE•oh), Europa (yu•ROH•puh), Callisto (kuh•LIS•toh), and Ganymede (GAN•uh•meed) are particularly large. In fact, Ganymede is larger than the planet Mercury.

Jupiter's moon Io is the most volcanically active place in the solar system. There are at least 400 active volcanoes on Io's surface. Jupiter's gravity tugs and pulls on Io. This causes the interior of Io to reach the temperature at which it melts. Lava erupts from Io's volcanoes, which throw tremendous geysers of sulfur compounds into space. Over time, the orbit of Io has become a ring of ejected gases that is visible to the Hubble Space Telescope.

Jupiter's moon Europa has an icy surface. Recent evidence suggests that an ocean of liquid water may lie beneath this surface. Because liquid water is essential for life, some scientists are hopeful that future spacecraft may discover life inside Europa.

6 Apply Io, Europa, Callisto, and Ganymede are known as the *Galilean moons*. The astronomer Galileo discovered these moons using one of the first telescopes. Why do you think that the Galilean moons were the first objects to be discovered with a telescope?

_____

_____

_____

Think Outside the Book

7 Model Select one of the following topics about weather on Jupiter to research: belts and zones; jet streams; storms. Present your findings to the rest of the class in the form of a model. Your model may be handcrafted, or may be an art piece, or may be a computer presentation.

King of the Rings!

What is known about Saturn?

Saturn (SAT•ern) is a near-twin to Jupiter. It is the second-largest gas giant planet and is made mostly of hydrogen and helium. About 800 Earths could fit inside the volume of Saturn. Amazingly, the planet's density is less than that of water.

Saturn Has a Large Ring System

The planetary ring system that circles Saturn's equator is the planet's most spectacular feature. A **planetary ring** is a disk of material that circles a planet and consists of orbiting particles. Saturn's ring system has many individual rings that form complex bands. Between bands are gaps that may be occupied by moons.

Saturn's rings span up to hundreds of kilometers in width, but they are only a few kilometers thick. They consist of trillions of small, icy bodies that are a few millimeters to several hundred meters in size. The rings are mostly pieces left over from the collision of Saturn's moons with comets and asteroids.

8 Identify As you read the text, underline important physical properties about the planet Saturn.

Statistics Table for Saturn

Distance from the sun	9.58 AU
Period of rotation	10 h 39 min
Period of revolution	29.5 y
Tilt of axis	26.73°
Diameter	120,536 km
Density	0.69 g/cm³
Mean surface temperature	−180 °C
Surface gravity	106% of Earth's gravity
Number of known satellites	53

Saturn's rings

Saturn's southern aurora

Saturn's Moon Enceladus Has Water Geysers

In the inner solar system, liquid rock erupts from volcanoes. In some parts of the outer solar system, liquid water erupts from volcanoes. When NASA's *Cassini* spacecraft explored Saturn's moon Enceladus (en•SEL•uh•duhs), it found an icy surface. Scientists believe that Enceladus has a liquid interior beneath this icy surface. Liquid water flows up through cracks in the moon's surface. It either freezes at the surface or forms spectacular water geysers. These geysers are the largest in the solar system.

Saturn's Moon Titan Has a Dense Atmosphere

Titan (TYT'in), the largest moon of Saturn, has an atmosphere that is denser than Earth's. The moon's atmosphere is composed mostly of nitrogen and has traces of compounds such as methane and ethane. Methane clouds form in Titan's atmosphere. From these clouds, methane rain may fall. Unlike Earth, Titan has a crust of ice, which is frozen at a temperature of −180 °C.

In 2005, the *Huygens* (HY•guhnz) Titan probe descended through Titan's atmosphere. It took pictures of a surface with lakes and ponds. The liquid that fills these lakes and ponds is mostly methane.

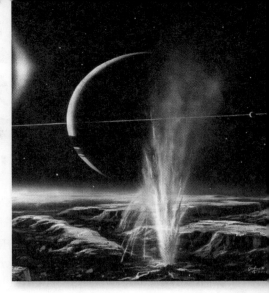

9 Explain In your own words, write a caption for this illustration of Saturn's moon Enceladus.

_____

_____

_____

Particles that make up Saturn's ring system

Cassini Division in Saturn's ring system

10 Describe Complete this table by writing a description of each structure in Saturn's ring system.

Structure	Description
ring	
gap	
ring particles	

Just Rollin' Along

How is Uranus unique?

11 Identify As you read the text, underline important physical properties of the planet Uranus.

The atmosphere of Uranus (YUR•uh•nuhs) is composed mostly of hydrogen and helium. However, the atmosphere also contains methane. The methane in Uranus's atmosphere absorbs red light, which gives the planet a blue-green color.

Uranus Is a Tilted World

Uranus's axis of rotation is tilted almost 98°. This means that unlike any other planet in the solar system, Uranus is tilted on its side as it orbits the sun. The planet's 27 moons all orbit Uranus's equator, just like the moons of other planets do. The ring system of Uranus also orbits the equator. Scientists are not sure what event caused Uranus's odd axial tilt. But computer models of the four gas giant planets as they were forming may offer an explanation. The huge gravities of Jupiter and Saturn may have caused the orbits of Uranus and Neptune to change. There may also have been many close encounters between Uranus and Neptune that could have tilted the axis of Uranus.

Statistics Table for Uranus

Distance from the sun	19.2 AU
Period of rotation	17 h 24 min (retrograde)
Period of revolution	84 y
Tilt of axis	97.8°
Diameter	51,118 km
Density	1.27 g/cm³
Mean surface temperature	−210 °C
Surface gravity	79% of Earth's gravity
Number of known satellites	27

12 Predict Earth has an axial tilt of 23.5°, whereas Uranus has an axial tilt of almost 98°. If Earth had the same axial tilt as Uranus, how would the conditions be different at Earth's North and South Poles?

_____

_____

_____

_____

_____

_____

_____

_____

_____

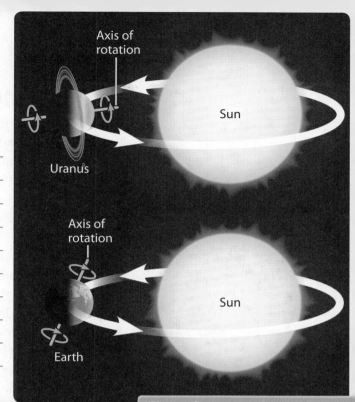

Think Outside the Book

13 Research Astronomers are discovering planets orbiting stars in other solar systems? Find out what kinds of planets astronomers are discovering in these solar systems.

Seasons on Uranus Last 21 Years

It takes Uranus 84 years to make a single revolution around the sun. For about 21 years of that 84-year period, the north pole faces the sun and the south pole is in darkness. About halfway through that 84-year period, the poles are reversed. The south pole faces the sun and the north pole is in darkness for 21 years. So, what are seasons like on Uranus? Except for a small band near the equator, every place on Uranus has winter periods of constant darkness and summer periods of constant daylight. But, during spring and fall, Uranus has periods of both daytime and nighttime just like on Earth.

Uranus's Moon Miranda Is Active

Miranda (muh•RAN•duh) is Uranus's fifth-largest moon. It is about 470 km in diameter. NASA's *Voyager 2* spacecraft visited Miranda in 1989. Data from *Voyager 2* showed that the moon is covered by different types of icy crust. What is the explanation for this patchwork surface? The gravitational forces of Uranus pull on Miranda's interior. This causes material from the moon's interior to rise to its surface. What we see on the surface is evidence of the moon turning itself inside out.

The surface of Uranus's moon Miranda

A Blue, Windy Giant

What is known about Neptune?

Neptune (NEP•toon) is the most distant planet from the sun. It is located 30 times farther from the sun than Earth is. So, sunlight on Neptune is 900 times fainter than sunlight on Earth is. High noon on Neptune may look much like twilight on Earth.

Neptune Is a Blue Ice Giant

Neptune is practically a twin to Uranus. Neptune is almost the same size as Uranus. It also has an atmosphere that is composed of hydrogen and helium, with some methane. The planet's bluish color is caused by the absorption of red light by methane. But because Neptune does not have an atmospheric haze like Uranus does, we can see deeper into the atmosphere. So, Neptune is blue, whereas Uranus is blue-green.

When *Voyager 2* flew by Neptune in 1989, there was a huge, dark area as large as Earth in the planet's atmosphere. This storm, which was located in Neptune's southern hemisphere, was named the *Great Dark Spot*. However, in 1994, the Hubble Space Telescope found no trace of this storm. Meanwhile, other spots that may grow larger with time have been sighted in the atmosphere.

Statistics Table for Neptune	
Distance from the sun	30.1 AU
Period of rotation	16 h 7 min
Period of revolution	164.8 y
Tilt of axis	28.5°
Diameter	49,528 km
Density	1.64 g/cm³
Mean surface temperature	−220 °C
Surface Gravity	112% of Earth's gravity
Number of known satellites	13

Great Dark Spot

Visualize It!

14 Predict The wind speeds recorded in Neptune's Great Dark Spot reached 2,000 km/h. Predict what kind of destruction might result on Earth if wind speeds in hurricanes approached 2,000 km/h.

_____

_____

_____

Triton

Neptune Has the Strongest Winds

Where does the energy come from that powers winds as fast as 2,000 km/h? Neptune has a warm interior that produces more energy than the planet receives from sunlight. Some scientists believe that Neptune's weather is controlled from inside the planet and not from outside the planet, as is Earth's weather.

Neptune's Moon Triton Has a Different Orbit Than Neptune's Other Moons

Triton (TRYT'in) is the largest moon of Neptune. Unlike the other moons of Neptune, Triton orbits Neptune in the opposite direction from the direction in which Neptune orbits the sun. One explanation for this oddity is that, long ago, there were several large moons that orbited Neptune. These moons came so close together that one moon was ejected. The other moon, Triton, remained behind but began traveling in the opposite direction.

Triton's days are numbered. The moon is slowly spiraling inward toward Neptune. When Triton is a certain distance from Neptune, the planet's gravitational pull will begin pulling Triton apart. Triton will then break into pieces.

A category 5 hurricane on Earth has sustained wind speeds of 250 km/h. Some effects of the winds of a category 5 hurricane can be seen in this image.

Inquiry

15 Conclude Complete the cause-and-effect chart by answering the question below.

Triton spirals inward toward Neptune.

↓

The gravitational pull of Neptune causes Triton to pull apart.

↓

Triton breaks into pieces.

What do you think will happen next?

_____

_____

_____

_____

_____

Visual Summary

To complete this summary, write the answers to the questions on the lines. Then use the key below to check your answers. You can use this page to review the main concepts of the lesson.

Properties
of Gas Giant Planets

Mercury Venus Earth Mars Jupiter Saturn Uranus Neptune

Terrestrial planets

Gas giant planets

Not to scale

Jupiter has cloud bands.

16 What causes cloud bands to form on Jupiter?

_____

_____

Saturn has a complex ring system.

17 What are Saturn's rings made up of?

_____

_____

Uranus is tilted on its side.

18 What is the tilt of Uranus's axis of rotation?

_____

_____

Neptune is a blue planet.

19 What gives Neptune its bluish color?

_____

_____

Answers: 16 The high winds on Jupiter circle the planet and cause cloud bands to form; 17 trillions of small, icy bodies; 18 almost 98° (97.8°); 19 the absorption of red light by methane in Neptune's atmosphere

20 Apply Compare the properties of the gas giant planets as a group with properties of Earth.

Lesson Review

Vocabulary

Fill in the blank with the term that best completes the following sentences.

1 A large planet that has a deep, massive atmosphere is called a _____.

2 A _____ is a disk of matter that circles a planet and consists of numerous particles in orbit that range in size from a few millimeters to several hundred meters.

Key Concepts

In the following table, write the name of the correct planet next to the property of that planet.

Properties	Planet
3 Identify Which planet has a density that is less than that of water?	
4 Identify Which planet has the strongest winds in the solar system?	
5 Identify Which planet is tilted on its side as it orbits the sun?	
6 Identify Which planet is the largest planet in the solar system?	

7 Compare How does the composition of Earth's atmosphere differ from the composition of the atmospheres of the gas giant planets?

_____

_____

_____

8 Compare How do the periods of rotation and revolution for the gas giant planets differ from those of Earth?

_____

_____

_____

_____

Critical Thinking

Use this diagram to answer the following questions.

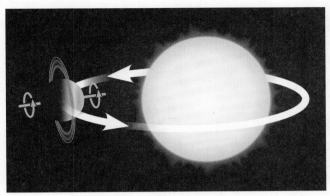

9 Identify Which planet is shown in the diagram? How do you know?

_____

_____

10 Analyze How does the axial tilt of this planet affect its seasons?

_____

_____

_____

_____

11 Analyze Why do you think the wind speeds on the gas giant planets are so much greater than the wind speeds on Earth?

_____

_____

_____

12 Compare List Earth and the gas giant planets in order from the hottest to the coldest planet. How does the temperature of each planet relate to its distance from the sun?

_____

_____

_____

_____

My Notes

Small Bodies in the Solar System

ESSENTIAL QUESTION

What is found in the solar system besides the sun, planets, and moons?

By the end of this lesson, you should be able to compare and contrast the properties of small bodies in the solar system.

Comet Hale-Bopp was discovered in 1995 and was visible from Earth for 18 months. It is a long-period comet that is thought to take about 2,400 years to orbit the sun.

Engage Your Brain

1 Predict Check T or F to show whether you think each statement is true or false.

T F

☐ ☐ Pluto is a planet.

☐ ☐ The Kuiper Belt is located beyond the orbit of Neptune.

☐ ☐ Comets are made of ice, rock, and dust.

☐ ☐ All asteroids have the same composition.

☐ ☐ Most meteoroids that enter Earth's atmosphere burn up completely.

2 Identify Can you identify the object that is streaking through the sky in the photograph? What do you think makes this object glow?

_____
_____
_____
_____
_____
_____

Active Reading

3 Apply Many scientific words, such as *belt,* also have everyday meanings. Use context clues to write your own definition for each meaning of the word *belt*.

Example sentence
I found a <u>belt</u> to go with my new pants.

belt:
_____
_____
_____

Example sentence
Short-term comets originate in the Kuiper <u>Belt</u>.

belt:
_____
_____
_____

Vocabulary Terms

• dwarf planet
• Kuiper Belt
• Kuiper Belt object
• comet
• Oort cloud
• asteroid
• meteoroid
• meteor
• meteorite

4 Apply As you learn the definition of each vocabulary term in this lesson, create your own definition or sketch to help you remember the meaning of the term.

Bigger is not better

Where are small bodies in the solar system?

Active Reading

5 Identify As you read the text, underline the names of different kinds of small bodies that are found in the solar system.

The sun, planets, and moons are not the only objects in the solar system. Scientists estimate that there are up to a trillion small bodies in the solar system. These bodies lack atmospheres and have weak surface gravity. The largest of the small bodies, the dwarf planets, are found in regions known as the *asteroid belt* and the *Kuiper Belt*. The Kuiper (KAHY•per) Belt is located beyond the orbit of Neptune. Kuiper Belt objects, as you might guess, are located in the Kuiper Belt. Comets, too, are found in the Kuiper Belt. However, comets are also located in the Oort cloud. The Oort (OHRT) cloud is a region that surrounds the solar system and extends almost halfway to the nearest star. Two other types of small bodies, asteroids and meteoroids, are located mostly between the orbits of Venus and Neptune.

Sizes and distances are not to scale.

Mercury Venus Earth Mars Ceres Jupiter

What are dwarf planets?

In 2006, astronomers decided that Pluto would no longer be considered a planet. It became the first member of a new group of solar system bodies called *dwarf planets*. Like planets, a **dwarf planet** is a celestial body that orbits the sun and is round because of its own gravity. However, a dwarf planet does not have the mass to have cleared other bodies out of its orbit around the sun.

Five dwarf planets, made of ice and rock, have been identified. Ceres (SIR•eez), located between the orbits of Mars and Jupiter, is about 950 km in diameter and travels at around 18 km/s. Pluto, Eris (IR•is), Haumea (HOW•may•uh), and Makemake (MAH•kay•MAH•kay) are located beyond the orbit of Neptune. They range in size from about 1,500 km (Haumea) to about 2,400 km (Eris). Their orbital periods around the sun range from 250 to 560 years. All travel at speeds of between 3 km/s and 5 km/s.

© Houghton Mifflin Harcourt Publishing Company • Image Credits: (inset) ©Lynette Cook/Photo Researchers, Inc., ©NASA, ESA, and A. Feild (STScI), ©NASA, ESA, and A. Feild (STScI), ©Lynette Cook/Photo Researchers, Inc.

Active Reading

6 Describe Describe two properties of dwarf planets.

_____

_____

_____

_____

_____

_____

_____

Saturn

Uranus

Neptune

Pluto   Haumea   Makemake   Eris

Visualize It!

7 Analyze Where in the solar system are most of the dwarf planets located?

_____

_____

_____

_____

KBOs

What are Kuiper Belt objects?

The **Kuiper Belt** is a region of the solar system that begins just beyond the orbit of Neptune and contains small bodies made mostly of ice. It extends outward to about twice the orbit of Neptune, a distance of about 55 astronomical units (AU). An AU is a unit of length that is equal to the average distance between Earth and the sun, or about 150,000,000 km. The Kuiper Belt is thought to contain matter that was left over from the formation of the solar system. This matter formed small bodies instead of planets.

A **Kuiper Belt object (KBO)** is any of the minor bodies in the Kuiper Belt outside the orbit of Neptune. Kuiper Belt objects are made of methane ice, ammonia ice, and water ice. They have average orbital speeds of between 1 km/s and 5 km/s. The first Kuiper Belt object was not discovered until 1992. Now, about 1,300 KBOs are known. Scientists estimate that there are at least 70,000 objects in the Kuiper Belt that have diameters larger than 100 km.

Quaoar is a KBO that orbits 43 AU from the sun. It is around 1,260 km in diameter and has one satellite.

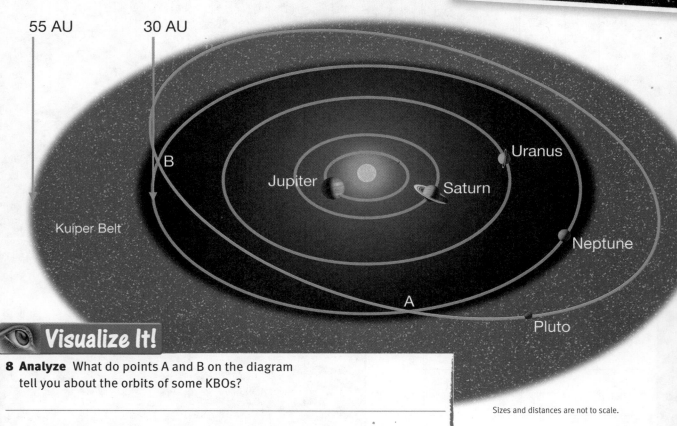

55 AU

30 AU

B

Jupiter

Uranus

Saturn

Neptune

Kuiper Belt

A

Pluto

Sizes and distances are not to scale.

Visualize It!

8 Analyze What do points A and B on the diagram tell you about the orbits of some KBOs?

_____

_____

Pluto: From Planet to KBO

From its discovery in 1930 until 2006, Pluto was considered to be the ninth planet in the solar system. However, beginning in 1992, a new group of small bodies called *Kuiper Belt objects*, or simply KBOs, began to be discovered beyond the orbit of Neptune. Not only are some of the KBOs close to Pluto in size, but some have a similar composition of rock and ice. Astronomers recognized that Pluto was, in fact, a large KBO and not the ninth planet. In 2006, Pluto was redefined as a "dwarf planet" by the International Astronomical Union (IAU).

Charon

Pluto

Pluto and Charon
At 2,306 km in diameter, Pluto is the second largest KBO. It is shown in this artist's rendition with Charon (KAIR•uhn), its largest satellite. Many large KBOs have satellites. Some KBOs and their satellites, such as Pluto and Charon, orbit each other.

The Kuiper Belt
The Kuiper Belt is located between 30 AU (the orbit of Neptune) and approximately 55 AU. However, most KBOs have been discovered between 42 and 48 AU, where their orbits are not disturbed by the gravitational attraction of Neptune.

Extend

Inquiry

9 Explain Why is Pluto no longer considered a planet?

10 Research Astronomer Clyde Tombaugh discovered Pluto in 1930. Research why Tombaugh was searching beyond Neptune for "Planet X" and how he discovered Pluto.

11 Debate Research the 2006 IAU decision to redefine Pluto as a "dwarf planet." Combine this research with your research on Pluto. With your classmates, debate whether Pluto should be considered a "dwarf planet" or return to being called the ninth planet in the solar system.

What do we know about comets?

Active Reading **12 Identify** As you read the text, underline the different parts of a comet and their properties.

A **comet** is a small body of ice, rock, and dust that follows a highly elliptical orbit around the sun. As a comet passes close to the sun, it gives off gas and dust in the form of a coma and a tail.

The speed of a comet will vary depending on how far from or how close to the sun it is. Far from the sun, a comet may travel at speeds as low as 0.32 km/s. Close to the sun, a comet may travel as fast as 445 km/s.

Comets Are Made of a Nucleus and a Tail

All comets have a *nucleus* that is composed of ice and rock. Most comet nuclei are between 1 km and 10 km in diameter. If a comet approaches the sun, solar radiation and heating cause the comet's ice to change to gas. A *coma* is a spherical cloud of gas and dust that comes off of the nucleus. The *ion tail* of a comet is gas that has been ionized, or stripped of electrons, by the sun. The solar wind—electrically charged particles expanding away from the sun—pushes the gas away from the comet's head. So, regardless of the direction a comet is traveling, its ion tail points away from the sun. A second tail made of dust and gas curves backward along the comet's orbit. This *dust tail* can be millions of kilometers long.

Visualize It!

13 Identify Use the write-on lines in the diagram to identify the structures of a comet.

Dust tail

(A)

(B)

(C)

Comets Come from the Kuiper Belt and the Oort Cloud

There are two regions of the solar system where comets come from. The first region is the Kuiper Belt, which is where short-period comets originate. The second region is the Oort cloud, which is where long-period comets originate.

Collisions between objects in the Kuiper Belt produce fragments that become comets. These comets are known as *short-period comets*. Short-period comets take less than 200 years to orbit the sun. Therefore, they return to the inner solar system quite frequently, perhaps every few decades or centuries. Short-period comets also have short life spans. Every time a comet passes the sun, it may lose a layer as much as 1 m thick.

Some comets originate in the Oort cloud. The **Oort cloud** is a spherical region that surrounds the solar system and extends almost halfway to the nearest star. Comets can form in the Oort cloud when two objects collide. Comets can also form when an object in the Oort cloud is disturbed by the gravity of a nearby star and is sent into the inner solar system. Comets that originate in the Oort cloud are called *long-period comets*. Long-period comets may take up to hundreds of thousands of years to orbit the sun.

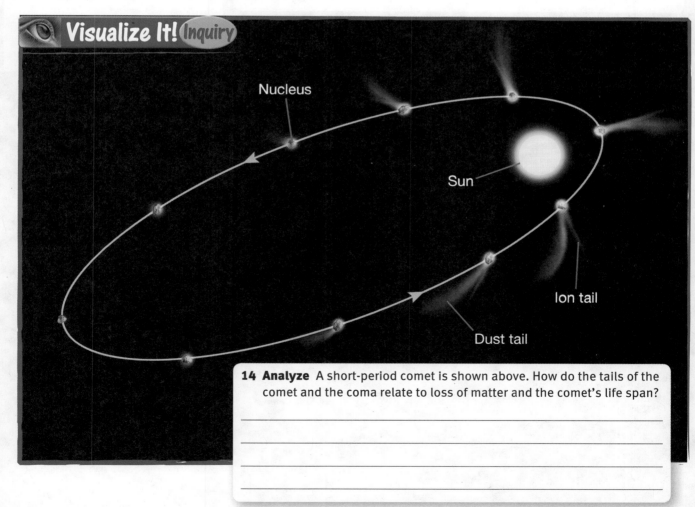

Visualize It! Inquiry

Nucleus

Sun

Ion tail

Dust tail

14 Analyze A short-period comet is shown above. How do the tails of the comet and the coma relate to loss of matter and the comet's life span?

_____

_____

_____

_____

On the rocks

What do we know about asteroids?

Active Reading **15 Identify** As you read the text, underline those places in the solar system where asteroids are located.

An **asteroid** is a small, irregularly shaped, rocky object that orbits the sun. Most asteroids are located between the orbits of Mars and Jupiter. This 300 million–km–wide region is known as the *asteroid belt*. The asteroid belt contains hundreds of thousands of asteroids, called *main-belt asteroids*. The largest main-belt asteroid by diameter is Pallas, which has a diameter of 570 km. The smallest asteroid is 4 m in diameter. Groups of asteroids are also located in the orbits of Jupiter and Neptune (called *Trojan asteroids*) and in the Kuiper Belt. Still other asteroids are called *near-Earth asteroids*. Some of these asteroids cross the orbits of Earth and Venus.

Asteroids in the asteroid belt orbit the sun at about 18 km/s and have orbital periods of 3 to 8 years. Although most asteroids rotate around their axis, some tumble end over end through space.

Visualize It!

16 Analyze Where is the asteroid belt located?

_____

_____

_____

_____

_____

_____

Asteroid Belt

Mars

Trojan Asteroids

Sizes and distances are not to scale.

Trojan Asteroids

Jupiter

Asteroids Have Different Compositions

The composition of asteroids varies. Many asteroids have dark surfaces. Scientists think that these asteroids are rich in carbon. Other asteroids are thought to be rocky and to have a core made of iron and nickel. Still other asteroids may have a rocky core surrounded largely by ice. Small, rocky asteroids have perhaps the strangest composition of all. They appear to be piles of rock loosely held together by gravity. Asteroid Itokawa (ee•TOH•kah•wah), shown below, is a rocky asteroid known as a "rubble-pile" asteroid.

Some asteroids contain economic minerals like those mined on Earth. Economic minerals that are found in asteroids include gold, iron, nickel, manganese, cobalt, and platinum. Scientists are now investigating the potential for mining near-Earth asteroids.

Itokawa is a rubble-pile asteroid. Astronomers think that the 500 m–long asteroid may be composed of two asteroids that are joined.

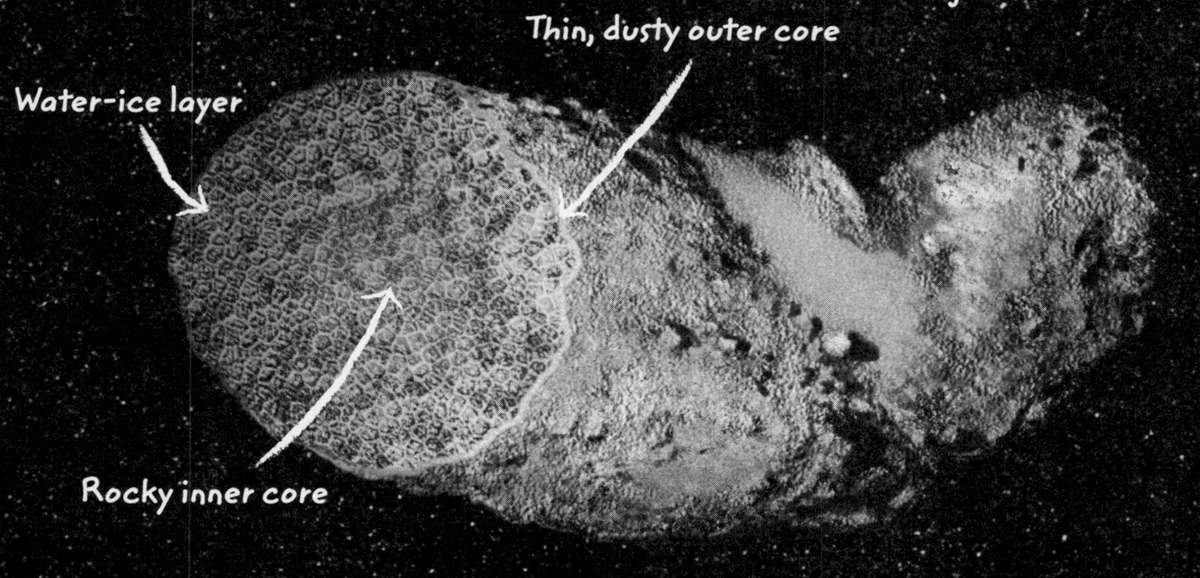

Thin, dusty outer core

Water-ice layer

Rocky inner core

Greetings from Eros!

Think Outside the Book

17 **Describe** Eros is a near-Earth asteroid that tumbles through space. Imagine that you are the first human to explore Eros. Write a postcard that describes what you found on Eros. Then research the asteroid and find out how close your description came to reality.

Burned Out

What do we know about meteoroids, meteors, and meteorites?

A sand grain- to boulder-sized, rocky body that travels through space is a **meteoroid**. Meteoroids that enter Earth's atmosphere travel at about 52 km/s, as measured by radar on Earth. Friction heats these meteoroids to thousands of degrees Celsius, which causes them to glow. The atmosphere around a meteoroid's path also gets hotter and glows because of friction between the meteoroid and air molecules. A bright streak of light that results when a meteoroid burns up in Earth's atmosphere is called a **meteor**. A **meteorite** is a meteoroid that reaches Earth's surface without burning up.

18 Identify Use the write-on lines below to identify the three objects that are shown.

A A small, rocky body that travels through space is a

_____

B The glowing trail of a body that is burning up in Earth's atmosphere is a _____

C A body that reaches Earth's surface without burning up is a _____

A meteorite 45 m across produced kilometer-wide Barringer Crater in Arizona about 50,000 years ago.

Meteorites Reach Earth

Meteoroids come from the asteroid belt, Mars, the moon, and comets. Most of the meteoroids that enter Earth's atmosphere do not reach Earth's surface. Many meteoroids explode in the upper atmosphere. These explosions are often recorded by military satellites in orbit around Earth. Other meteoroids skip back into space after briefly crossing the upper atmosphere. However, some large meteoroids that enter Earth's lower atmosphere or strike Earth's surface can be destructive. Scientists estimate that a destructive meteorite impact occurs every 300 to 400 years.

Meteorites Have Different Compositions

Meteorites can be divided into three general groups. The first group of meteorites are the stony meteorites. They are the most common form of meteorite. Stony meteorites are made of silicate minerals, just like rocks on Earth. Some stony meteorites also contain small amounts of organic matter. A much smaller group of meteorites are the iron meteorites. Iron meteorites are composed of iron and nickel. The rarest group of meteorites are stony-iron meteorites. Stony-iron meteorites are composed of both silicate minerals and iron and nickel. All three groups of meteorites can originate from asteroids. However, some stony meteorites come from the moon and Mars.

Visualize It!

19 Describe In the boxes below, describe the composition and origin of each group of meteorite. Also, indicate how common each group of meteorite is.

Stony meteorite

_____
_____
_____
_____
_____

Iron meteorite

_____
_____
_____
_____
_____

Stony-iron meteorite

_____
_____
_____
_____
_____

Visual Summary

To complete this summary, answer the questions below. Then use the key below to check your answers. You can use this page to review the main concepts of the lesson.

Small Bodies in the Solar System

Small bodies are found throughout the solar system.

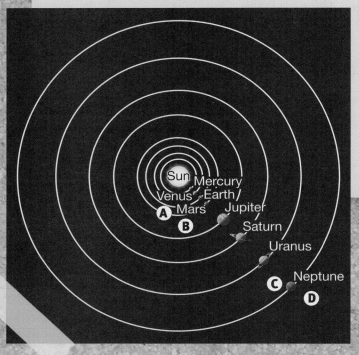

Sun
Mercury
Venus Earth
Mars Jupiter
A
B
Saturn
Uranus
C Neptune
D

Answers: 20 asteroids A, B, C; dwarf planets B, D; KBOs C, D; 21 F, F, T

20 Enter the correct letter or letters that indicate a location for each small body in the solar system.

Asteroids	
Dwarf planets	
Kuiper Belt objects	

21 Check true or false to answer the questions below.

T	F	
☐	☐	Comets originate in the asteroid belt and the Kuiper Belt.
☐	☐	Three groups of asteroids are stony, iron, and stony-iron.
☐	☐	Most meteoroids that enter Earth's atmosphere burn up.

22 Compare Make a table in which you compare and contrast comets and asteroids in terms of composition, location in the solar system, and size.

Lesson Review

Vocabulary

Fill in the blank with the term that best completes the following sentences.

1 The _____ is a spherical region that surrounds the solar system and extends almost halfway to the nearest star.

2 A region of the solar system that extends from the orbit of Neptune to about twice the orbit of Neptune is the _____.

3 Most _____ are located between the orbits of Mars and Jupiter.

4 A meteoroid that reaches Earth's surface without burning up is a _____.

Key Concepts

In the following table, write the name of the correct body next to the property of that body.

Property	Body
5 Identify What is a minor body that orbits outside the orbit of Neptune?	
6 Identify What is a small body that follows a highly elliptical orbit around the sun?	
7 Identify What is the largest of the small bodies that are found in the solar system?	
8 Identify What is the glowing trail that results when a meteoroid burns up in Earth's atmosphere?	

Critical Thinking

Use this table to answer the following questions.

Comet	Orbital Period (years)
Borrelly	6.9
Halley	76
Hale-Bopp	2,400
Hyakutake	100,000

9 Apply Which of the comets in the table are short-period comets?

_____

_____

10 Apply Which of the comets in the table most likely originated in the Oort cloud?

_____

_____

11 Infer Why do you think that the speeds of comets increase as they near the sun?

_____

_____

_____

_____

12 Predict Why do you think that some asteroids tumble end over end through space while other asteroids rotate around their axis?

_____

_____

_____

_____

My Notes

Unit 2 〉 Big Idea 〉 Planets and a variety of other bodies form a system of objects orbiting the sun.

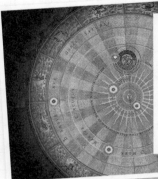

Lesson 1
ESSENTIAL QUESTION
How have people modeled the solar system?

Compare various historical models of the solar system.

Lesson 4
ESSENTIAL QUESTION
What is known about the terrestrial planets?

Describe some of the properties of the terrestrial planets and how the properties of Mercury, Venus, and Mars differ from the properties of Earth.

Lesson 2
ESSENTIAL QUESTION
Why is gravity important in the solar system?

Explain the role that gravity played in the formation of the solar system and in determining the motion of the planets.

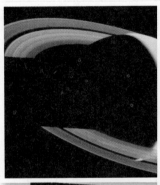

Lesson 5
ESSENTIAL QUESTION
What is known about the gas giant planets?

Describe some of the properties of the gas giant planets and how these properties differ from the physical properties of Earth.

Lesson 3
ESSENTIAL QUESTION
What are the properties of the sun?

Describe the structure and rotation of the sun, energy production and energy transport in the sun, and solar activity on the sun.

Lesson 6
ESSENTIAL QUESTION
What is found in the solar system besides the sun, planets, and moons?

Compare and contrast the properties of small bodies in the solar system.

Connect ESSENTIAL QUESTIONS
Lessons 4 and 5

1 Synthesize Explain why the planet Jupiter has more moons than the planet Mars.

_____

_____

_____

_____

Think Outside the Book

2 Synthesize Choose one of these activities to help synthesize what you have learned in this unit.

☐ Using what you learned in lessons 4 and 5, write a short essay explaining where in the solar system besides Earth life could exist.

☐ Using what you learned in lessons 2, 3, and 4, make a poster showing why comets are the fastest-moving bodies in the solar system.

Unit 2 Review

Name _____

Vocabulary

Fill in each blank with the term that best completes the following sentences.

1 _____ is the process in which energy is released as the nuclei of small atoms combine to form a larger nucleus.

2 The solar system formed from a _____, which is a rotating cloud of gas and dust that formed into the sun and planets.

3 When an object looks as if the position has shifted when it is viewed from different locations, this is referred to as _____.

4 Earth, Venus, Mars, and Mercury are considered _____, which are highly dense planets nearest the sun.

5 A(n) _____ is a small, rocky object that orbits the sun; many of these objects are located in a band between the orbits of Mars and Jupiter.

Key Concepts

Read each question below, and circle the best answer.

6 This diagram illustrates a historical model of the solar system.

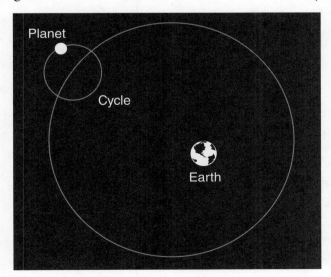

Which type of model is shown?

A geocentric model

C Copernican model

B heliocentric model

D Aristarchan model

7 Galileo Galilei showed that Earth was not the center of our solar system. By which method did he do this?

A calculating mathematical models

B using a telescope to see four moons orbiting Jupiter and the phases of Venus

C observing the sun

D assuming that all pre-existing astronomic theories were incorrect

8 The Kuiper Belt, pictured below, is generally thought to contain leftover bits from the formation of the solar system.

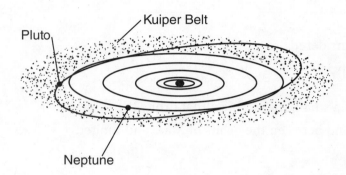

Which of the following describes Kuiper Belt objects?

A often larger than some planets in the solar system

B extremely hot

C minor planet-sized objects that orbit the sun in a flat belt beyond Neptune's orbit

D 100 AU wide

9 Suppose the comets in the table orbited the sun.

Comet Name	Comet Size (km)	Comet Speed (km/h)
Rasmussen	1	750,000
Zigler	10	2
Schier	5	1.5 million
Brant	3	3,700

Using what you know about comets, which comet is in the closest orbit to the sun?

A Rasmussen

B Zigler

C Schier

D Brant

10 Which of the following is a list of the gas giant planets?

A Jupiter, Saturn, Uranus, and Neptune

B Earth, Mars, and Venus

C Pluto, Saturn, and Jupiter

D Earth, Jupiter, Neptune, and Saturn

11 Below is an illustration of the planet Saturn. Saturn is one of the four gas giant planets.

Saturn

Which of the four statements below is not true about Saturn?

A It travels around the Sun once every 29.5 years.

B It is the only planet with a ring system.

C It is composed mostly of hydrogen and helium gas.

D It has a large number of moons.

12 Earth, Mercury, and Venus are all classified as terrestrial planets. When compared to Earth, which of the following is true of Mercury and Venus?

A Mercury and Venus have a higher surface gravity than Earth.

B Mercury and Venus have a longer period of revolution than Earth.

C Mercury and Venus have slower periods of rotation (longer days) than Earth.

D Mercury and Venus are farther away from the sun than Earth.

13 Which of the following lists accurately relates which terrestrial planets have moons and how many moons they have?

  A Mercury and Venus (no moons), Earth (one moon), and Mars (two moons)

  B Mercury, Venus, and Earth (one moon each), and Mars (two moons)

  C Mercury and Venus (no moons), Earth (two moons), and Mars (two moons)

  D Mercury and Venus (no moons), Earth (one moon), and Mars (three moons)

14 Why is nuclear fusion possible in the cores of stars?

  A Hydrogen exists only in the cores of stars.

  B Hydrogen and helium nuclei require a lot of light to bond together.

  C High temperatures and pressures, which are required for fusion to occur, occur in the cores of stars.

  D $E = mc^2$ only works in the cores of stars.

15 The sunspot cycle is a period of about 11 years during which the number of sunspots rises and falls. What are sunspots?

  A a light area on the sun's corona that is hotter than surrounding areas

  B a darker area on the photosphere that is cooler than surrounding areas

  C a spot with a weaker magnetic field

  D a spot easily seen without a telescope

16 Which describes an effect of centripedal force?

  A objects break apart in space

  B objects burn at very high temperatures

  C objects move in a circular path

  D objects move in an elliptical path

17 What does Kepler's first law of planetary motion state?

A the orbit of a planet around the sun is an ellipse with the sun at one focus

B the orbit of a planet is dependent on heat

C the difference between centripedal force and elliptical force

D the orbital period is infinite

Critical Thinking

Answer the following questions in the space provided.

18 Explain the difference between a meteoroid, a meteor, and a meteorite. Which one would you most likely see on the surface of Earth?

_____

_____

_____

_____

_____

_____

19 Name three characteristics of gas giants that make them different from terrestrial planets.

_____

_____

_____

_____

20 Study the diagrams below.

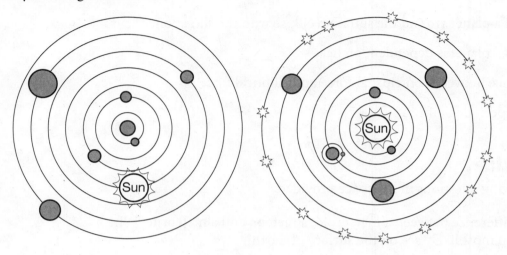

Explain what the two diagrams show. What is significant about them? How were these models developed and by whom? How do the models affect the way we study and think about our solar system?

_____

_____

_____

_____

_____

_____

Connect **ESSENTIAL QUESTIONS**
Lessons 2, 3, 4, 5, and 6

Answer the following question in the space provided.

21 Discuss gravitational force in our universe and how it works. Why is it critical to our universe? Name at least three instances of gravitational forces at work in our solar system.

_____

_____

_____

_____

_____

_____

_____

The Earth-Moon-Sun System

Big Idea

Earth and the moon move in predictable ways and have predictable effects on each other as they orbit the sun.

What do you think?

Earth is affected by its sun and moon. The sun provides light and energy. The sun and moon regulate Earth's tides. How do tides affect life on Earth?

Tidal pool exposed by low tide

Unit 3
The Earth-Moon-Sun System

Measuring Shadows

One way to learn more about Earth's rotation and orbit is to study the shadows created by the sun throughout the year. Help students with an ongoing research project, called the Sun Shadows Project. The results are presented at the American Geophysical Union's Annual Conference every year.

1 Think About It

Students at James Monroe Middle School in Albuquerque, New Mexico, asked the following questions: The seasons change, but do the length of shadows? How could this be measured? What do you think?

_____

_____

_____

Scientists in Antarctica measure shadows.

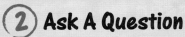

② Ask A Question

What effects do seasons have on the lengths of shadows in your area?

As a class, come up with a prediction. Then, research what students at James Monroe Middle School are doing to gather information.

Things to Consider

Some parts of the world participate in Daylight Savings Time. People move their clocks forward by an hour in the spring and back by an hour in the fall. Daylight Savings Time may affect the way that you will need to collect data in comparison to students at James Monroe Middle School. Make sure to take your measurements when shadows are shortest.

③ Apply Your Knowledge

A List the materials your class will need in order to make and record the measurements to gather the information needed by the students at James Monroe Middle School.

_____

_____

_____

_____

B Decide on a time frame for your class project. Will you participate for an entire season? What factors influence your decision?

_____

_____

_____

_____

_____

C Track the information gathered by your class and draw your own preliminary conclusions.

_____

_____

_____

_____

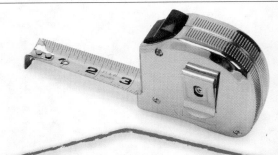

Take It Home

Who else is participating in the Sun Shadows Project? Research the various national and international groups taking part, such as the U.S. Antarctic Program. See *ScienceSaurus*® for more information about the motions of the Earth and the moon.

Earth's Days, Years, and Seasons

ESSENTIAL QUESTION

How are Earth's days, years, and seasons related to the way Earth moves in space?

By the end of this lesson, you should be able to relate Earth's days, years, and seasons to Earth's movement in space.

In many parts of the world, blooming flowers are one of the first signs that spring has arrived. Spring flowers start blooming with the warmer temperatures of spring, even if there is still snow on the ground.

Lesson Labs

Quick Labs
• Earth's Rotation and Revolution
• Seasons Model

Field Lab
• Sunlight and Temperature

Engage Your Brain

1 Predict Check T or F to show whether you think each statement is true or false.

T   F

☐   ☐   A day is about 12 hours long.

☐   ☐   A year is about 365 days long.

☐   ☐   When it is summer in the Northern Hemisphere, it is summer all around the world.

2 Apply Write your own caption for this photo of leaves in the space below.

_____

_____

_____

_____

_____

_____

Active Reading

3 Synthesize The term *rotation* can be tricky to remember because it is used somewhat differently in science than it is in everyday life. In baseball, a pitching *rotation* lists the order of a team's starting pitchers. The order starts over after the last pitcher on the list has played. On the lines below, write down any other examples you can think of that use the term *rotation*.

rotation:

_____

_____

_____

_____

Vocabulary Terms

• rotation   • season
• day   • equinox
• revolution   • solstice
• year

4 Apply As you learn the definition of each vocabulary term in this lesson, create your own definition or sketch to help you remember the meaning of the term.

Spinning in

What determines the length of a day?

Each planet spins on its axis. Earth's axis (ACK•sis) is an imaginary straight line that runs from the North Pole to the South Pole. The spinning of a body, such as a planet, on its axis is called **rotation**. The time it takes a planet to complete one full rotation on its axis is called a **day**.

Active Reading

5 Identify As you read, underline the places on Earth's surface at which the ends of Earth's axis would be.

The Time It Takes for Earth to Rotate Once

Earth rotates in a counterclockwise motion around its axis when viewed from above the North Pole. This means that as a location on Earth's equator rotates from west to east, the sun appears to rise in the east. The sun then appears to cross the sky and set in the west.

As Earth rotates, only one-half of Earth faces the sun at any given time. People on the half of Earth facing the sun experience daylight. This period of time in daylight is called *daytime*. People on the half of Earth that faces away from the sun experience darkness. This period of time in darkness is called *nighttime*.

Earth's rotation is used to measure time. Earth completes one rotation on its axis in 24 hours, or in one day. Most locations on Earth's surface move through daylight and darkness in that time.

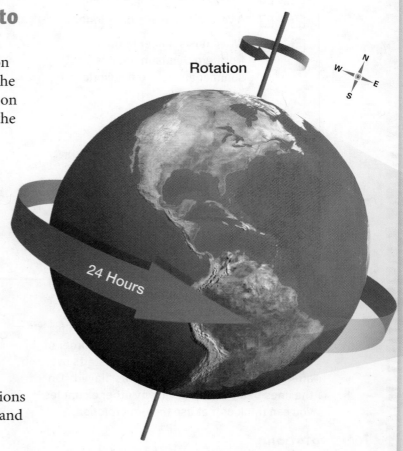

Rotation

24 Hours

Earth's motion is used to measure the length of an Earth day.

Circles

What determines the length of a year?

As Earth rotates on its axis, Earth also revolves around the sun. Although you cannot feel Earth moving, it is traveling around the sun at an average speed of nearly 30 km/s. The motion of a body that travels around another body in space is called **revolution** (reh•vuh•LOO•shun). Earth completes a full revolution around the sun in 365 ¼ days, or about one **year**. We have divided the year into 12 months, each month lasting from 28 to 31 days.

Earth's orbit is not quite a perfect circle. In January, Earth is about 2.5 million kilometers closer to the sun than it is in July. You may be surprised that this distance makes only a tiny difference in temperatures on Earth.

Visualize It!

7 Apply Imagine that Earth's current position is at point A below. Write the label B to show Earth's position 6 months from now in the same diagram.

This drawing is not to scale.

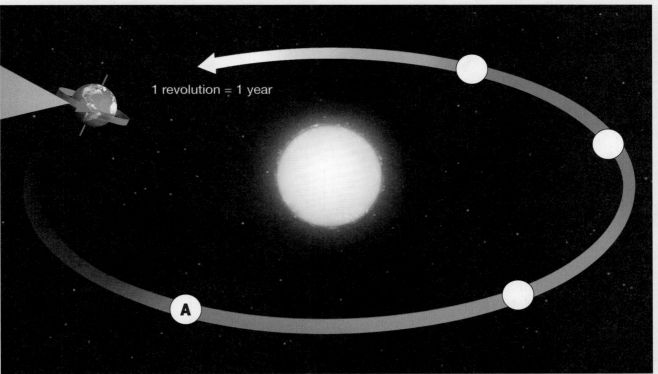

1 revolution = 1 year

Tilt-a-Whirl

What conditions are affected by the tilt of Earth's axis?

Earth's axis is tilted at 23.5°. Earth's axis always points toward the North Star as Earth revolves around the sun. Thus, during each revolution, the North Pole may be tilted toward the sun or away from the sun, as seen below. When the North Pole is tilted toward the sun, the Northern Hemisphere (HEHM•ih•sfeer) has longer periods of daylight than does the Southern Hemisphere. When the North Pole is tilted away from the sun, the opposite is true.

The direction of tilt of Earth's axis remains the same throughout Earth's orbit around the sun.

23.5°

23.5°

orbit

This drawing is not to scale.

Temperature

The angle at which the sun's rays strike each part of Earth's surface changes as Earth moves in its orbit. When the North Pole is tilted toward the sun, the sun's rays strike the Northern Hemisphere more directly. Thus, the region receives a higher concentration of solar energy and is warmer. When the North Pole is tilted away from the sun, the sun's rays strike the Northern Hemisphere less directly. When the sunlight is less direct, the solar energy is less concentrated and the region is cooler.

The spherical shape of Earth also affects how the sun warms up an area. Temperatures are high at point A in the diagram. This is because the sun's rays hit Earth's surface at a right angle and are focused in a small area. Toward the poles, the sun's rays hit Earth's surface at a lesser angle. Therefore, the rays are spread out over a larger area and the temperatures are cooler.

Visualize It!

8 Apply Which location on the illustration of Earth below receives more direct rays from the sun?
- [ ] A
- [ ] B
- [ ] They receive equal amounts.

9 Identify Which location is cooler?_____

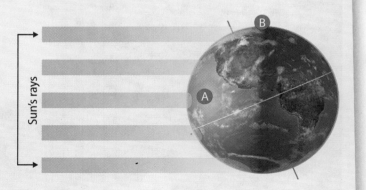

Sun's rays

Daylight Hours

All locations on Earth experience an *average* of 12 hours of light a day. However, the *actual* number of daylight hours on any given day of the year varies with location. Areas around Earth's equator receive about 12 hours of light a day. Areas on Earth's surface that are tilted toward the sun have more hours of daylight. These areas travel a longer path through the lit part of Earth than areas at the equator. Areas on Earth's surface that are tilted away from the sun have less than 12 hours of light a day. These areas travel a shorter path through the lit part of Earth, as shown below.

This drawing is not to scale.

Sun's Rays

During summer in the Northern Hemisphere, a person has already had many daylight hours by the time a person in the Southern Hemisphere reaches daylight.

About twelve hours later, the person in the Northern Hemisphere is close to daylight again, while the person in the Southern Hemisphere still has many hours of darkness left.

Midnight Sun

When it is summer in the Northern Hemisphere, the time in each day that it is light increases as you move north of the equator. Areas north of the Arctic Circle have 24 hours of daylight, called the "midnight sun," as seen in the photo. At the same time, areas south of the Antarctic Circle receive 24 hours of darkness, or "polar night." When it is winter in the Northern Hemisphere, conditions in the polar areas are reversed.

Visualize It! Inquiry

10 Synthesize Why isn't the area in the photo very warm even though the sun is up all night long?

_____

_____

_____

This composite image shows that the sun never set on this Arctic summer day.

Seasons change...

What causes seasons?

Most locations on Earth experience seasons. Each **season** is characterized by a pattern of temperature and other weather trends. Near the equator, the temperatures are almost the same year-round. Near the poles, there are very large changes in temperatures from winter to summer. We experience seasons due to the changes in the intensity of sunlight and the number of daylight hours as Earth revolves around the sun. So, both the tilt of Earth's axis and Earth's spherical shape play a role in Earth's changing seasons.

As Earth travels around the sun, the area of sunlight in each hemisphere changes. At an **equinox** (EE•kwuh•nahks), sunlight shines equally on the Northern and Southern Hemispheres. Half of each hemisphere is lit, and half is in darkness. As Earth moves along its orbit, the sunlight reaches more of one hemisphere than the other. At a **solstice** (SAHL•stis), the area of sunlight is at a maximum in one hemisphere and at a minimum in the other hemisphere.

- **September Equinox** When Earth is in this position, sunlight shines equally on both poles.
- **December Solstice** About three months later, Earth has traveled a quarter of the way around the sun, but its axis still points in the same direction into space. The North Pole leans away from the sun and is in complete darkness. The South Pole is in complete sunlight.
- **March Equinox** After another quarter of its orbit, Earth reaches another equinox. Half of each hemisphere is lit, and the sunlight is centered on the equator.
- **June Solstice** This position is opposite to the December solstice. Now the North Pole leans toward the sun and is in complete sunlight, and the south pole is in complete darkness.

Visualize It!

The amount of sunlight an area on Earth receives changes during the year. These changes are due to Earth's tilt and position in its orbit around the sun. Equinoxes and solstices mark certain points in the range of sunlight each of Earth's hemispheres receives.

This drawing is not to scale.

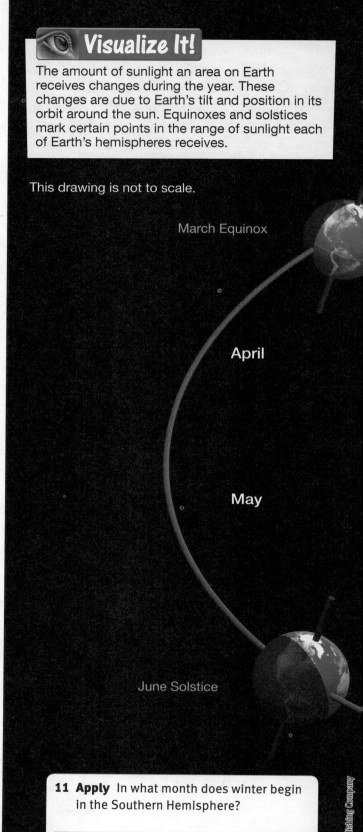

March Equinox

April

May

June Solstice

11 Apply In what month does winter begin in the Southern Hemisphere?

_____

12 Infer During which solstice would the sun be at its highest point in the sky in the Northern Hemisphere?

_____

Solstices

The seasons of summer and winter begin on days called *solstices*. Each year on June 21 or 22, the North Pole's tilt toward the sun is greatest. This day is called the *June solstice*. This solstice marks the beginning of summer in the Northern Hemisphere. By December 21 or 22, the North Pole is tilted to the farthest point away from the sun. This day is the December solstice.

December Solstice

February

January

November

October

July

August

September Equinox

13 Infer In which parts of the world is an equinox most different from other days of the year?

_____

_____

Equinoxes

The seasons fall and spring begin on days called *equinoxes*. The hours of daylight and darkness are approximately equal everywhere on Earth on these days. The *September equinox* occurs on September 22 or 23 of each year. This equinox marks the beginning of fall in the Northern Hemisphere. The March equinox on March 20 or 21 of each year marks the beginning of spring.

Visual Summary

To complete this summary, circle the correct word. Then use the key below to check your answers. You can use this page to review the main concepts of the lesson.

The length of a day is determined by Earth's rotation.

14 It takes Earth 24 seconds/hours to make one rotation on its axis.

The length of a year is determined by Earth's revolution around the sun.

15 It takes Earth about 365 hours/days to revolve around the sun.

Earth's
Days, Years, and Seasons

Earth's tilt affects temperatures and daylight hours at different locations on Earth.

Sun's rays

16 Earth's temperatures and hours of daylight stay the most constant at the equator/poles.

This diagram shows how seasons change in the Northern Hemisphere as Earth orbits the sun.

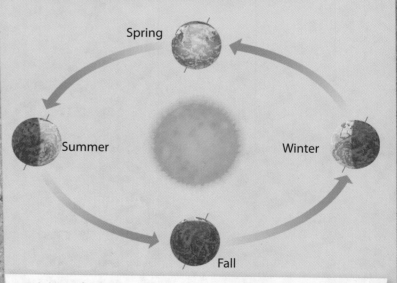

Spring

Summer

Winter

Fall

17 When it is summer in the Northern Hemisphere, it is summer/winter in the Southern Hemisphere.

Answers: 14 hours; 15 days; 16 equator; 17 winter

18 Predict How would conditions on Earth change if Earth stopped rotating on its axis?

Lesson Review

Vocabulary

In the space provided below, describe how each set of words are related.

1 revolution, year

_____

_____

2 rotation, day

_____

_____

3 season, equinox, solstice

_____

_____

_____

_____

_____

Key Concepts

4 Identify About how many days are in an Earth year? And how many hours in an Earth day?

_____

5 Describe How does the tilt of Earth's axis affect how the sun's rays strike Earth?

_____

_____

_____

_____

6 Synthesize How does the tilt of Earth's axis affect the number of daylight hours and the temperature of a location on Earth?

_____

_____

_____

_____

Critical Thinking

Use this image to answer the questions below.

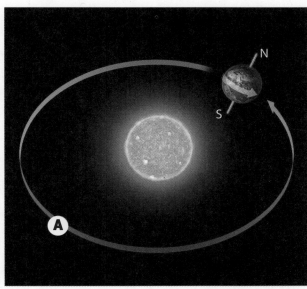

This drawing is not to scale.

7 Identify What season is the Northern Hemisphere experiencing in the image above?

_____

8 Explain How do the tilt of Earth's axis and Earth's movements around the sun cause seasons?

_____

_____

_____

_____

_____

_____

_____

_____

_____

_____

9 Describe If the Earth moves to point A in the image above, what season will the Northern Hemisphere experience?

_____

_____

My Notes

Analyzing Scientific Explanations

Scientists use different methods to develop scientific explanations in different fields of study. Scientists base their explanations on data collected through observation and measurement. After scientists make observations and collect data, they analyze current explanations for what they observed. If a new observation doesn't fit an existing explanation, scientists might work to revise the explanation or to offer a new one.

Tutorial

The text below describes how Ptolemy, a Greek astronomer in the second century C.E., described the universe. Consider the following steps as you analyze scientific explanations.

As Aristotle put forth, Earth is at the center of the universe. All other planets and the Sun revolve around Earth, each on its own sphere. The spheres follow this order outward from Earth: Mercury, Venus, the Moon, the Sun, Mars, Jupiter, Saturn, and the Fixed Stars. Each sphere turns at its own steady pace. Bodies do appear to move backward during their wanderings, but that does not mean the spheres do not keep a steady pace. This is explained by the movement of the bodies along smaller spheres that turn along the edge of the larger spheres. My calculations and models agree with and predict the motions of the spheres. The constant turning of the spheres also moves the bodies closer to Earth and farther from Earth, which explains why the bodies appear brighter or darker at different times. Thus, the heavens remain perfect. This perfection leads to music in the heavens, created by the spheres.

Identify the evidence that supports the explanation. At least two different lines of evidence are needed to be considered valid.

Identify any evidence that does not support the explanation. A single line of evidence can disprove an explanation. Often, new evidence makes scientists reevaluate an explanation. By the 1500s, Ptolemy's model was not making accurate predictions. In 1543, Copernicus, a Polish astronomer, proposed a new explanation of how planets move.

Identify any additional lines of evidence that should be considered. They might point to additional investigations to further examine the explanation. The gravitational force between objects was not known in Ptolemy's time. However, it should be considered when explaining the motion of planets.

Decide whether the original explanation is supported by enough evidence. An alternative explanation might better explain the evidence or might explain a wider range of observations.

If possible, propose an alternative explanation that could fit the evidence. Often, a simpler explanation is better if it fits the evidence. Copernicus explained the apparent backward movement and changing brightness of planets by placing the sun at the center of the solar system with the planets revolving around it.

You Try It!

In 2006, an official definition of a planet was determined. Read and analyze the information below concerning the classification of the largest Main Belt asteroid, Ceres.

The members of the International Astronomical Union (IAU) voted for the official definition of a planet to be a celestial body that

1. orbits the sun,
2. has enough mass so that its gravity helps it to maintain a nearly round shape,
3. has cleared the neighborhood around its orbit.

A group suggests that Ceres be considered a planet under the new definition. As the largest Main Belt asteroid, Ceres orbits the sun along with thousands of smaller asteroids. Images of Ceres clearly show its nearly round shape. These points, says the group's leader, should qualify Ceres as a planet.

1 Making Observations Underline lines of evidence that support the explanation.

2 Evaluating Data Circle any lines of evidence that do not support the proposed explanation. Explain why this evidence does not support the classification.

_____

_____

_____

_____

_____

3 Applying Concepts Identify any additional evidence that should be considered when evaluating the explanation.

_____

_____

_____

_____

4 Communicating Ideas If possible, propose an alternative explanation that could fit the evidence.

_____

_____

_____

_____

_____

_____

_____

Take It Home

Pluto was recently reclassified. What was it changed to and why? Identify the evidence that supported the decision. How does this compare to the proposed reclassification of Ceres? List similarities of the two explanations in a chart.

Moon Phases and Eclipses

ESSENTIAL QUESTION

How do Earth, the moon, and the sun affect each other?

By the end of this lesson, you should be able to describe the effects the sun and the moon have on Earth, including gravitational attraction, moon phases, and eclipses.

Why is part of the moon orange? Because Earth is moving between the moon and the sun, casting a shadow on the moon.

Engage Your Brain

1 Identify Fill in the blanks with the word or phrase you think correctly completes the following sentences.

We can see the moon because it _____ the light from the sun.

The moon's _____ affects the oceans' tides on Earth.

The impact craters on the moon were created by collisions with _____, meteorites, and asteroids.

2 Describe Write your own caption for this photo in the space below.

_____

_____

_____

_____

_____

_____

Active Reading

3 Synthesize You can often define an unknown word if you know the meaning of its word parts. Use the word parts and sentence below to make an educated guess about the meaning of the word *penumbra*.

Word part	Meaning
umbra	shade or shadow
pen-, from the Latin *paene*	almost

Example sentence
An observer in the <u>penumbra</u> experiences only a partial eclipse.

Vocabulary Terms
- satellite
- gravity
- lunar phases
- eclipse
- umbra
- penumbra

4 Apply As you learn the definition of each vocabulary term in this lesson, create your own definition or sketch to help you remember the meaning of the term.

penumbra:

_____

_____

_____

'Round and 'Round They Go!

How are Earth, the moon, and the sun related in space?

Earth not only spins on its axis, but like the seven other planets in our solar system, Earth also orbits the sun. A body that orbits a larger body is called a **satellite** (SAT'l•yt). Six of the planets in our solar system have smaller bodies that orbit around each of them. These natural satellites are also called moons. Our moon is Earth's natural satellite.

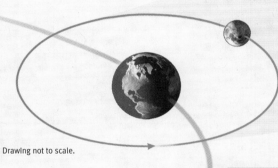

Earth revolves around the sun as the moon revolves around Earth.

Drawing not to scale.

Active Reading

5 Identify As you read, underline the reason that the moon stays in orbit around Earth.

Earth and the Moon Orbit the Sun

All bodies that have mass exert a force that pulls other objects with mass toward themselves. This force is called **gravity.** The mass of Earth is much larger than the mass of the moon, and therefore Earth's gravity exerts a stronger pull on the moon than the moon does on Earth. It is Earth's gravitational pull that keeps the moon in orbit around Earth, forming the Earth–moon system.

The Earth–moon system is itself in orbit around the sun. Even though the sun is relatively far away, the mass of the sun exerts a large gravitational pull on the Earth–moon system. This gravitational pull keeps the Earth–moon system in orbit around the sun.

The Moon Orbits Earth

The pull of Earth's gravity keeps the moon, Earth's natural satellite, in orbit around Earth. Even though the moon is Earth's closest neighbor in space, it is far away compared to the sizes of Earth and the moon themselves.

The distance between Earth and the moon is roughly 383,000 km (238,000 mi)—about a hundred times the distance between New York and Los Angeles. If a jet airliner could travel in space, it would take about 20 days to cover a distance that huge. Astronauts, whose spaceships travel much faster than jets, need about 3 days to reach the moon.

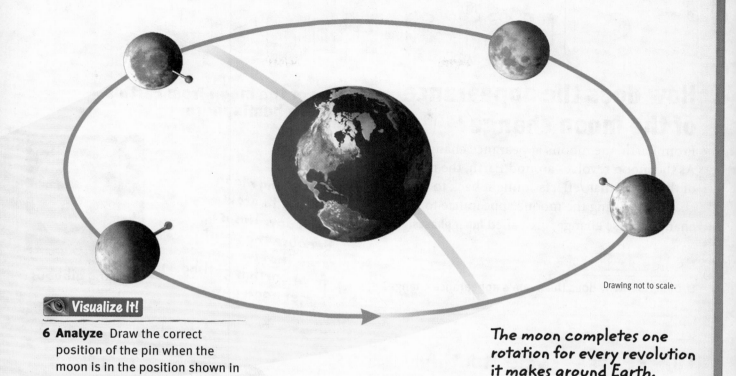

Drawing not to scale.

 Visualize It!

6 Analyze Draw the correct position of the pin when the moon is in the position shown in the top right corner of this figure.

The moon completes one rotation for every revolution it makes around Earth.

What does the moon look like from Earth?

The moon is only visible from Earth when it reflects the sunlight that reaches the moon. Although the moon is most easily seen at night, you have probably also seen it during daytime on some days. In the daytime, the moon may only be as bright as a thin cloud and can be easily missed. On some days you can see the moon during both the daytime and at night, whereas on other days, you may not see the moon at all.

When you can look at the moon, you may notice darker and lighter areas. Perhaps you have imagined them as features of a face or some other pattern. People around the world have told stories about the animals, people, and objects they have imagined while looking at the light and dark areas of the moon. The dark and light spots do not change over the course of a month because only one side of the moon faces Earth, often called the near side of the moon. This is because the moon rotates once on its own axis each time it orbits Earth. The moon takes 27.3 days or about a month to orbit Earth once.

Inquiry

7 Analyze How would the moon appear to an observer on Earth if the moon did not rotate?

_____

_____

_____

_____

It's Just a Phase!

How does the appearance of the moon change?

From Earth, the moon's appearance changes. As the moon revolves around Earth, the portion of the moon that reflects sunlight back to Earth changes, causing the moon's appearance to change. These changes are called **lunar phases.**

 **Active Reading**

8 Describe Why does the moon's appearance change?

_____

_____

Lunar Phases Cycle Monthly

The cycle begins with a new moon. At this time, Earth, the moon, and the sun are lined up, such that the near side of the moon is unlit. And so there appears to be no moon in the sky.

As the moon moves along its orbit, you begin to see the sunlight on the near side as a thin crescent shape. The crescent becomes thicker as the moon waxes, or grows. When half of the near side of the moon is in the sunlight, the moon has completed one-quarter of its cycle. This phase is called the *first quarter.*

More of the moon is visible during the second week, or the *gibbous* (GIB•uhs) *phase.* This is when the near side is more than half lit but not fully lit. When the moon is halfway through its cycle, the whole near side of the moon is in sunlight, and we see a full moon.

During the third week, the amount of the moon's near side in the sunlight decreases and it seems to shrink, or wane. When the near side is again only half in sunlight, the moon is three-quarters of the way through its cycle. The phase is called the *third quarter.*

In the fourth week, the area of the near side of the moon in sunlight continues to shrink. The moon is seen as waning crescent shapes. Finally, the near side of the moon is unlit—*new moon.*

Views of the moon from Earth's northern hemisphere

The waxing moon appears to grow each day. This is because the sunlit area that we can see from Earth is getting larger each day.

Waxing gibbous

Full moon

Waning gibbous

Think Outside the Book

9 Apply Look at the night sky and keep a moon journal for a series of nights. What phase is the moon in now?

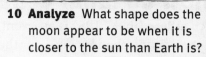

10 Analyze What shape does the moon appear to be when it is closer to the sun than Earth is?

First quarter

Waxing crescent

Drawing not to scale.

New moon

Waning crescent

Third quarter

The waning moon appears to shrink each day. When the moon is waning, the sunlit area is getting smaller. Notice above that even as the phases of the moon change, the total amount of sunlight that the moon gets remains the same. Half the moon is always in sunlight, just as half of Earth is always in sunlight. The moon phases have a period of 29.5 days.

Exploring Eclipses

How do lunar eclipses occur?

An **eclipse** (ih•KLIPS) is an event during which one object in space casts a shadow onto another. On Earth, a lunar eclipse occurs when the moon moves through Earth's shadow. There are two parts of Earth's shadow, as you can see in the diagram below. The **umbra** (UHM•bruh) is the darkest part of a shadow. Around it is a spreading cone of lighter shadow called the **penumbra** (pih•NUHM•bruh). Just before a lunar eclipse, sunlight streaming past Earth produces a full moon. Then the moon moves into Earth's penumbra and becomes slightly less bright. As the moon moves into the umbra, Earth's dark shadow seems to creep across and cover the moon. The entire moon can be in darkness because the moon is small enough to fit entirely within Earth's umbra. After an hour or more, the moon moves slowly back into the sunlight that is streaming past Earth. A total lunar eclipse occurs when the moon passes completely into Earth's umbra. If the moon misses part or all of the umbra, part of the moon stays light and the eclipse is called a partial lunar eclipse.

You may be wondering why you don't see solar and lunar eclipses every month. The reason is that the moon's orbit around Earth is tilted—by about 5°—relative to the orbit of Earth around the sun. This tilt is enough to place the moon out of Earth's shadow for most full moons and Earth out of the moon's shadow for most new moons.

This composite photo shows the partial and total phases of a lunar eclipse over several hours.

Lunar eclipse

Visualize It!

11 Identify Fill in the boxes with the type of eclipse that would occur if the moon were in the areas being pointed to.

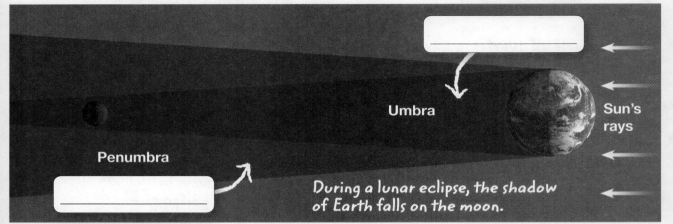

Umbra

Sun's rays

Penumbra

During a lunar eclipse, the shadow of Earth falls on the moon.

Drawing not to scale.

How do solar eclipses occur?

When the moon is directly between the sun and Earth, the shadow of the moon falls on a part of Earth and causes a solar eclipse. During a total solar eclipse, the sun's light is completely blocked by the moon, as seen in this photo. The umbra falls on the area of Earth that lies directly in line with the moon and the sun. Outside the umbra, but within the penumbra, people see a partial solar eclipse. The penumbra falls on the area that immediately surrounds the umbra.

The umbra of the moon is too small to make a large shadow on Earth's surface. The part of the umbra that hits Earth during an eclipse, is never more than a few hundred kilometers across, as shown below. So, a total eclipse of the sun covers only a small part of Earth and is seen only by people in particular parts of Earth along a narrow path. A total solar eclipse usually lasts between one to two minutes at any one location. A total eclipse will not be visible in the United States until 2017, even though there is a total eclipse somewhere on Earth about every one to two years.

Solar eclipse

During a solar eclipse, the moon passes between the sun and Earth so that the sun is partially or totally obscured.

12 Explain Why is it relatively rare to observe a solar eclipse?

_____

_____

_____

_____

Visualize It!

13 Describe Explain what happens during a solar eclipse.

_____

_____

_____

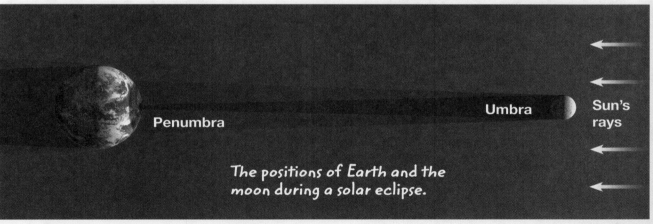

Penumbra

Umbra

Sun's rays

The positions of Earth and the moon during a solar eclipse.

Drawing not to scale.

Visual Summary

To complete this summary, circle the correct word. Then use the key below to check your answers. You can use this page to review the main concepts of the lesson.

Moon Phases and Eclipses

The Earth–moon system orbits the sun.

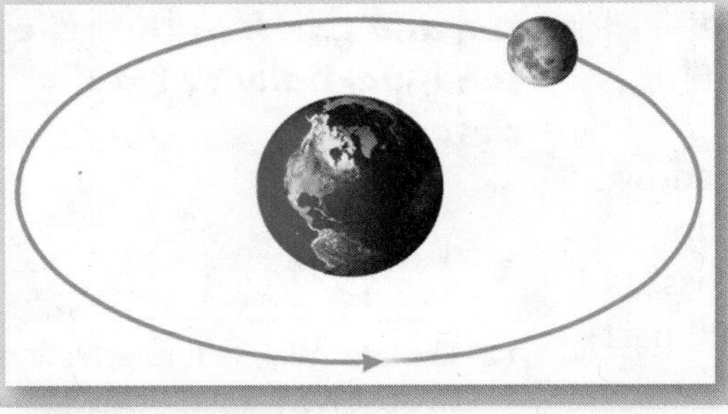

14 The moon takes about one day/month/year to orbit Earth.

Shadows in space cause eclipses.

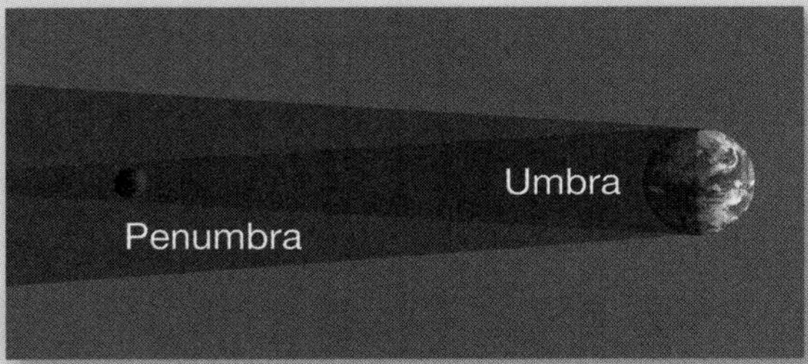

15 When the moon is in Earth's umbra, a total solar/lunar eclipse is occurring.

The appearance of the moon depends on the positions of the sun, the moon, and Earth.

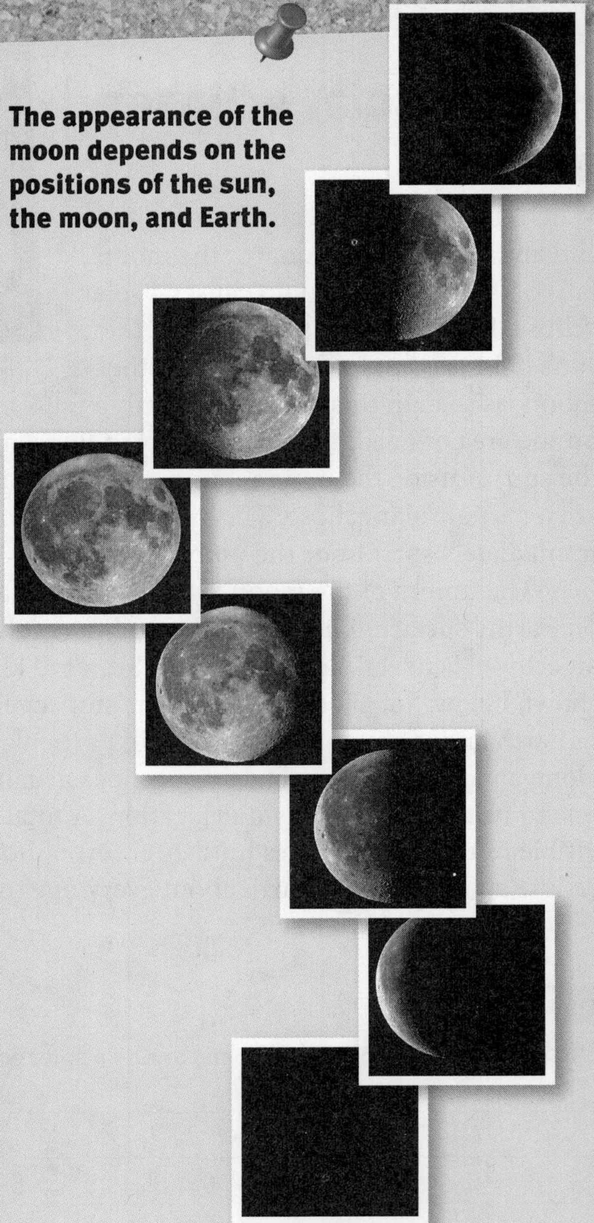

16 The fraction of the moon that receives sunlight always/never changes.

Answers: 14 month; 15 lunar; 16 never

17 Describe What causes the lunar phases that we see from Earth?

© Houghton Mifflin Harcourt Publishing Company • Image Credits: (all) ©Larry Landolfi/Photo Researchers, Inc.

Lesson Review

Vocabulary

In your own words, define the following terms.

1 gravity

_____

_____

_____

2 satellite

_____

_____

3 umbra

_____

_____

Key Concepts

4 Describe What are two phases of a waxing moon, and how do they appear?

_____

_____

_____

_____

_____

_____

_____

5 Identify Explain why the moon can be seen from Earth.

_____

_____

_____

6 Describe What is the relationship between Earth, the sun, and the moon in space?

_____

_____

_____

_____

_____

Critical Thinking

Use the image below to answer the following question.

7 Identify What type of eclipse is shown in the diagram?

_____

_____

8 Describe Where is the moon in its orbit at the time of a solar eclipse?

_____

9 Infer What phase is the moon in when there is a total solar eclipse?

_____

_____

10 Predict Which shape of the moon will you never see during the daytime, after sunrise and before sunset? *Hint:* Consider the directions of the sun and moon from Earth.

_____

11 Synthesize If you were an astronaut in the middle of the near side of the moon during a full moon, how would the ground around you look? How would Earth, high in your sky look? Describe what is in sunlight and what is in darkness.

_____

_____

_____

_____

_____

_____

My Notes

Engineering Design Process

Skills
Identify a need
Conduct research
Brainstorm solutions
✓ Select a solution
✓ Design a prototype
✓ Build a prototype
✓ Test and evaluate
✓ Redesign to improve
✓ Communicate results

Objectives

- Explain several advantages of tidal energy over conventional energy sources.
- Design a technological solution to harnessing changing water levels.
- Test and modify a prototype to raise a mass as water levels change.

Harnessing Tidal Energy

Our society uses a lot of electrical energy. If the energy is generated by nuclear power plants or by burning fossil fuels, the waste products tend to harm the environment. However, in many places, these methods of obtaining energy are still used.

Scientists and engineers have been investigating alternative energy sources, such as solar, wind, and tidal energy. Tidal energy is energy from *tides,* the daily, predictable changes in the level of ocean water. The mechanical energy of the moving water can be transformed to other forms of energy that are useful in human activities. Tidal power facilities have less of an impact on nature and have low operating costs. And unlike fossil fuels or the uranium ore used in nuclear power plants, water is not used up in the generation of tidal energy. Generating electrical energy from tides and other alternative energy sources can be less harmful to the environment, but challenges must still be overcome.

Barrage tidal power facility at La Rance, France

1 **Compare** What are some advantages of generating electrical energy from tides instead of from fossil fuels?

_____

_____

_____

Types of Tidal Power Generators

There are three main types of tidal energy generators. One type is a system that uses a dam with turbines. The dam is called a *barrage*. The barrage allows water in during high tide and releases water during low tide. Barrage tidal power stations can affect marine life behind the barrage. Also, silt settles behind the barrage and must be dredged up and hauled out to sea. This is an older system of generating electrical energy from tides.

The other two types of tidal power generators are *horizontal-axis turbines* and *vertical-axis turbines*. These systems are like huge underwater fans turned by tidal currents instead of by wind. Because water is denser than air, slow-moving water can still produce a lot of power. These facilities have fewer effects on the environment.

2 Compare What is an advantage of using horizontal-axis turbines and vertical-axis turbines instead of barrage tidal power stations?

_____

_____

_____

_____

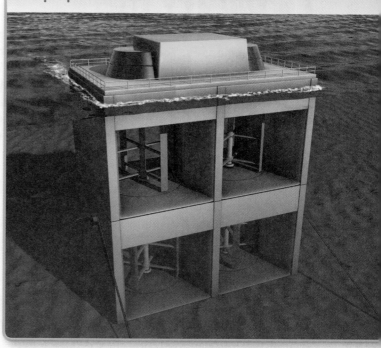

Four vertical-axis tidal power turbines are seen here. The blades rotate on an axis perpendicular to the ocean floor.

Two horizontal-axis tidal power turbines are seen here. The blades rotate on an axis parallel to the ocean floor.

✋ You Try It! ⟶

Now it's your turn to design and build a tidal power device.

You Try It!

Now it's your turn to design and build a tidal power device that will lift two masses. You will lift the masses by harnessing energy from the changing water levels in a sink or tub. Adding water to the sink or tub will simulate a rising tide, and removing water will simulate a falling tide. One mass must be raised when the tide rises, and the other mass must be raised when the tide falls. Both masses must be outside the sink or tub.

(1) Select a Solution

A How will you use the falling tide to raise a mass?

_____

_____

_____

B How will you use the rising tide to raise a mass?

_____

_____

_____

_____

(2) Design a Prototype

In the space below, draw and label a prototype of your tidal power device. You may have one idea for harnessing the falling tide and a different idea for harnessing the rising tide.

You Will Need

✓ block, wooden or foam

✓ bucket

✓ dowels, wooden

✓ duct tape

✓ masses, 50 g or 100 g (2)

✓ milk jug, 1 gallon, empty

✓ siphon hose

✓ string

✓ tub, plastic or sink

✓ water

③ Build a Prototype

Now build your tidal power device. As you built your device, were there some aspects of your design that could not be assembled as you had predicted? What aspects did you have to revise as you were building the prototype?

_____

_____

_____

_____

④ Test and Evaluate

Place your device in the tub. Add water to the tub to simulate a rising tide. Then drain water from the tub. Observe the motion of the masses as the tide rises and falls, and record your observations.

_____

_____

_____

_____

⑤ Redesign to Improve

Keep making revisions, one at a time, until your tidal power device can lift both masses. Describe the revisions you made.

_____

_____

_____

⑥ Communicate Results

Were you able to raise a mass more easily when the simulated tide was rising or falling? Why do you think that was? Record your ideas below. Then, compare your results with those of your classmates.

_____

_____

_____

_____

_____

_____

Earth's Tides

ESSENTIAL QUESTION

What causes tides?

By the end of this lesson, you should be able to explain what tides are and what causes them in Earth's oceans and to describe variations in the tides.

You may wonder why this boat is sitting in such shallow water. This photo was taken at low tide, when the ocean water is below average sea level.

© Houghton Mifflin Harcourt Publishing Company • Image Credits: ©Robin Whalley/LOOP IMAGES/Loop Images/Corbis

🧠 Engage Your Brain

1 Describe Fill in the blank with the word that you think correctly completes the following sentences.

The motion of the _____ around Earth is related to tides.

The daily rotation of _____ is also related to tides.

During a _____ tide, the water level is higher than the average sea level.

During a _____ tide, the water level is lower than the average sea level.

2 Label Draw an arrow to show where you think high tide might be.

Low tide ▶

✏️ Active Reading

3 Synthesize The word *spring* has different meanings. Use the meanings of the word *spring* and the sentence below to make an educated guess about the meaning of the term *spring tides*.

Meanings of *spring*
the season between winter and summer
a source of water from the ground
jump, or rise up
a coiled piece of metal

Example Sentence
During spring tides, the sun, the moon, and Earth are in a straight line, resulting in very high tides.

spring tides:

_____

_____

_____

Vocabulary Terms
- tide
- tidal range
- spring tide
- neap tide

4 Apply As you learn the definition of each vocabulary term in this lesson, create your own definition or sketch to help you remember the meaning of the term.

A Rising Tide of Interest

What causes tides?

The photographs below show the ocean at the same location at two different times. **Tides** are daily changes in the level of ocean water. Tides are caused by the difference in the gravitational force of the sun and the moon across Earth. This difference in gravitational force is called the *tidal force*. The tidal force exerted by the moon is stronger than the tidal force exerted by the sun because the moon is much closer to Earth than the sun is. So, the moon is mainly responsible for tides on Earth.

How often tides occur and how tidal levels vary depend on the position of the moon as it revolves around Earth. The gravity of the moon pulls on every particle of Earth. But because liquids move more easily than solids do, the pull on liquids is much more noticeable than the pull on solids is. The moon's gravitational pull on Earth decreases with the moon's distance from Earth. The part of Earth facing the moon is pulled toward the moon with the greatest force. So, water on that side of Earth bulges toward the moon. The solid Earth is pulled more strongly toward the moon than the ocean water on Earth's far side is. So, there is also a bulge of water on the side of Earth farthest from the moon.

At low tide, the water level is low, and the boats are far below the dock.

At high tide, the water level has risen, and the boats are close to the dock.

What are high tides and low tides?

The bulges that form in Earth's oceans are called high tides. *High tide* is a water level that is higher than the average sea level. Low tides form in the areas between the high tides. *Low tide* is a water level that is lower than the average sea level. At low tide, the water levels are lower because the water is in high-tide areas.

As the moon moves around Earth and Earth rotates, the tidal bulges move around Earth. The tidal bulges follow the motion of the moon. As a result, many places on Earth have two high tides and two low tides each day.

 **Visualize It!**

6 Identify Label the areas where high tides form and the area where the other low tide forms.

Note: Drawing is not to scale.

Moon

A _____

B _____

Earth

Low tide

C _____

This grizzly bear in Alaska is taking advantage of low tide by digging for clams.

7 Predict What happens to the bear when high tide comes in?

_____

_____

Tide Me Over

What are two kinds of tidal ranges?

Active Reading

8 Identify As you read, underline the two kinds of tidal range.

Tides are due to the *tidal force,* the difference between the force of gravity on one side of Earth and the other side of Earth. Because the moon is so much closer to Earth than the sun is, the moon's tidal force is greater than the sun's tidal force. The moon's effect on tides is twice as strong as the sun's effect. The combined gravitational effects of the sun and the moon on Earth result in different tidal ranges. A **tidal range** is the difference between the levels of ocean water at high tide and low tide. Tidal range depends on the positions of the sun and the moon relative to Earth.

Spring Tides: The Largest Tidal Range

Tides that have the largest daily tidal range are **spring tides**. Spring tides happen when the sun, the moon, and Earth form a straight line. So, spring tides happen when the moon is between the sun and Earth and when the moon is on the opposite side of Earth, as shown in the illustrations below. In other words, spring tides happen during the new moon and full moon phases, or every 14 days. During these times, the gravitational effects of the sun and moon add together, causing one pair of very large tidal bulges. Spring tides have nothing to do with the season.

Note: Drawings are not to scale.

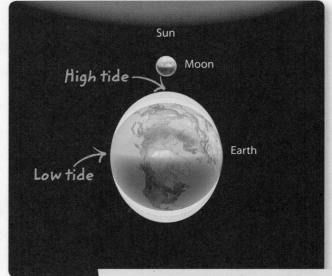
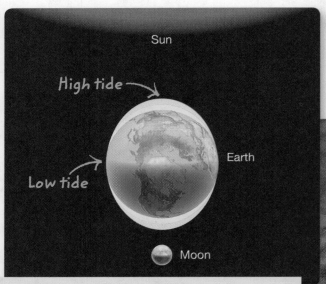

During spring tides, the tidal force of the sun on Earth adds to the tidal force of the moon. The tidal range increases.

Inquiry

9 Inquire Explain why spring tides happen twice a month.

_____

_____

Neap Tides: The Smallest Tidal Range

Tides that have the smallest daily tidal range are **neap tides**. Neap tides happen when the sun, Earth, and the moon form a 90° angle, as shown in the illustrations below. During a neap tide, the gravitational effects of the sun and the moon on Earth do not add together as they do during spring tides. Neap tides occur halfway between spring tides, during the first quarter and third quarter phases of the moon. At these times, the sun and the moon cause two pairs of smaller tidal bulges.

Note: Drawings are not to scale.

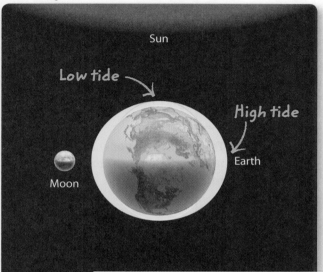

During neap tides, the gravitational effects of the sun and the moon on Earth do not add together. The tidal range decreases.

10 Compare Fill in the Venn diagram to compare and contrast spring tides and neap tides.

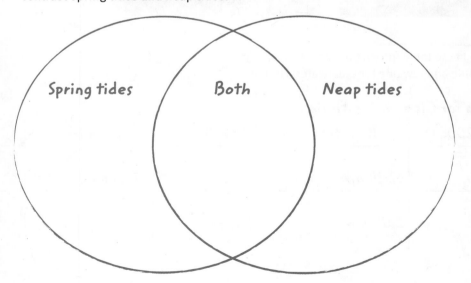

Spring tides   Both   Neap tides

What causes tidal cycles?

The rotation of Earth and the moon's revolution around Earth determine when tides occur. Imagine that Earth rotated at the same speed that the moon revolves around Earth. If this were true, the same side of Earth would always face the moon. And high tide would always be at the same places on Earth. But the moon revolves around Earth much more slowly than Earth rotates. A place on Earth that is facing the moon takes 24 h and 50 min to rotate to face the moon again. So, the cycle of high tides and low tides at that place happens 50 min later each day.

In many places there are two high tides and two low tides each day. Because the tide cycle occurs in 24 h and 50 min intervals, it takes about 6 h and 12.5 min (one-fourth the time of the total cycle) for water in an area to go from high tide to low tide. It takes about 12 h and 25 min (one-half the time of the total cycle) to go from one high tide to the next high tide.

Note: Drawings are not to scale.

Tuesday 11:00 a.m.

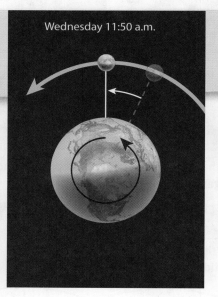

Wednesday 11:50 a.m.

The moon moves only a fraction of its orbit in the time that Earth rotates once.

Think Outside the Book Inquiry

11 Inquire Draw a diagram of Earth to show what Earth's tides would be like if the moon revolved around Earth at the same speed that Earth rotates.

12 Predict In the table, predict the approximate times of high tide and low tide for Clearwater, Florida.

Tide Data for Clearwater, Florida

Date (2009)	High tide	Low tide	High tide	Low tide
August 19	12:14 a.m.		12:39 p.m.	
August 20	1:04 a.m.	7:17 a.m.		
August 21				

Extreme Living Conditions

Some organisms living along ocean coastlines must be able to tolerate extreme living conditions. At high tide, much of the coast is under water. At low tide, much of the coast is dry. Some organisms must also survive the constant crashing of waves against the shore.

Barnacle Business

Barnacles must be able to live in water as well as out of water. They must also tolerate the air temperature, which may differ from the temperature of the water.

Ghostly Crabs

Ghost crabs live near the high tide line on sandy shores. They scurry along the sand to avoid being underwater when the tide comes in. Ghost crabs can also find cover between rocks.

Stunning Starfish

Starfish live in tidal pools, which are areas along the shore where water remains at low tide. Starfish must be able to survive changes in water temperature and salinity.

Extend

Inquiry

13 Identify Describe how living conditions change for two tidal organisms.

14 Research and Record List the names of two organisms that live in the high tide zone or the low tide zone along a coastline of your choice.

15 Describe Imagine a day in the life of an organism you researched in question 14 by doing one of the following:
- make a poster
- write a play
- record an audio story
- make a cartoon

Visual Summary

To complete this summary, fill in the blanks with the correct word. Then use the key below to check your answers. You can use this page to review the main concepts of the lesson.

In many places, two high tides and two low tides occur every day.

16 The type of tide shown here is

_____

The gravitational effects of the moon and the sun cause tides.

17 Tides on Earth are caused mainly by the

_____

Moon

Earth

Tides on Earth

Note: Drawings are not to scale.

There are two kinds of tidal ranges: spring tides and neap tides.

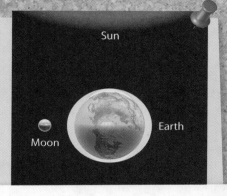

Sun

Moon

Earth

Sun

Earth

Moon

18 During a spring tide, the sun, moon, and Earth are in a/an

_____

19 During a neap tide, the sun, moon, and Earth form a/an

_____

Answers: 16 low tide; 17 moon; 18 straight line; 19 90° angle

20 Describe State how the moon causes tides.

_____

Lesson Review

Vocabulary

Answer the following questions in your own words.

1 Use *tide* and *tidal range* in the same sentence.

_____

_____

_____

2 Write an original definition for *neap tide* and for *spring tide*.

_____

_____

_____

_____

Key Concepts

3 Describe Explain what tides are. Include *high tide* and *low tide* in your answer.

_____

_____

_____

_____

_____

4 Explain State what causes tides on Earth.

_____

_____

_____

5 Identify Write the alignment of the moon, the sun, and Earth that causes a spring tide.

_____

_____

6 Describe Explain why tides happen 50 min later each day.

_____

_____

_____

Critical Thinking

Use this diagram to answer the next question.

Note: Drawing is not to scale.

Last quarter moon

7 Analyze What type of tidal range will Earth have when the moon is in this position?

_____

_____

8 Apply How many days pass between the minimum and the maximum of the tidal range in any given area? Explain your answer.

_____

_____

_____

_____

_____

9 Apply How would the tides on Earth be different if the moon revolved around Earth in 15 days instead of 30 days?

_____

_____

_____

_____

_____

_____

My Notes

Lesson 1

ESSENTIAL QUESTION

How are Earth's days, years, and seasons related to the way Earth moves in space?

Relate Earth's days, years, and seasons to Earth's movement in space.

Lesson 2

ESSENTIAL QUESTION

How do Earth, the moon, and the sun affect each other?

Describe the effects the sun and the moon have on Earth, including gravitational attraction, moon phases, and eclipses.

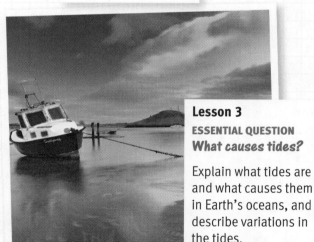

Lesson 3

ESSENTIAL QUESTION

What causes tides?

Explain what tides are and what causes them in Earth's oceans, and describe variations in the tides.

Think Outside the Book

2 Synthesize Choose one of these activities to help synthesize what you have learned in this unit.

☐ Using what you learned in lessons 2 and 3, make a flipbook showing the importance of the alignment of Earth, the moon, and the sun in the Earth-moon-sun system.

☐ Using what you learned in lessons 1, 2, and 3, describe the hierarchical relationship of gravitational attraction in the Earth-moon-sun system using a poster presentation.

Connect ESSENTIAL QUESTIONS
Lessons 1, 2, and 3

1 Synthesize Name the natural cycles that occur as a result of the Earth-moon-sun system.

_____

_____

_____

_____

Unit 3 Review

Name _____

Vocabulary

Fill in each blank with the term that best completes the following sentences.

1 A _____ is the periodic rise and fall of the water level in the oceans and other large bodies of water.

2 A _____ is the motion of a body that travels around another body in space.

3 The force of _____ keeps Earth and other planets of the solar system in orbit around the sun and keeps the moon in orbit around Earth.

4 A natural or artificial body that revolves around a celestial body that is greater in mass is called a _____ .

5 _____ is the counterclockwise spin of a planet or moon as seen from above a planet's north pole.

Key Concepts

Read each question below, and circle the best answer.

6 Look at the table of tide information.

Date	High tide time	High tide height (m)	Low tide time	Low tide height (m)
June 3	6:04 a.m.	6.11	12:01 a.m.	1.76
June 4	6:58 a.m.	5.92	12:54 a.m.	1.87
June 5	7:51 a.m.	5.80	1:47 a.m.	1.90
June 6	8:42 a.m.	5.75	2:38 a.m.	1.87
June 7	9:30 a.m.	5.79	3:27 a.m.	1.75
June 8	10:16 a.m.	5.90	4:13 a.m.	1.56
June 9	11:01 a.m.	6.08	4:59 a.m.	1.32
June 10	11:46 a.m.	6.28	5:44 a.m.	1.05
June 11	12:32 p.m.	6.47	6:30 a.m.	0.78

What was the tidal range on June 9?

A 4.76 m   **C** 6.08 m

B 7.40 m   **D** 4.76 ft

7 Aside from Earth's tilt, what other factor contributes to Earth's seasons?

   A the time of the day

   B the energy as heat from the moon

   C the angle of the sun's rays and the number of hours of daylight

   D cold or warm air blowing from the oceans

8 Ann is looking at the night sky. There is a first-quarter moon. What does she see?

   A a moon shaped like a crescent

   B a moon shaped like a half circle

   C a moon shaped like a circle, shining brightly

   D no moon in the sky

9 Which is a similarity between a neap tide and a spring tide?

   A Neap tides occur once a year in fall and spring tides once a year in spring.

   B Each occurs twice a year and relates to the phases of the moon.

   C A neap tide occurs at night, and a spring tide occurs during the day.

   D Each tide occurs twice a month, and is determined by the pull of gravity of the moon.

10 The diagram below shows the relative positions of the sun, the moon, and Earth.

What does the diagram show?

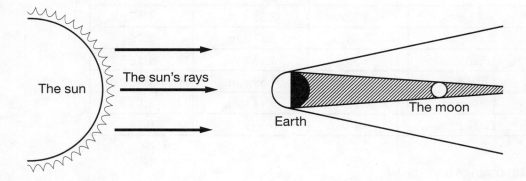

   A a solar eclipse   **C** a first-quarter moon

   B a lunar eclipse   **D** a third-quarter moon

11 During equinox, the sun's rays strike Earth at a 90-degree angle along the equator. What is the result of the equinox?

A the hours of daylight and the hours of darkness are about the same

B the hours of daylight are longer than the hours of darkness

C the hours of darkness are longer than the hours of daylight

D an unseasonably warm day in the midst of winter

12 Examine the diagram below.

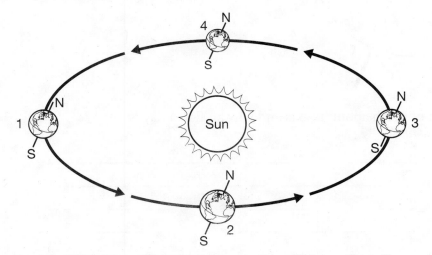

The position labeled "1" represents the season of summer in—

A the Southern Hemisphere.   **C** the Eastern Hemisphere.

B Antarctica.   **D** the Northern Hemisphere.

Critical Thinking

Answer the following questions in the space provided.

13 Janais lives near the ocean. How do Earth, the sun, and the moon interact to affect Janais's life?

_____

_____

_____

_____

_____

_____

14 Look at the diagram of Earth.

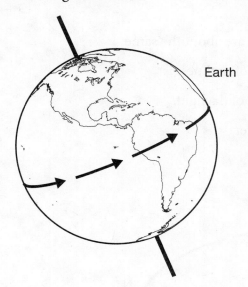

Earth

Describe the rotation of Earth about its axis and why an Earth day is 24 hours long.

_____

_____

_____

_____

_____

_____

_____

Connect **ESSENTIAL QUESTIONS**
Lessons 2 and 3

Answer the following question in the space provided.

15 Explain what causes tides on Earth and why high and low tides occur.

_____

_____

_____

_____

_____

_____

_____

_____

Exploring Space

Big Idea

People develop and use technology to explore and study space.

What do you think?

Probes send information about the outer solar system back to scientists on Earth. How might humans benefit from space exploration?

Exploring Space!

The exploration of space began in 1957 with the launch of Sputnik I. Since 1957, humans have walked on the moon, rovers have investigated the surface of Mars, and spacecraft have flown by the most distant planets in the solar system.

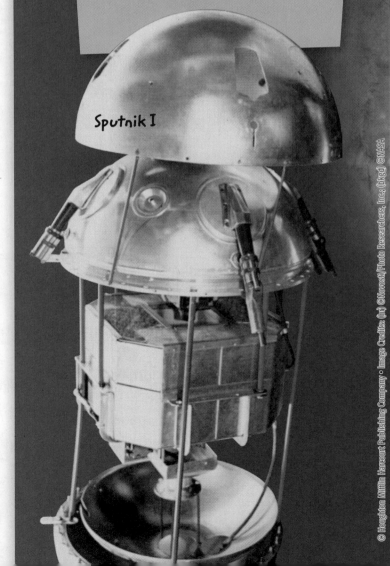

Sputnik I, 1957
On October 4, 1957, the successful launch of the Russian satellite Sputnik I kicked off the race for space.

Sputnik I

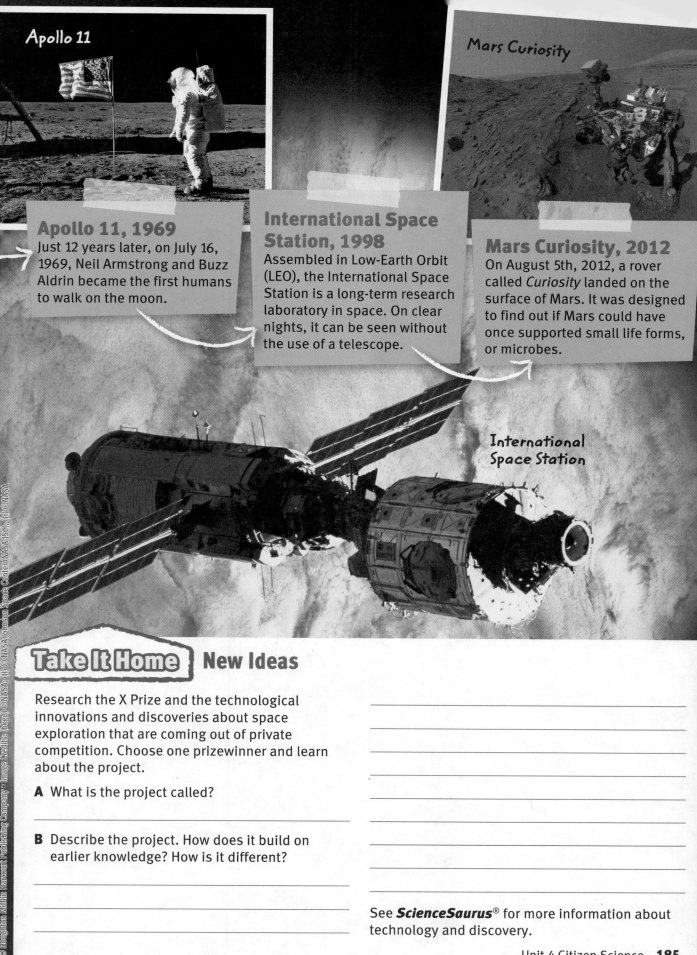

Apollo 11

Mars Curiosity

Apollo 11, 1969
Just 12 years later, on July 16, 1969, Neil Armstrong and Buzz Aldrin became the first humans to walk on the moon.

International Space Station, 1998
Assembled in Low-Earth Orbit (LEO), the International Space Station is a long-term research laboratory in space. On clear nights, it can be seen without the use of a telescope.

Mars Curiosity, 2012
On August 5th, 2012, a rover called *Curiosity* landed on the surface of Mars. It was designed to find out if Mars could have once supported small life forms, or microbes.

International Space Station

Take It Home New Ideas

Research the X Prize and the technological innovations and discoveries about space exploration that are coming out of private competition. Choose one prizewinner and learn about the project.

A What is the project called?

B Describe the project. How does it build on earlier knowledge? How is it different?

See *ScienceSaurus*® for more information about technology and discovery.

Images from Space

ESSENTIAL QUESTION

What can we learn from space images?

By the end of this lesson, you should be able to describe ways of collecting information from space and analyze how different wavelengths of the electromagnetic spectrum provide different information.

This blue object is the sun. The image was not produced using visible light.

Lesson Labs

Quick Labs
- Using Invisible Light
- A Model of the Universe
- Splitting White Light

S.T.E.M. Lab
- Making a Telescope

Engage Your Brain

1 Predict Check T or F to show whether you think each statement is true or false.

T F

☐ ☐ Visible light is a type of electromagnetic radiation.

☐ ☐ Artificial satellites can produce images of Earth only.

☐ ☐ Earth's atmosphere blocks all ultraviolet radiation from space.

☐ ☐ Optical telescopes are used to study objects in the universe.

2 Identify Look at the picture below. Write a caption that explains what the picture shows.

_____

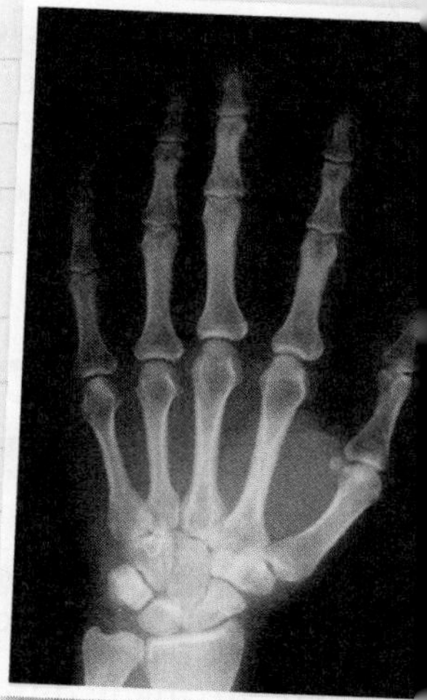

_____

_____

_____

_____

_____

Active Reading

3 Synthesize You can often define an unknown word if you know the meaning of its word parts. Use the word parts and sentence below to make an educated guess about the meaning of the word *microwave*.

Word part	Meaning
micro-	small
-wave	a movement of up or down or back and forth

Example sentence
Microwaves can be used to heat food.

microwave:

_____

_____

Vocabulary Terms

- wavelength
- electromagnetic spectrum
- spectrum

4 Apply As you learn the definition of each vocabulary term in this lesson, create your own definition or sketch to help you remember the meaning of the term.

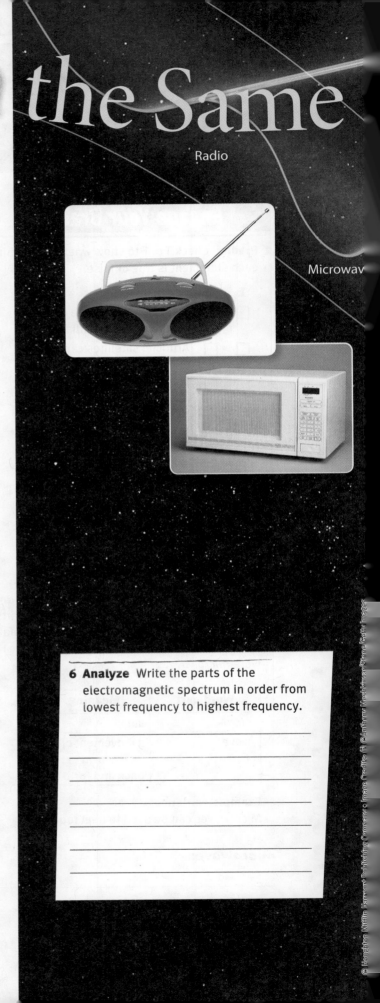

On the Same

Radio

Microwave

What is electromagnetic radiation?

Energy traveling as electromagnetic waves is called *electromagnetic radiation*. Waves can be described by either their wavelength or frequency. **Wavelength** is the distance between two adjacent crests or troughs of a wave. *Frequency* measures the number of waves passing a point per second. Higher-frequency waves have a shorter wavelength. Energy carried by electromagnetic radiation depends on both the wavelength and the amount of radiation at that wavelength. A higher-frequency wave carries higher energy than a lower-frequency wave.

How is electromagnetic radiation classified?

Active Reading **5 Identify** As you read, underline the name of each part of the electromagnetic spectrum.

There are many different wavelengths and frequencies of electromagnetic radiation. All these wavelengths and frequencies make up what is called the **electromagnetic spectrum**. A **spectrum** is a continuous range of a single feature, in this case wavelength. The form of electromagnetic radiation with the longest-wavelength and the lowest-frequency is radio waves. Radios and televisions receive radio waves. These receivers then produce sound waves. Sound waves are not electromagnetic radiation. Microwaves have shorter wavelengths and higher frequencies than radio waves. The next shorter wavelength radiation is called infrared. Infrared is sometimes called "heat radiation." Visible light has a shorter wavelength than infrared. You see an object when visible light from the object reaches your eyes. Images produced in visible light are the only images we can see without computer enhancement. Even shorter in wavelength is ultraviolet radiation. The shortest wavelengths belong to x-rays and gamma rays.

6 Analyze Write the parts of the electromagnetic spectrum in order from lowest frequency to highest frequency.

_____

_____

_____

_____

_____

_____

Wavelength?

Infrared

Visible light

Ultraviolet

7 Complete Electromagnetic _____
that has a shorter wavelength has a _____
frequency.

X-rays

Gamma rays

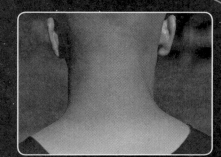

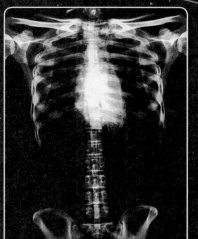

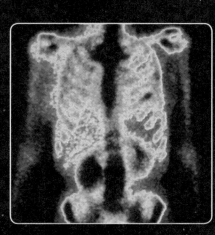

The Better to See You With

What are some characteristics of electromagnetic radiation?

Electromagnetic waves can be generated by devices such as cell phones, microwave ovens, and flashlights. Electromagnetic radiation is also generated by heat. Very cool material radiates, or emits energy, mostly as radio waves. Warmer objects may radiate mainly in the infrared. To emit visible light, an object must be hot. Light bulbs are good examples of hot objects that emit light.

Different portions of the electromagnetic spectrum interact differently with matter. Radio waves pass easily through space and the atmosphere. Using special equipment, infrared radiation allows someone to see room-temperature objects, even at night. Microwaves penetrate a small distance into many materials, where they are absorbed. The energy is released as heat. A microwave oven uses this property to cook food. Ultraviolet rays can cause materials to fluoresce (flu•RES), or glow. This property is used for many purposes, from criminal investigation to document protection. For example, documents can be protected against counterfeiting (KOUN•ter•fit•ing) if they use symbols that are detectable only by special lamps. X-rays pass through flesh easily but less easily through bone. Physicians and other doctors can use x-rays to examine the insides of your body.

In small amounts, electromagnetic radiation can be very useful. Large amounts of any type of radiation can cause problems because of the total amount of energy carried. For example, ultraviolet radiation can cause skin cancer. Gamma rays are especially dangerous to living organisms.

Active Reading

8 Identify As you read, underline five ways that people can use electromagnetic radiation.

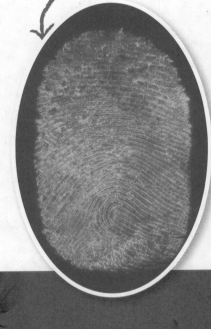

Under an ultraviolet lamp, fingerprints glow.

9 Explain Describe an example of how nonvisible radiation can be used.

_____

_____

_____

_____

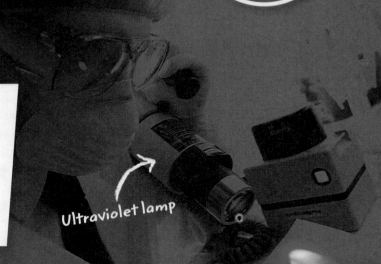

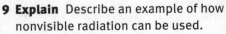

Ultraviolet lamp

Visible

Radio   Microwave   Infrared   ↓   Ultraviolet   X-ray   Gamma rays

What electromagnetic radiation reaches Earth?

If Earth had no atmosphere, energy from the entire electromagnetic spectrum would reach Earth's surface. But not all wavelengths of the electromagnetic spectrum reach Earth's surface, as shown in the illustration above. In the atmosphere, atoms and molecules reflect some of the incoming radiation back into space. Atoms and molecules can also absorb some forms of electromagnetic radiation. For example, water vapor and carbon dioxide molecules absorb much of the infrared and microwave radiation. Most visible light and radio radiation reach Earth's surface.

The higher frequencies of ultraviolet radiation are absorbed by ozone in the atmosphere. Oxygen and nitrogen atoms absorb x-rays and gamma rays. X-rays and gamma rays have high enough energies to damage living tissue and other materials. Fortunately, they are absorbed by molecules in the atmosphere. Therefore, x-rays and gamma rays from space do not reach Earth's surface.

Inquiry

10 Analyze Why are x-ray telescopes and gamma-ray telescopes in space?

_____

_____

_____

_____

To See or Not to See

How do people detect electromagnetic radiation from objects in space?

Visible light from the sun, moon, planets, and stars can be detected by the human eye or a camera to form an image. Images of objects in space can tell us about their positions and properties. Telescopes are one way to learn about objects in space. They can be placed on mountain tops. Telescopes are also placed in space to collect radiation that does not reach Earth's surface.

All forms of electromagnetic radiation from space can be collected by telescopes. However, special detectors must be used to form images from radiation other than visible light. A radio receiver is used for radio waves. Infrared, x-ray, and gamma-ray detectors are used for those regions of the electromagnetic spectrum.

With Optical Telescopes

Active Reading 11 **Identify** As you read, underline two types of optical telescopes.

Optical telescopes collect visible light with a mirror or a lens. A mirror reflects light, and a lens changes the direction of light rays as they pass through the lens. A telescope that uses a mirror to collect light is called a *reflecting telescope*. A telescope that uses a lens to collect light is a called a *refracting telescope*. The larger the lens or mirror, the more light that can be collected. With more light, the observer can view fainter objects. The light collected is then detected by the eye or other detector, such as a camera.

A reflecting telescope uses a mirror to gather and focus light.

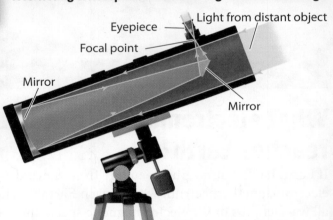

Light from distant object
Eyepiece
Focal point
Mirror
Mirror

A refracting telescope uses a lens to gather and focus light.

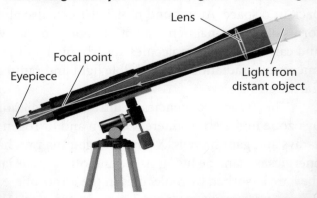

Lens
Focal point
Eyepiece
Light from distant object

The Keck Observatory is on top of Mauna Kea, in Hawaii.

Houghton Mifflin Harcourt Publishing Company • Image Credits: ©David Nunuk/Photo Researchers, Inc.

With Non-Optical Telescopes

Active Reading **12 Identify** As you read, underline one example of electromagnetic radiation that non-optical telescopes detect.

The first telescopes were used to collect visible light. Today, however, astronomers use telescopes to observe in all parts of the electromagnetic spectrum. Most radio telescopes use metal mirrors to reflect radio waves. Radio waves are reflected onto a radio receiver at the focus. A satellite dish is an example of this kind of radio telescope. Radio waves have long wavelengths. Therefore, many radio telescopes are very large.

Telescopes are often used to produce images. First, the electromagnetic radiation that is collected must reach a detector that is sensitive to that wavelength, just like x-rays that pass through your teeth must reach a material sensitive to x-rays. Then the electromagnetic radiation is collected and processed through a computer to produce an image that we can see.

The computer software also adds color, called *false color*. The addition of false color highlights important details. For example, an image might be colored so that areas emitting low energy are dark and areas emitting high energy are bright. The brightness of an object tells the scientists how much energy that object is producing.

Visualize It!

14 Analyze Compare the mirror in the reflecting telescope with the radio telescope. In what way is a radio telescope like a reflecting telescope?

_____

_____

_____

_____

_____

This array of radio telescopes is in New Mexico.

Think Outside the Book **Inquiry**

13 Apply Choose a wavelength from the electromagnetic spectrum other than visible light or x-rays. Imagine that you could look at an image of your hand produced using that wavelength. Then draw a picture of what you think your hand would look like.

An artist's depiction of the Chandra X-ray Observatory in front of a nebula

Focus

The View from Above

The satellite scans the surface of the Earth.

The satellite transmits the data to a station on the ground.

How can people observe Earth from space?

Active Reading **15 Identify** As you read, underline three examples of satellite orbits.

Observations of Earth from space—called *remote sensing*—are made from satellites. Satellites orbit Earth at different altitudes and in different directions. A satellite at a low altitude is in low Earth orbit. Low Earth orbit is a few hundred kilometers above Earth's surface. Satellites that monitor the atmosphere are in low Earth orbits. They take about 90 min to orbit Earth once.

A satellite about 35,700 km above the equator takes 24 h to orbit Earth once. This type of satellite is called a *geosynchronous* (jee•oh•SINGK•kruh•nuhs) *satellite*. It always remains above the same location on the ground as Earth rotates below. Most weather and remote-sensing observations are made from satellites in this orbit. Television signals picked up by satellite dishes also come from geosynchronous satellites.

Some satellites pass over the North and South Poles on every orbit. These satellites look straight down as Earth rotates below. This allows a good look at all areas of the surface, allowing mapping and other observations.

What can you learn about Earth from satellite images?

Images from remote-sensing satellites provide a variety of information. They show evidence of human activity, such as cities. Remote-sensing images of the same place taken on different dates show how things change over time. For example, images of populated areas can show how development has changed over several years, as shown in the two images below of Las Vegas.

The lights seen in images taken at night indicate populated areas and highways. Infrared images can show forests and cleared areas, because trees appear cooler than bare land in infrared images. Images can also show forest fires and can be used to warn people of the danger. Weather satellites provide images of clouds and storms, such as hurricanes. Other images can show features in the atmosphere, such as the aurora and ozone variations.

Visualize It!

17 Analyze Describe one change in urbanization between 1973 and 2006 that you see with these two images.

_____

_____

1973

2006

These false-color images of Las Vegas were produced by a satellite called Landsat. The green represents vegetation, and the lines represent city streets.

Seeing Is Believing

What can you learn from space images?

Visible light allows you to see the surfaces of planets and how other objects in space might look. Different types of radiation can be used to produce images to reveal features not visible to the eye. For example, infrared radiation can reveal the temperature of objects. Dust blocks visible light, but some wavelengths of infrared pass through dust, so scientists can see objects normally hidden by dust clouds in space. High-energy objects may be very bright in x-ray or gamma-ray radiation, although difficult to see at longer wavelengths. The four images of the Andromeda galaxy on the right were produced using wavelengths other than visible light, so the colors are all false colors.

Visualize It!

18 Analzye Compare one image of the Andromeda galaxy on the opposite page with the image in visible light on this page.

_____

_____

_____

_____

_____

_____

_____

The Andromeda galaxy in visible light

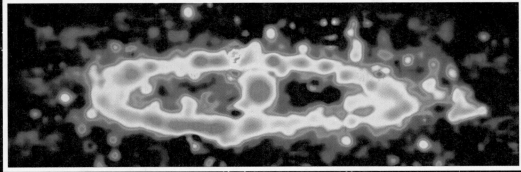

This image of the Andromeda galaxy was produced using radio waves. The reddish-orange color in the center and in the ring represents a source of radio waves. New stars are forming in the ring area.

In this infrared image of the Andromeda galaxy, you can see more detail in the structure of the galaxy. The dark areas within the bright rings are dust. The dust is so thick in some areas that radiation behind the dust is not getting through.

This image of the Andromeda galaxy was produced with a combination of ultraviolet and infrared radiation. The blue areas represent large, young, hot stars. The green areas represent older stars. The bright yellow spot at the very center of the galaxy represents an extremely dense area of old stars.

Visual Summary

To complete this summary, fill in the blanks with the correct word or phrase. Then use the key below to check your answers. You can use this page to review the main concepts of the lesson.

Images from Space

The electromagnetic spectrum is all the wavelengths and frequencies of electromagnetic radiation.

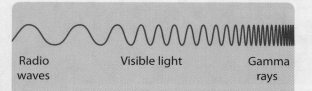

Radio waves   Visible light   Gamma rays

19 Two parts of the electromagnetic spectrum between visible light and gamma rays are

_____

_____

Different types of telescopes are used to detect different ranges of electromagnetic radiation.

20 Optical telescopes detect

_____

Telescopes are available for every portion of the electromagnetic spectrum. Different types of radiation reveal various features not visible to the eye.

21 These two images of Saturn are different because they were made using different wavelengths of

_____

_____

Answers: 19 ultraviolet; x-rays; 20 visible light; 21 electromagnetic radiation

22 **Explain** Describe how images from space of Earth and other objects are useful.

Lesson Review

Vocabulary

Fill in the blank with the term that best completes the following sentences.

1 The distance between two adjacent crests of a wave is called its _____.

2 The _____ is all the wavelengths of electromagnetic radiation.

3 A _____ is a continuous range of a single feature, such as wavelength.

Key Concepts

4 Explain State why telescopes that detect non-optical radiation are useful for studying objects in space. Give an example.

_____
_____
_____
_____

5 Identify List three examples of telescopes that detect different types of electromagnetic radiation.

_____
_____
_____
_____

6 Explain Describe how wavelength, frequency, and energy are related.

_____
_____
_____
_____

7 Explain Describe one type of electromagnetic radiation that can cause harm to humans.

_____
_____
_____

Critical Thinking

Use this diagram to answer the following questions.

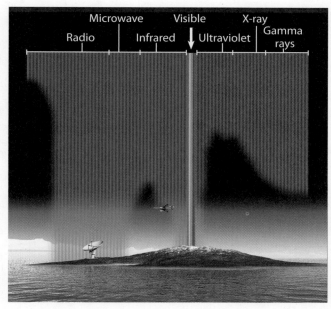

8 Analyze Some infrared radiation reaches Earth, and some does not. Which part does reach Earth—longer wavelength infrared or shorter wavelength infrared?

_____
_____
_____

9 Analyze List two other types of electromagnetic radiation that reach Earth's surface.

_____
_____
_____

10 Apply Describe how remote-sensing satellites can help people stay safe from massive fires.

_____
_____
_____
_____
_____
_____
_____

My Notes

Sandra Faber

ASTRONOMER

What do you do when you send a telescope into space and then find out that it is broken? You call Dr. Sandra Faber, a professor of astronomy at the University of California, Santa Cruz (UCSC). In April 1990, after the *Hubble Space Telescope* went into orbit, scientists found that the images the telescope collected were not turning out as expected. Dr. Faber's team at UCSC was in charge of a device on *Hubble* called the *Wide Field Planetary Camera*. Dr. Faber and her team decided to test the telescope to determine what was wrong.

To perform the test, they centered *Hubble* onto a bright star and took several photos. From those photos, Dr. Faber's team created a model of what was wrong. After reporting the error to NASA and presenting the model they had developed, Dr. Faber and a group of experts began to correct the problem. The group's efforts were a success and put *Hubble* back into operation so that astronomers could continue researching stars and other objects in space.

The **Hubble Space Telescope** orbits 569 km above Earth.

Language Arts Connection

Suppose you are a journalist preparing to interview Dr. Sandra Faber. List four questions you would ask her.

ton Mifflin Harcourt Publishing Company • Image Credits: (bkgd, b) ©NASA; (t) ©R.R. Jones, Hubble Deep field team, NASA

JOB BOARD

Astronautical Engineer

What You'll Do: Work on spacecraft that operate outside of Earth's atmosphere, like satellites or space shuttles. Other tasks include planning space missions, determining orbits of spacecraft, and designing rockets and communications systems.

Where You Might Work: Most likely with space agencies. You may also find jobs with aerospace companies or the military.

Education: All engineers must have a four-year college degree in aerospace or astronautical engineering. Many engineers go on to earn a master's degree and a doctorate. Basic engineering classes include algebra, calculus, physics, and computer programming.

Other Job Requirements: You should be able to work well with a team. You should be very careful and exact in your calculations and measurements.

Robotics Technician

What You'll Do: Help engineers build and operate robots, and work with robotic engineers on robotic tools for spacecraft. Use software to solve problems and to test equipment as part of your daily routine.

Where You Might Work: Government space agencies such as NASA, the auto industry, schools, laboratories, and manufacturing plants.

Education: Most technicians complete a two-year technical certificate. Technicians should have a strong interest in math and science. Professional certification is offered to technicians who have at least four years of work experience.

Other Job Requirements: You may also be asked to read blueprints, use microcomputers, and use oscilloscopes.

Technology for Space Exploration

ESSENTIAL QUESTION

How do we explore space?

By the end of this lesson, you should be able to analyze the ways people explore space, and assess the role of technology in these efforts.

Space probes, like the artist's rendition shown here, visit distant planets in our solar system and transmit data back to Earth.

Lesson Labs

Quick Labs
- Analyzing Satellite Images
- Design a Spacecraft

S.T.E.M. Lab
- Build a Rocket

 Engage Your Brain

1 Predict Check T or F to show whether you think each statement is true or false.

T	F
☐	☐ Astronauts can travel to distant planets in the solar system.
☐	☐ The space shuttle orbits the moon.
☐	☐ Artificial satellites in space can help you find locations on Earth.
☐	☐ Rovers explore the surfaces of planets and moons.

2 Describe Write your own caption to this photo.

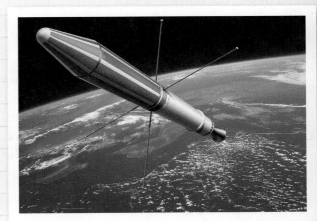

_____

_____

_____

Active Reading

3 Apply Use context clues to write your own definition for the words *analyze* and *transmit*.

Example sentence
Some spacecraft carry technology that can <u>analyze</u> soil and rock samples from objects in space.

analyze:

_____

_____

Example sentence
Satellites <u>transmit</u> data back to Earth.

transmit:

_____

_____

Vocabulary Terms

- space shuttle
- probe
- orbiter
- lander
- rover
- artificial satellite

4 Identify As you read, place a question mark next to any words that you don't understand. When you finish reading the lesson, go back and review the text that you marked. If the information is still confusing, consult a classmate or a teacher.

Beyond the Clouds

How do people travel to space?

On April 12, 1961, Yuri Gagarin became the first human to orbit Earth. Since then, people have continued to travel into space. Large rockets were the first method used to transport humans into space. The space shuttle was developed later and allowed people more time to live and work in space.

With Rockets

To travel away from Earth, large rockets must overcome the pull of Earth's gravity. A *rocket* is a machine that uses gas, often from burning fuel, to escape Earth's gravitational pull. Rockets launch both crewed and uncrewed vehicles into space. During early space missions, the capsules that contained the crews detached from the rockets. The rockets themselves burned up. The capsules "splashed down" in the ocean and were recovered but not reused.

With Space Shuttles

A **space shuttle** is a reusable spacecraft that launches with the aid of rocket boosters and liquid fuel. The shuttle glides to a landing on Earth like an airplane. It carries astronauts and supplies back and forth into orbit around Earth. *Columbia*, the first space shuttle in a fleet of six, was launched in 1981. Since then, more than 100 shuttle missions have been completed. Two white, solid rocket boosters (SRBs) help the shuttle reach orbit. These booster rockets detach and are reused.

> ✈ **Active Reading** 5 **Explain** What is the purpose of SRBs?

_____

_____

How do people live in space?

People live and work in space on space stations. A *space station* is a long-term crewed spacecraft on which scientific research can be carried out. Currently, the *International Space Station* (ISS) is the only space station in Earth orbit. Six-member crews live aboard the ISS for an average of six months. Because crews live in a constant state of weightlessness, the ISS is the perfect place to study the effects of weightlessness on the human body. Many other scientific experiments are conducted as well. Observations of Earth and earth systems are also made from the ISS.

Booster rockets launch the space shuttle. Following launch, they detach and fall into the ocean. They are retrieved for use again.

What are some challenges people face in space?

6 Identify As you read, underline challenges humans face when traveling in space.

Astronauts have traveled to the moon, but no human has yet traveled to more distant objects in the solar system. There are many technological challenges to overcome, such as having the fuel necessary for a long return voyage. Other challenges include having sufficient supplies of air, food, and water available for a long journey. Also, the spacecraft must be insulated from the intense cold of space as well as harmful radiation from the sun.

Spacesuits protect astronauts when they work outside a spacecraft. But astronauts still face challenges inside a spacecraft. In space, everything seems weightless. Simple tasks like eating and drinking become difficult. Astronauts must strap themselves to their beds to avoid floating around. The human body experiences problems in a weightless environment. Bones and muscles weaken. So, astronauts must exercise daily to strengthen their bodies.

Visualize It!

Spacesuits protect astronauts from extreme temperatures and from micrometeoroid strikes in space. They provide oxygen to astronauts and remove excess carbon dioxide.

7 Identify What are some technologies humans use to survive outside in space?

A life support pack supplies oxygen and removes carbon dioxide.

Pressurized suits protect the astronaut from the vacuum of space.

The astronaut is tethered to the shuttle at the waist.

The helmet contains communication gear and a protective visor.

The Hubble Space Telescope took this amazing image of Supernova SN1987A in the Large Magellanic Cloud and transmitted the image back to Earth.

Looking Up

What uncrewed technologies do people use to explore space?

Most objects in space are too far away for astronauts to visit. Scientists and engineers have developed uncrewed technologies to gather information about these objects. These technologies include space telescopes, probes, orbiters, landers, and rovers.

Telescopes in Space

Earth's atmosphere distorts light that passes through it. This makes it difficult to obtain clear images of objects in deep space. So some telescopes are placed in Earth orbit to obtain clearer images. Computers in the telescopes gather data and transmit it back to Earth. For example, the *Hubble Space Telescope* is a reflecting telescope that was placed in orbit in 1990. It detects visible light, and ultraviolet and infrared radiation as well. It has greatly expanded our knowledge of the universe.

Other space telescopes collect data using different types of electromagnetic radiation. The *Chandra X-Ray Observatory* and *Compton Gamma-Ray Observatory* were placed in space because Earth's atmosphere blocks most X-rays and gamma rays.

Active Reading **8 Relate** What is one advantage of placing a telescope in space?

_____

_____

_____

Space Probes

A space **probe** is an uncrewed vehicle that carries scientific instruments to distant objects in space. Probes carry a variety of data-collecting instruments, and on-board computers handle data, which are sent back to Earth.

Probes have been especially useful for studying the atmospheres of the gas giant planets. An atmospheric entry probe is dropped from a spacecraft into a planet's atmosphere. These probes relay atmospheric data back to the spacecraft for a short period of time before they are crushed in the planet's atmosphere. Remember, the gas giant planets do not have solid surfaces on which to land, and the pressure within their atmospheres is much greater than the atmospheric pressure on Earth.

Some probes can collect and return materials to Earth. In 2004, NASA's *Stardust* probe collected dust samples as it flew by a comet. The particles were returned to Earth for analysis two years later. It was the first time samples from beyond the moon were brought back to Earth!

The **Mars Curiosity** rover is searching for evidence of past life. This photo shows the rover's tracks across a sand dune.

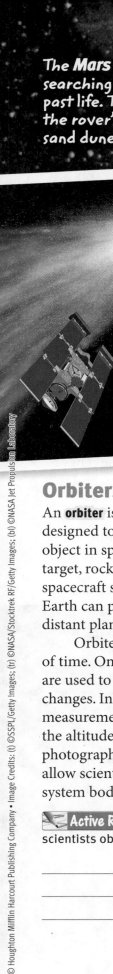

This artist's rendition shows the encounter of the space probe **Stardust** with Comet Wild 2 in 2004.

9 Compare How are probes and landers alike? How are they different?

_____

_____

_____

_____

Orbiters

An **orbiter** is an uncrewed spacecraft that is designed to enter into orbit around another object in space. As an orbiter approaches its target, rocket engines are fired to slow down the spacecraft so it can go into orbit. Controllers on Earth can place a spacecraft into orbit around a distant planet or its moons.

Orbiters can study a planet for long periods of time. On-board cameras and other technology are used to monitor atmospheric or surface changes. Instruments are also used to make measurements of temperature and to determine the altitudes of surface features. Orbiters can photograph an entire planet's surface. The data allow scientists to create detailed maps of solar system bodies.

Active Reading **10 Describe** What information can scientists obtain from orbiters?

_____

_____

_____

Landers and Rovers

Orbiters allow astronomers to create detailed maps of planets. They do not touch down on a planet or moon, however. That task is accomplished by landers that are controlled by scientists from Earth. A **lander** is a craft designed to land on the surface of a body in space. Landers have been placed successfully on the moon, Venus, Mars, and on Saturn's moon Titan. Some, such as the *Mars Pathfinder*, transmitted data for years. The images taken by a lander are more detailed than those taken by an orbiter.

In addition, a lander may carry a rover. A **rover** is a small vehicle that comes out of the lander and explores the surface of a planet or moon beyond the landing site. Both landers and rovers may have mechanical arms for gathering rock, dust, and soil samples.

In 2004, the rovers *Spirit* and *Opportunity* landed on Mars. They found evidence that water and wind once shaped Mars' surface. In 2012, *Curiosity* landed on Mars. After analyzing rock on the surface, *Curiosity* found that Mars likely had suitable conditions for life to have begun in the past.

Looking Down

How are satellites used to observe Earth?

A satellite is any object in space that orbits another object. An **artificial satellite** is any human-made object placed in orbit around a body in space. Some examples of artificial satellites include remote-sensing satellites, navigation satellites, weather satellites, and communications satellites. Artificial satellites orbit Earth and send data about our planet back to ground stations.

To Study Earth's Features

Scientists use remote-sensing satellites to study Earth. Remote sensing is a way to collect information about something without physically being there. Remote-sensing satellites map and monitor Earth's resources. For example, these satellites identify sources of pollution and monitor crops to track the spread of disease. They also monitor global temperatures, ocean and land heights, and the amount of freshwater ice and sea ice.

Astronauts in the *International Space Station* have photographed volcanoes during different stages of eruption. These photos from space are valuable because scientists can see and study views that are not possible from Earth.

Using satellites, scientists can study images of Earth's features taken from space, such as the eruption of the Gaua volcano in the South Pacific.

To Monitor Changes in Earth Systems

Remote-sensing data provide valuable information on how Earth systems change over time. For example, for more than 30 years, satellites have been observing Arctic sea ice. Images from the European Space Agency's ENVISAT satellite show that a large decline in Arctic sea ice has occurred over the past several years. By analyzing these images, scientists can better determine why the changes are happening.

Images taken by remote-sensing Landsat satellites show changes in the Mississippi River delta over time. When comparing an image taken in 1973 with an image taken in 2003, scientists can see how the delta has changed shape. They can also keep track of changes in the amount of land that is underwater.

To Collect Weather Data

It is difficult to imagine life without reliable weather forecasts. Every day, millions of people make decisions based on information provided by weather satellites. Weather satellites give scientists a big-picture view of Earth's atmosphere. These satellites constantly monitor the atmosphere for events that lead to severe weather conditions. For example, weather satellites are able to provide images of hurricanes. These images help scientists predict the path of the hurricane. People living in the projected pathway can be warned to move to a safer place until the hurricane passes.

Weather satellites also monitor changes in cloud formation and in energy coming from Earth. Information from weather satellites helps airplanes avoid dangerous weather and provides farmers with information that can help them to grow their crops.

Mississippi River

The blue shows the shape of the delta in 1973. The green shows the land surface.

This image shows the shape of the delta in 2003. The black represents the water in the Gulf of Mexico.

Visualize It!

13 Analyze Identify changes in the land surface along the Mississippi River delta using the photos.

_____

_____

_____

_____

Weather satellites monitor the path of Hurricane Igor churning over the Atlantic Ocean in 2010.

For Search and Rescue Operations

The U.S. National Oceanic and Atmospheric Administration (NOAA) has many different satellites. NOAA's environmental satellites carry an instrument package called *SARSAT*. The SARSAT instruments detect distress signals from emergency beacons (BEE•kuhnz). Many ships, airplanes, and individuals on land have emergency beacons. The beacons can be used anywhere in the world, at any time of day. Once the distress signals are received, the satellites relay the signals to a network of ground stations, as shown in the illustration. In the end, the signals go to the U.S. Mission Control Center in Maryland. The Mission Control Center processes the emergency and puts the search and rescue operation into action.

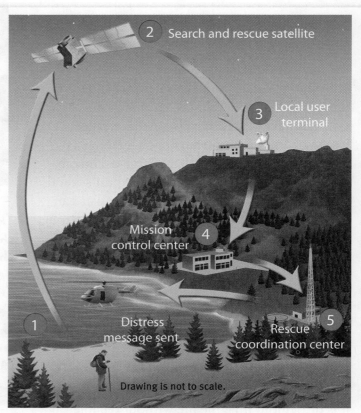

2 Search and rescue satellite

3 Local user terminal

Mission control center

4

1 Distress message sent

5 Rescue coordination center

Drawing is not to scale.

Steps involved in a search and rescue operation

The white areas indicate the most light.

To Provide Composite Images

Data from satellites can be combined to form one image that shows more complete information. The combined image is called a *composite* image. Composite satellite images can give very detailed information about an area's surface features and other features. For example, satellite images can be combined to produce a dramatic image that shows where most of the sources of artificial light are located, as shown here. In this false-color image, data were combined to produce the different colors. A composite image that shows artificial light sources would include images of Earth with no cloud cover.

Think Outside the Book

14 **Research** Investigate a satellite map that shows surface features for your town or city. What kinds of data does this map contain?

Exploring the Ocean

NEW FRONTIERS

They may not seem related, but deep-sea exploration and space exploration have something in common. Both use advanced technologies to observe locations that are difficult or dangerous for humans to explore.

Ocean Submersibles

Both marine scientists and space scientists investigate areas most humans will never visit. Ocean submersibles can be crewed or uncrewed.

Black Smokers

Hydrothermal vents are on the ocean floor where the pressure is too great for humans to withstand.

Tube Worms

In the 1970s, scientists aboard a submersible discovered giant tube worms living near an ocean vent. NASA scientists examine the extreme conditions of Mars and other planets for any signs of life.

Extend

Inquiry

15 Identify List two similarities between deep-sea exploration and space exploration.

16 Research and Record List some features of an ocean submersible, for example, *Alvin*. How is the submersible's structure similar to that of spacecraft?

17 Recommend Support more funding for deep-sea exploration by doing one of the following:
- write a letter
- design an ad for a science magazine
- write a script for a radio commercial

For Communication

Communications satellites relay data, including Internet service and some television and radio broadcasts. They are also used to relay long-distance telephone calls. One communications satellite can relay thousands of telephone calls or several television programs at once. Communications satellites are in use continuously.

Communications satellites relay television signals to consumers.

Active Reading **18 Identify** As you read, number the sequence of steps required to get a television signal to your television set.

For Relaying Information to Distant Locations on Earth

How do you send a television signal to someone on the other side of Earth? The problem is that Earth is round, and the signals travel in a straight line. Communications satellites are the answer. A television signal is sent from a point on Earth's surface to a communications satellite. Then the satellite sends the signal to receivers in other locations, as shown in the diagram. Small satellite dishes on the roofs of houses or outside apartments collect the signals. The signals are then sent to the customer's television set.

19 Explain State one reason satellites are useful for communication.

_____

_____

_____

_____

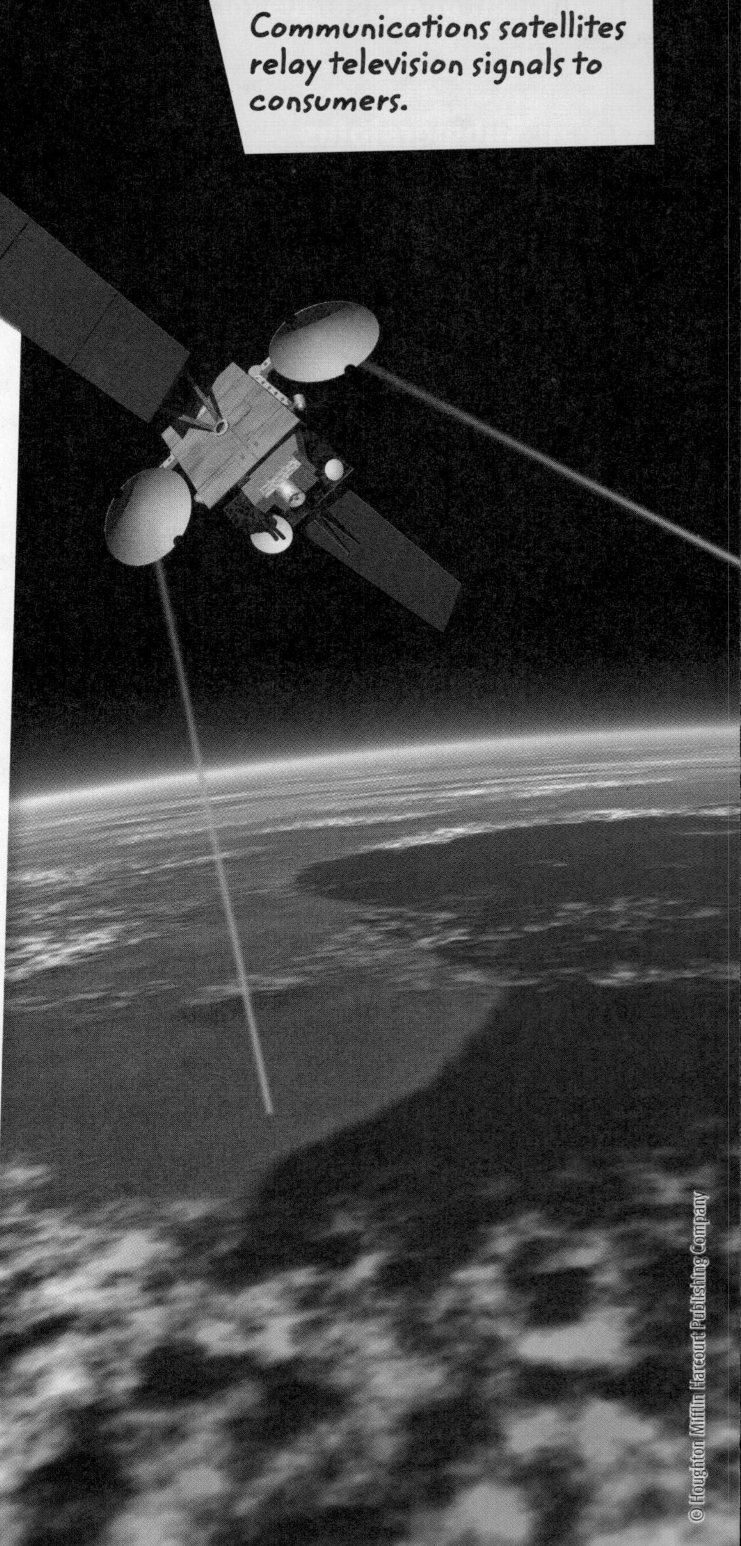

Drawing is not to scale.

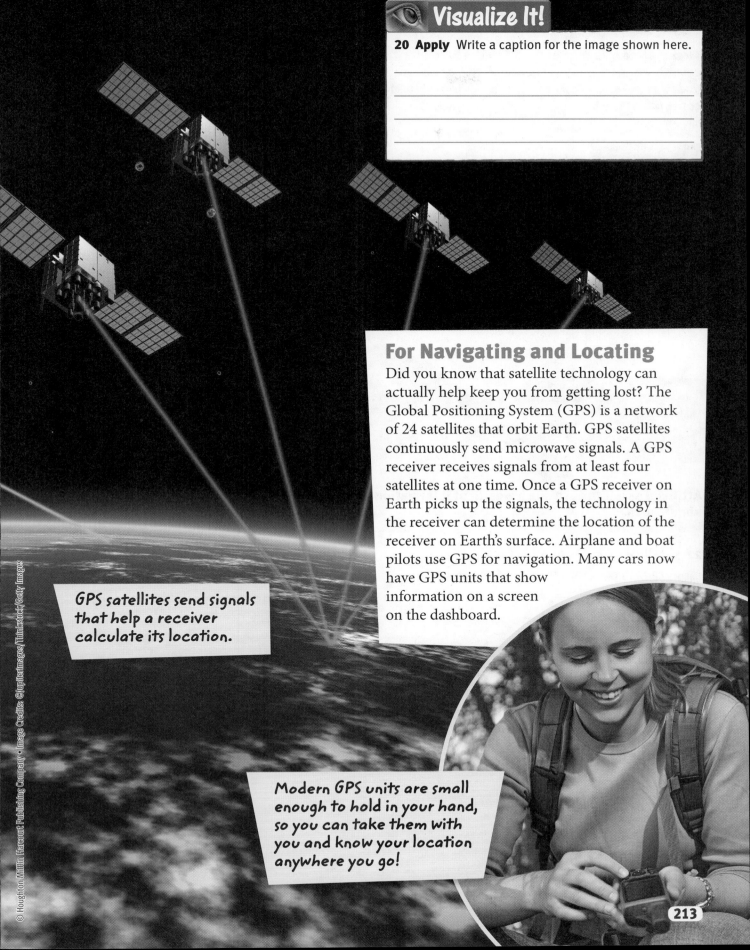

20 Apply Write a caption for the image shown here.

_____

_____

_____

_____

For Navigating and Locating

Did you know that satellite technology can actually help keep you from getting lost? The Global Positioning System (GPS) is a network of 24 satellites that orbit Earth. GPS satellites continuously send microwave signals. A GPS receiver receives signals from at least four satellites at one time. Once a GPS receiver on Earth picks up the signals, the technology in the receiver can determine the location of the receiver on Earth's surface. Airplane and boat pilots use GPS for navigation. Many cars now have GPS units that show information on a screen on the dashboard.

GPS satellites send signals that help a receiver calculate its location.

Modern GPS units are small enough to hold in your hand, so you can take them with you and know your location anywhere you go!

213

Visual Summary

To complete this summary, fill in the blanks with the correct word or phrase. Then, use the key below to check your answers. You can use this page to review the main concepts of the lesson.

Technology for Space Exploration

Humans use crewed technology to travel to and from space.

21 To escape from Earth's gravity, the space shuttle uses liquid fuel and _____

Telescopes in space study different types of electromagnetic radiation.

23 To obtain clearer images, space telescopes orbit above _____

Artificial satellites provide a wealth of information about Earth.

22 Satellites provide images for military purposes, remote sensing, communications, navigation, and _____

Uncrewed spacecraft can explore distant planets.

24 Examples of uncrewed spacecraft include probes, orbiters, landers, and _____

Answers: 21 solid rocket boosters; 22 weather; 23 Earth's atmosphere; 24 rovers

25 Provide Give examples of the kind of information scientists can obtain from each type of uncrewed spacecraft.

_____

_____

_____

Lesson Review

Vocabulary

Circle the term that best completes the following sentences.

1 A *rocket / space shuttle* is a reusable crewed spacecraft.

2 A(n) *lander / orbiter* is a kind of artificial satellite.

3 A(n) *orbiter / rover* often has mechanical arms to gather rock samples.

4 A(n) *orbiter / probe* is more suited to the long-term study of a planet or moon.

5 A *rocket / space shuttle* had detachable capsules that contained the crew.

Key Concepts

6 List Give an example of how satellites are used for communication.

_____

_____

7 Explain Why is most space exploration accomplished with spacecraft that do not have crews on board?

_____

_____

_____

8 Apply How could you benefit from using a GPS unit in your daily life?

_____

_____

_____

9 Explain What is one advantage of using an orbiter to study objects in space?

_____

_____

_____

Critical Thinking

Use the diagram to answer the following questions.

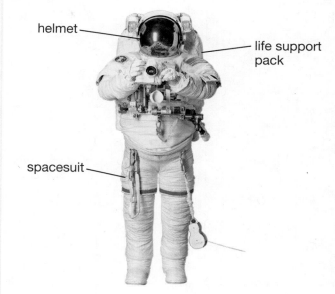

helmet — life support pack

spacesuit —

10 Identify Which spacesuit feature provides oxygen to an astronaut?

_____

11 Infer How is the spacesuit designed to protect the astronaut outside of a spacecraft?

_____

_____

_____

12 Infer Why do you think it's important to map a planet's surface before planning a lander mission?

_____

_____

_____

13 Conclude Could a lander be used to study the surface of Saturn? Explain.

_____

_____

My Notes

Testing and Modifying Theories

When scientists develop a theory, they use experiments to investigate the theory. The results of experiments can support or disprove theories. If the results of several experiments do not support a theory, it may be modified.

Tutorial

Read below about the Tomatosphere Project to find out more about how theories are tested and modified. This project exposes tomato seeds to simulated Martian conditions to observe later seed germination.

Theory → Prediction → Experiment → Observation (cycle diagram)

A theory is created/ modified.
Sometimes, two well-supported theories explain a single phenomenon. A theory might be modified based on new data. Scientists can figure out how to supply long-term space missions with food, water, oxygen, and other life-support needs.

A prediction is made.
Predictions are based on prior knowledge. Scientists might predict that if tomato seeds are exposed to Martian conditions, they will still be able to germinate and grow into healthy, fruit-bearing plants.

Observations are made.
Scientists evaluate their observations to see whether or not the results support their hypothesis. If any data disprove the original prediction, scientists may have to modify their theory. The results of the blind studies are gathered and analyzed to see whether exposure to harsh conditions affected the germination of the seeds.

Experiments are done.
Setting up the proper scientific procedure to test the prediction is important. In the Tomatosphere Project, a set of exposed seeds, along with a control group of regular seeds, are planted in thousands of classrooms. At least 20 of each type were planted, to ensure a large enough sample size. The type of seeds were not revealed, as part of a blind study.

You Try It!

Two scientists describe theories that try to explain the motion of galaxies. Use the information provided to answer the questions that follow.

Background

Any objects that have mass, such as Earth and you, exert a gravitational force that pulls them toward each other. An unexpected motion of an object in space, such as a galaxy, could be the result of an unseen object pulling on it. Scientists use electromagnetic radiation, such as visible, infrared, and ultraviolet light, to detect and study visible matter. However, dark matter is a hypothetical material that does not give off electromagnetic radiation that we can detect.

Scientist A

There is more dark matter than visible matter in galaxies. There is just too little visible matter to exert the force that would explain how the galaxies move. The additional force exerted by dark matter would explain the motion we see without having to change our understanding of gravitational force.

Scientist B

We must change our understanding of gravitational force. The farther away from the center of a galaxy you go, the stronger (not weaker) the gravitational force becomes. With this change, the amount of visible matter is enough to explain how the galaxies move. Dark matter is not needed.

1 Predicting Outcomes How would proof that dark matter exists affect each scientist's theory?

_____

_____

_____

_____

2 Predicting Outcomes If experiments fail to detect dark matter, does Scientist A's theory need to be modified? Explain why.

_____

_____

_____

_____

_____

_____

3 Making Inferences What evidence would require both scientists to modify their theories?

_____

_____

_____

_____

Take It Home

Using the Internet, research a scientific theory that has been reproduced in two different experiments. Write a short report that explains how the observations helped develop the theory. How else could this theory could be investigated?

History of Space Exploration

ESSENTIAL QUESTION

What are some milestones of space exploration?

By the end of this lesson, you should understand some of the achievements of space exploration.

In 1993, astronauts walked in space to repair the damaged Hubble Space Telescope.

Engage Your Brain

1 Describe Write a word beginning with each letter of the acronym NASA that describes space exploration.

N _____

A _____

S _____

A _____

2 Describe Write your own caption to this photo.

Cape Canaveral, 1961

_____

_____

_____

Active Reading

3 Apply Use context clues to write your own definition for the word *challenge*.

Example sentence:
Visiting other planets is a <u>challenge</u> for humans given their great distances from Earth.

challenge:

_____

_____

Vocabulary Terms
- NASA

4 Identify As you read, place a question mark next to any words that you don't understand. When you finish reading the lesson, go back and review the text that you marked. If the information is still confusing, consult a classmate or a teacher.

Space: The Final Frontier

How did space exploration begin?

Active Reading

5 Identify As you read, underline the four words that make up the acronym NASA.

6 Infer Why might people continue to pursue space exploration in the future?

_____

_____

_____

_____

Have you ever looked into the night sky and wondered what exists beyond Earth? If so, you are not alone. People have been curious about space since ancient times. This curiosity and the desire to understand the unknown paved the way for space exploration.

In October of 1957, the Soviet Union launched the first satellite, _Sputnik I_, into low Earth orbit. Though it was a sphere only 585 mm in diameter that contained a 3.5 kg radio transmitter, _Sputnik I_ was the first step in space exploration beyond Earth. It was the start of the "Space Age."

The United States clearly understood the advantages of placing technology in space. In response to the Soviet launch of _Sputnik I_, the U.S. launched its first satellite, _Explorer I_, on January 31, 1958. This started what became known as the Space Race between the two nations, which would continue for several decades. In the same year, the National Aeronautics and Space Administration, or **NASA**, was formed. Its purpose was to head up a program of research and development for the "conquest of space."

1950   1960   1970

1957: The Space Age began when the Soviet Union launched the first artificial satellite, _Sputnik I_, into low Earth orbit.

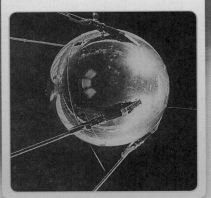

1961: The first human to orbit Earth was cosmonaut Yuri A. Gagarin of the Soviet Union, shown below. In the same year, Alan Shepard became the first American in space.

1961–1966: Mission control monitors a Gemini space flight below. During this period, projects Mercury and Gemini focused on launching spacecraft that would prepare for journeys to the moon.

© Houghton Mifflin Harcourt Publishing Company • Image Credits: (bg) ©Purestock/Photolibrary; (b) ©OFF/AFP/Getty Images; (tc) ©Bettmann/Corbis; (br) ©NASA Johnson Space Center

The space shuttle **Atlantis** heads into orbit around Earth.

1998–present: Numerous countries have participated in the construction and use of the *International Space Station*, a long-term research laboratory that orbits Earth.

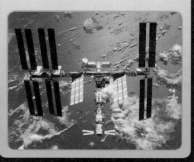

2000

1990

1981: Shuttle flights began in 1981. The space shuttle launched and retrieved satellites from Earth orbit. The space shuttle later flew to the *International Space Station*.

1980

1971: *Salyut 1*, the world's first space station, was launched into orbit by the Soviet Union. Its first crew arrived in the *Soyuz 11* spacecraft and remained on board for 24 days.

1968–1972: Six missions to the moon carried three astronauts each. The first moon landing was *Apollo 11* in 1969. The last moon landing was *Apollo 17* in 1972. A total of 12 astronauts walked on the moon.

Visualize It!

7 Interpret How has space exploration changed over time?

_____

_____

_____

_____

From Earth to the Moon

Alan Shepard prepares for launch in 1961.

Astronauts emerge from the **Gemini 8** capsule after splashdown in 1966.

Valentina Tereshkova of the Soviet Union became the first woman in space in 1963.

How have people explored space?

It was not until the 1960s that the first rockets capable of launching space capsules were built and tested. All that was needed to explore space was to place astronauts inside these capsules.

By Using Suborbital Crewed Exploration

Suborbital crewed spacecraft do not orbit Earth because they do not reach the required speed and altitude. So, these flights spend only a very short time in space. The first crewed suborbital spaceflight missions were NASA's Mercury project in 1961. On May 5, 1961, a Redstone rocket launched astronaut Alan B. Shepard, Jr., aboard a capsule called *Freedom 7*. Shepard flew safely for 15 minutes before returning to Earth. The second suborbital flight, which took place on July 21, 1961, was that of astronaut Virgil I. Grissom. Although the capsule sank shortly after splashdown in the Atlantic Ocean, Grissom was rescued safely.

By Using Orbital Crewed Exploration

Orbital crewed spacecraft completely orbit Earth. The first crewed orbital space flight was made on April 12, 1961, by Soviet air force pilot Yuri A. Gagarin (guh•GAR•in) aboard *Vostok 1*. Gagarin orbited Earth for 108 minutes before parachuting safely to Earth. On July 21, 1961, John H. Glenn, Jr., observed Earth from space as he became the first American to orbit Earth. Glenn completed three orbits of Earth in a little less than five hours. On June 16, 1963, cosmonaut Valentina V. Tereshkova became the first woman in space. She orbited Earth 48 times over a three-day period.

Meanwhile, the United States was developing plans for a two-person, crewed Gemini program. Ten crewed Gemini missions would follow. One goal of the Gemini program was to see if astronauts could spend longer periods of time in space. The Soviet Union responded with their own multiperson spaceflights as part of their existing Vostok program. Another milestone took place on March 18, 1965, when Soviet cosmonaut Alexei A. Leonov performed the first walk in space. The first American to walk in space was Edward H. White II on June 3, 1965.

8 Compare How are suborbital and orbital space exploration alike and different?

_____

_____

_____

© Houghton Mifflin Harcourt Publishing Company • Image Credits: (t) ©Bettmann/Corbis; (c) ©Bettmann/Corbis; (b) ©Hutton-Deutsch Collection/Corbis

By Landing on the Moon

The race to the moon began in the 1960s. On September 12, 1962, President John F. Kennedy committed the United States to "landing a man on the moon and returning him safely to Earth" before the decade ended. The key requirement for a successful moon landing is to travel fast enough to escape Earth's gravity and slow enough to land safely on the moon's surface.

The United States would be the only nation to send astronauts to the moon. Six moon landings took place during the Apollo program of the late 1960s and early 1970s. In 1969, the *Apollo 11* spacecraft took astronauts Neil Armstrong, Edwin "Buzz" Aldrin, and Michael Collins to the moon. While Collins orbited the moon in the lunar spacecraft, Armstrong and Aldrin descended to the moon's surface in the lunar module, named the *Eagle*. The *Eagle* landed in the Sea of Tranquility on July 20, 1969. Millions of people heard Armstrong's breathtaking transmission from the lunar surface, "Tranquility Base here. The *Eagle* has landed." Soon after, Neil Armstrong became the first person to set foot on the moon's surface. Six of the 11 Apollo missions landed on the moon. In total, 12 astronauts walked on the moon.

9 Infer Why was landing on the moon such an important moment in American history?

_____

_____

_____

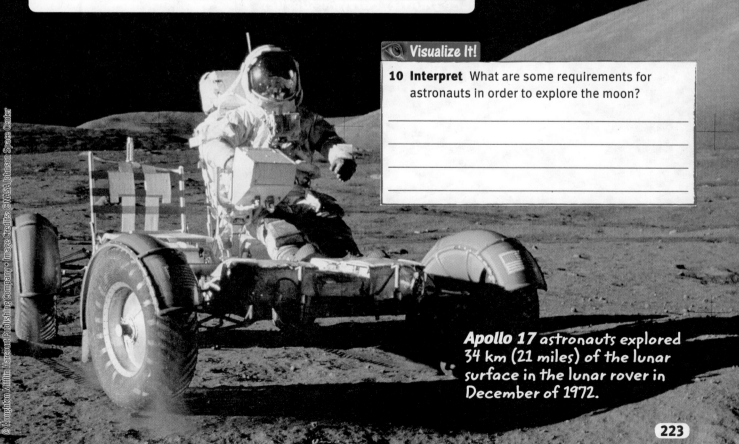

Visualize It!

10 Interpret What are some requirements for astronauts in order to explore the moon?

_____

_____

_____

Apollo 17 astronauts explored 34 km (21 miles) of the lunar surface in the lunar rover in December of 1972.

Where have people lived and worked in space?

Active Reading **11 Assess** As you read, underline different uses of space shuttle technology.

As you might imagine, rocket technology is potentially dangerous. Rockets are also expensive, considering that they cannot be reused. Beginning in the 1970s, NASA made plans to build spacecraft that were not only habitable but also reusable.

In Space Shuttles

Space shuttles are crewed space vehicles that lift off with the aid of rocket boosters and land like airplanes. Both the space shuttle and its rocket boosters are reusable. Space shuttles orbit Earth while in space. Missions aboard shuttles have been an important way to gather data, launch satellites, and transport materials. Space shuttles have also docked with the *International Space Station*.

Missions using space shuttles began with the launch of the shuttle *Columbia* in 1981. Six shuttles—*Enterprise, Columbia, Challenger, Discovery, Atlantis,* and *Endeavour*—have completed a total of more than 100 missions. The *Challenger* and its crew were lost when the shuttle broke apart minutes after liftoff in 1986. An accident also led to the fatal explosion of the *Columbia* in 2003.

Space shuttles carrying supplies have traveled to and docked with the ***International Space Station***.

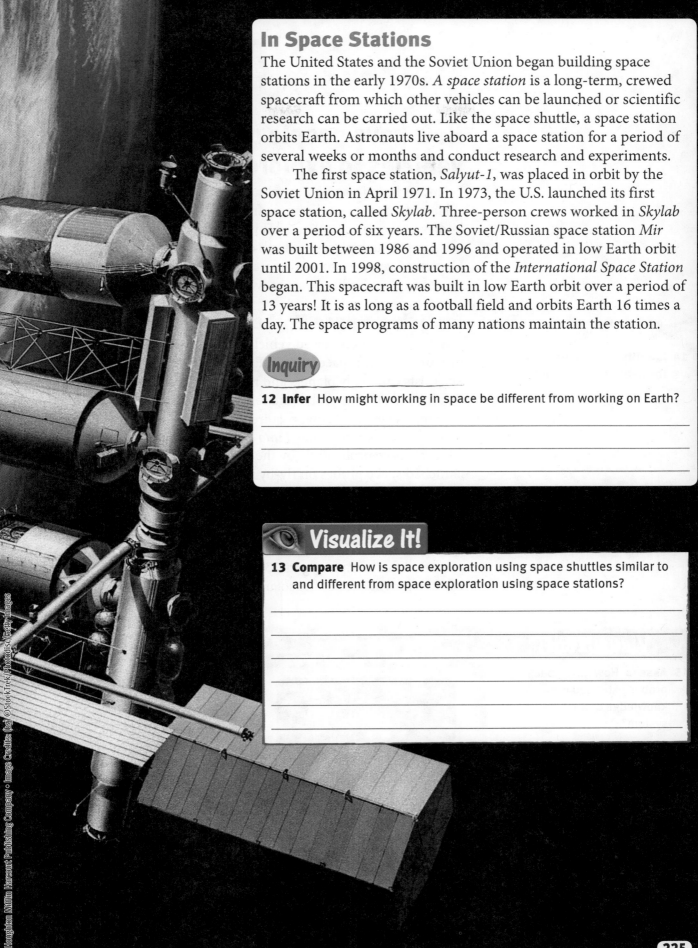

In Space Stations

The United States and the Soviet Union began building space stations in the early 1970s. *A space station* is a long-term, crewed spacecraft from which other vehicles can be launched or scientific research can be carried out. Like the space shuttle, a space station orbits Earth. Astronauts live aboard a space station for a period of several weeks or months and conduct research and experiments.

The first space station, *Salyut-1*, was placed in orbit by the Soviet Union in April 1971. In 1973, the U.S. launched its first space station, called *Skylab*. Three-person crews worked in *Skylab* over a period of six years. The Soviet/Russian space station *Mir* was built between 1986 and 1996 and operated in low Earth orbit until 2001. In 1998, construction of the *International Space Station* began. This spacecraft was built in low Earth orbit over a period of 13 years! It is as long as a football field and orbits Earth 16 times a day. The space programs of many nations maintain the station.

Inquiry

12 Infer How might working in space be different from working on Earth?

_____

_____

_____

Visualize It!

13 Compare How is space exploration using space shuttles similar to and different from space exploration using space stations?

_____

_____

_____

_____

_____

_____

Just Passing By

How have people used uncrewed vehicles to explore space?

Scientists have imagined traveling to planets, moons, and even solar systems at great distances from Earth. But reaching other bodies in the solar system takes years or even decades. Crewed missions to such places are both difficult and dangerous. Uncrewed vehicles, such as space probes and orbiters, are a safe way to explore bodies in space without using people.

By Using Space Probes

Space probes are uncrewed vehicles that carry scientific instruments into space beyond Earth's orbit to collect data. Scientists can study planets and moons at great distances from Earth, as data from probes are sent to Earth. Space probes are used to complete missions that require years of travel time in space.

The first space probe, *Luna 1*, was launched in 1959. It was the first space probe to fly by the moon. Since then, scientists have launched space probes on fly-by missions to Mercury and Venus. Some space probes were designed to land on distant planets, such as the landings of *Viking 1* and *Viking 2* on Mars in 1976. Other space probes have been used to explore the far reaches of the solar system. In 1977, *Voyager 2* was launched to explore the gas giant planets. After completing its 33-year mission, the probe is now close to moving out of the solar system and into interstellar space.

14 Identify As you read, underline the uses of space probes.

Visualize It!

15 Assess How have space probes extended our knowledge of the solar system?

_____

_____

_____

_____

_____

_____

_____

1950   1960   1970

In 1962, *Mariner 2* successfully passed within 35,000 km of Venus and returned data from the planet. Here, technicians attach solar panels that powered the probe.

In 1972, *Pioneer 10* was the first space probe to travel through the asteroid belt and make observations of Jupiter.

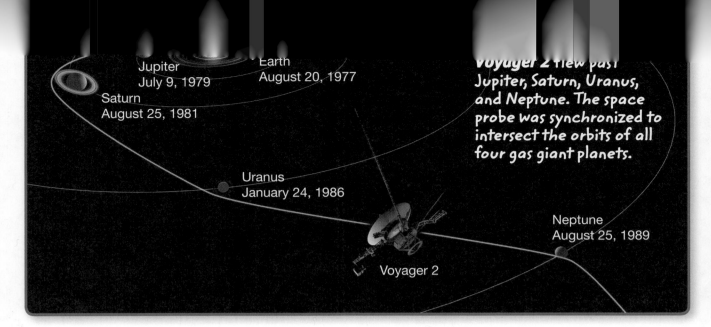

Jupiter
July 9, 1979

Earth
August 20, 1977

Saturn
August 25, 1981

Voyager 2 flew past Jupiter, Saturn, Uranus, and Neptune. The space probe was synchronized to intersect the orbits of all four gas giant planets.

Uranus
January 24, 1986

Neptune
August 25, 1989

Voyager 2

By Using Orbiters

An *orbiter* is a spacecraft that travels to a planet and goes into orbit around it. Several orbiters have explored the planetary features of Mars. The first of these orbiters, *Mars Odyssey* (AHD•ih•see), was launched in 2001. It entered the orbit of Mars after a seven-month journey through space. Two of the missions of the *Mars Odyssey* are to make maps of the Martian surface and to collect data about the chemical makeup of the planet. It was still in service as of 2011.

Launched in 2003, the European Space Agency's *Mars Express* is being used to look for signs of water on Mars. It has also played a role in mapping the surface of Mars and studying the composition of the planet's atmosphere. In 2006, NASA's *Mars Reconnaissance Orbiter* arrived at Mars. It has the most powerful camera ever sent to view another planet. The camera can be used to guide future spacecraft to make precise landings on the Martian surface.

Think Outside the Book

16 **Research** Investigate a particular space probe or orbiter and its mission. What did it discover?

1980	1990	2000	2010

Space probe *Galileo* was deployed from the space shuttle *Atlantis* in 1989 to study Jupiter and its moons. It flew by Jupiter in 1995.

In 1997, the *Cassini-Huygens* space probe was launched to study the planet Saturn and its moons, including Enceladus and Titan.

Comet Temple 1 was the target of the *Deep Impact* space probe, which released an impactor into the comet in 2005 to study the composition of its interior.

© Houghton Mifflin Harcourt Publishing Company • Image Credits: (bl) ©NASA/Science Photo Library; (bc) ©NASA/Jet Propulsion Laboratory; (br) ©NASA/JPL/UMD

This photograph from 1958 shows scientists examining the prototype for **Explorer I**, the first United States satellite in space.

By Using Landers and Rovers

Imagine being able to view a planet's surface from Earth. Robotic exploration on the surface of planets and other bodies in space is done by using landers. A *lander* is designed to land on the surface of a planet and send data back to Earth. A *rover* is a mobile vehicle that is used to physically explore the surface by moving about. The chief advantage of landers and rovers is that they can conduct experiments on soil and rocks. They can also directly record surface conditions, such as temperature and wind flow.

The *Mars Pathfinder*, a lander launched in 1996, placed the Mars rover called *Sojourner* on the planet's surface in 1997. In 2003, NASA sent two more rovers, called *Spirit* and *Opportunity*, to explore Mars. In 2012, the *Mars Curiosity* rover was sent to further explore the red planet.

Active Reading

17 List As you read, underline the advantages of using landers and rovers in the exploration of a planet's surface.

Visualize It!

18 Assess How have we learned about Mars from landers and rovers?

_____
_____
_____
_____
_____
_____
_____
_____
_____

1950   1960   1970

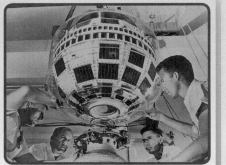

In 1962, technicians joined the *Telstar* satellite to a Delta rocket for launch. *Telstar* was the first satellite to transmit TV signals.

Viking 2 landed on Mars in 1976 and took more than 16,000 images of the Martian surface. The lander stopped working in 1978.

Telstar

Receiver

Transmitter

Satellites allow us to communicate around the world and help make the world a global village.

With Artificial Satellites

When you turn on a TV or a cell phone, a satellite high in the atmosphere often makes this communication possible. An *artificial satellite* is any human-made object placed in orbit around a body in space. Satellites orbit Earth at high speeds. Each satellite has a unique function such as collecting weather data, relaying TV and radio signals, assisting in navigation, and studying Earth's surface.

The *Echo I* satellite was one of the very first communication satellites. It was launched by the United States in 1960. In that same year, the first weather satellite was launched. It carried a video camera to record observations of Earth's atmosphere. A system of orbiting global navigation satellites has been operated by the U.S. since 1978. These satellite systems are used to determine precise locations on Earth. Hundreds of active satellites orbit Earth.

Visualize It!

19 Infer How do satellites transmit data to Earth?

_____

_____

_____

_____

_____

_____

1980   1990   2000   2010

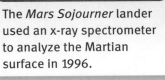

The *Mars Sojourner* lander used an x-ray spectrometer to analyze the Martian surface in 1996.

Between 2004 and 2009, NASA sent three rovers to explore the surface of Mars.

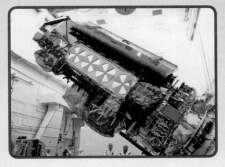

NOAA and NASA established the Joint Polar Satellite System in 2011. One of its goals is to help scientists better predict severe weather.

Visual Summary

To complete this summary, check the box that indicates true or false. Then, use the key below to check your answers. You can use this page to review the main concepts of the lesson.

Crewed orbital space exploration takes place in a piloted spacecraft that orbits Earth or travels to the moon.

T F

20 ☐ ☐ The first crewed orbital spaceflight mission took place aboard NASA's project Gemini in 1961.

Space probes are uncrewed vehicles that carry scientific instruments into space beyond Earth's orbit to collect data.

T F

21 ☐ ☐ Space probes can travel on the surface of a planet.

A space station is a long-term orbiting crewed spacecraft from which other vehicles can be launched or scientific research can be carried out.

T F

22 ☐ ☐ Space stations are a place where humans can live their daily lives, such as eating, sleeping, and working.

Answers: 20 F; 21 F; 22 T

23 **Compare** What are some advantages and disadvantages of crewed and uncrewed missions?

Lesson Review

Vocabulary

Fill in the blank with the term that best completes the following sentences.

1 A/An _____ is a human-made object that is placed in orbit around a body in space.

2 _____ is a government agency that runs the space program in the United States.

3 A vehicle that is designed to move about and collect data from the surface of a planet is called a _____

Key Concepts

4 List Identify four ways in which people can directly explore space.

_____

_____

_____

5 Identify What are five ways in which people can explore and study space without physically going there?

_____

_____

_____

_____

_____

6 Summarize Describe three achievements in space exploration that involved the United States.

_____

_____

_____

_____

_____

Critical Thinking

Use the image to answer the following question.

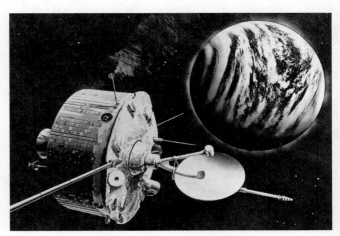

7 Infer Is this an image of an orbiter or a rover? How do you know?

_____

_____

_____

8 Relate How is preparing for a space mission similar to planning for a camping trip? How is it different?

_____

_____

_____

_____

_____

_____

9 Assess What type of technology would you want to use to study the gas giant plants?

_____

_____

_____

_____

_____

My Notes

Unit 4 Big Idea People develop and use technology to explore and study space.

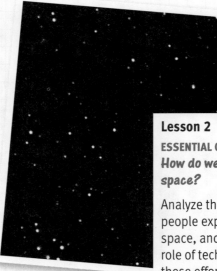

Lesson 1

ESSENTIAL QUESTION
What can we learn from space images?

Describe ways of collecting information from space, and analyze how different wavelengths of the electromagnetic spectrum provide different information.

Lesson 2

ESSENTIAL QUESTION
How do we explore space?

Analyze the ways people explore outer space, and assess the role of technology in these efforts.

Lesson 3

ESSENTIAL QUESTION
What are some milestones of space exploration?

Understand some of the achievements of space exploration.

Connect ESSENTIAL QUESTIONS
Lessons 1 and 3

1 Synthesize Explain how electromagnetic radiation can be dangerous to humans who are exploring space.

_____

_____

_____

_____

Think Outside the Book

2 Synthesize Choose one of these activities to help synthesize what you have learned in this unit.

☐ Using what you learned in lessons 1 and 2, write a short essay explaining why weather satellites are placed in polar orbits.

☐ Using what you learned in lessons 2 and 3, create a graphic novel to show some of the limitations of human space exploration.

Unit 4 Review

Name _____

Vocabulary

Fill in each blank with the term that best completes the following sentences.

1 A(n) _____ is any human-made object placed in orbit around a body in space, either with or without a crew.

2 _____ is the United States agency that explores space through crewed and uncrewed missions.

3 The _____ refers to all of the frequencies or wavelengths of electromagnetic radiation.

4 _____ provide information about weather, temperature, land use, and changes on Earth over time.

5 A mobile, uncrewed vehicle that is used to explore the surface of another planet is called a _____.

Key Concepts

Read each question below, and circle the best answer.

6 Satellites in orbit around Earth are used for various purposes. For which one of the following purposes are satellites not used?

A transmitting signals over large distances to remote locations

B monitoring changes in Earth's environment over time

C transporting materials to space stations

D collecting different types of weather data

7 What is the most important reason why astronauts who live on a space station have to exercise every day?

A There is not much else to do, and exercising passes the time.

B It prevents their bones and muscles from weakening.

C Astronauts need to stay in good shape.

D It helps them to sleep better at night.

8 Which one of the following is not an example of technology used in crewed space exploration?

   A a space shuttle   **C** a space telescope

   B a space station   **D** a rocket

9 Look at the diagram of the electromagnetic spectrum.

The Electromagnetic Spectrum

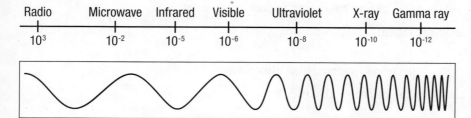

What characteristic determines the different kinds of radiation in the electromagnetic spectrum?

   A length of the wave   **C** whether the wave is visible or not

   B color   **D** name of the wave

10 Optical telescopes are used to study wavelengths from a certain portion of the electromagnetic spectrum. Which is true of optical telescopes?

   A Optical telescopes are used to study objects in space using ultraviolet radiation.

   B Optical telescopes are used to receive radio waves from objects in space.

   C Optical telescopes are used to study objects in space using infrared radiation.

   D Optical telescopes are used to study visible light from objects in space.

11 The chart below lists four waves and their wavelengths.

Wave	Wavelength
Radio	10^3 m
Visible	10^{-6} m
X-ray	10^{-10} m
Gamma ray	10^{-12} m

Which wave will have the highest frequency?

A radio waves

C x-rays

B visible waves

D gamma rays

12 How are telescopes used in space science?

A Telescopes are used to transmit visible light over long distances.

B Telescopes help in looking at cells.

C Telescopes help to gather data about space for use by astronomers.

D Telescopes are used to communicate over long distances.

Critical Thinking

Answer the following questions in the space provided.

13 Outline a brief history of space exploration, and discuss some problems humans encounter when they explore space.

_____

_____

_____

_____

_____

_____

_____

14 Satellites provide us with various forms of communication.

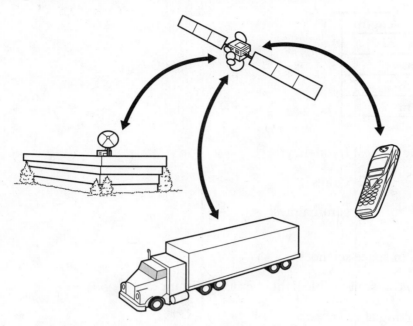

Describe how satellites can aid in communication.

_____

_____

_____

_____

_____

Connect **ESSENTIAL QUESTIONS**
Lessons 1, 2, and 3

Answer the following question in the space provided.

15 Explain the distinction between astronomy and space exploration, and elaborate on the significance of space exploration in our society.

_____

_____

_____

_____

_____

_____

_____

(br) ©NASA

21st Century Skills
⟨Technology⟩
and Coding

This breathtaking image of Earth was taken from the International Space Station, an international laboratory orbiting Earth. The operation of the International Space Station is controlled by 52 computers and millions of lines of computer code. Its many high-tech features include solar panels that power the laboratory and a human-like robotic astronaut.

This is Robonaut 2, a robot designed to do routine maintenance at the International Space Station.

Data Driven

What is computer science?

If you like computer technology and learning about how computers work, computer science might be for you. *Computer science* is the study of computer technology and how data is processed, stored, and accessed by computers. Computer science is an important part of many other areas, including science, math, engineering, robotics, medicine, game design, and 3D animation.

Computer technology is often described in terms of *hardware*, which are the physical components, and *software*, which are the programs or instructions that a computer runs. Computer scientists must understand how hardware and software work together. Computer scientists may develop new kinds of useful computer software. Or they may work with engineers to improve existing computer hardware.

The first electronic computer, the computer ENIAC (Electronic Numerical Integrator And Computer), was developed at the University of Pennsylvania in 1946.

The integrated circuit (IC), first developed in the 1950s, was instrumental in the development of small computer components.

The development of the IC made it possible to reduce the overall size of computers and their components and to increase their processing speed.

How has computer technology changed over time?

Modern digital computer technology is less than 100 years old. Yet in that short amount of time, it has advanced rapidly. The earliest digital computers could perform only a limited number of tasks and were the size of an entire room. Over the decades, engineers continued to develop smaller, faster, and more powerful computers. Today's computers can process hundreds of millions of instructions per second!

Computer scientists and engineers think about what people want or need from computer technology. The most advanced hardware is not useful if people do not know how to use it. So computer scientists and engineers work to create software that is reliable, useful, and easy to use. Today's tablet computers, cell phones, and video game consoles can be used without any special training.

Advances in digital computer technology have help make computers cheaper and easier to operate, which has allowed many more people to work and play with them.

1 Compare Are modern computers simpler or more complex than early computers? Explain.

_____

_____

Computer Logic

What do computer scientists do?

Many people enjoy developing computer technology for fun. Learning how to create mobile phone games or Internet-enabled gadgets can be rewarding hobbies. For some people, that hobby may one day become a career in computer science. Working in computer science is a bit like solving a puzzle. Applying knowledge of how computers work to solve real-world problems requires collaboration, creativity, and logical step-by-step thinking.

This is a kayak folded up.

They collaborate across many disciplines

Computers are valuable tools in math and science because they can perform complex calculations very quickly. Computers are useful to many other fields, too. For example, animators use computer technology to create realistic lighting effects in 3D animated films. Mechanics use computers to diagnose problems in car systems. For every field that relies on special software or computer technology, there is an opportunity for computer scientists and engineers to collaborate and develop solutions for those computing needs. Computer scientists must be able to define and understand the problems presented to them and to communicate and work with experts in other fields to develop the solutions.

Computational origami is a computer program used to model the ways in which different materials, including paper, can be folded. It combines computer science and the art of paper folding to create new technologies, such as this kayak.

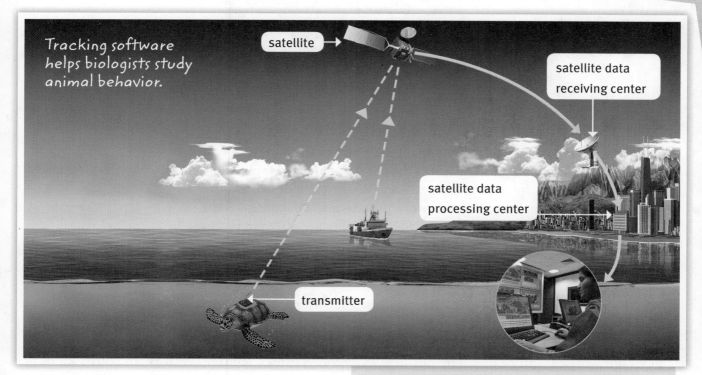

Tracking software helps biologists study animal behavior.

satellite

satellite data receiving center

satellite data processing center

transmitter

They help solve real-world problems

Some computer scientists carry out theoretical research. Others apply computer science concepts to develop software. Theoretical computer science and practical software development help solve real-world problems. For example, biologists need ways to safely and accurately track endangered animals. Computer science theories on artificial intelligence and pattern recognition have been applied to advanced animal-tracking technologies, such as satellite transmitters and aerial cameras. New kinds of image processing software now allow biologists to analyze the collected data in different ways.

They use logical, step-by-step thinking

Computers perform tasks given to them, and they do this very well. But in order to get the results they expect, computer scientists and programmers must write very accurate instructions. Computer science and programming requires logical thinking, deductive reasoning, and a good understanding of cause-and-effect relationships. When designing software, computer scientists must consider every possible user action and how the computer should respond to each action.

2 Explain How is computer science helping this scientist do her research?

_____

_____

_____

_____

Transmitters can be attached to animals to help track their movements.

Up to <Code>

How is computer software created?

Imagine that you are using a computer at the library to learn more about the history of electronic music. You use the library's database application to start searching for Internet resources. You also do a search to look for audio recordings. Finally, you open a word processor to take notes on the computer. Perhaps without realizing it, you've used many different pieces of software. Have you ever wondered how computer software is created?

Computer software is designed to address a need

Computer software can help us to learn more about our world. It can be useful to business. Or it can simply entertain us. Whatever its purpose, computer software should fulfill some human want or need. The first steps in creating software are precisely defining the need or want being addressed and planning how the software will work.

Computer software source code is written in a programming language

The instructions that tell a computer how to run video games, word processors, and other kinds of software are not written in a human language. They are written in a special programming language, or *code*. Javascript, C++, and Python are examples of programming languages. Programming languages—like human languages—must follow certain rules in order to be understood by the computer. A series of instructions written in a programming language is called *source code*.

Identifying what need a computer program addresses is one of the first development steps.

Source code is revised

Sometimes, programmers make mistakes in their code. Many programming environments have a feature that alerts the programmer to certain errors, such as spelling mistakes in commands, missing portions of code, or logical errors in the sequence of instructions. However, many mistakes go undetected, too. Some errors may cause the program to function incorrectly or not at all. When this happens, the programmer must identify the error, correct it, and test the software again.

Computer software is user tested, and revised

Once the software is created, it must be tested thoroughly to make sure it does not fail or behave in unexpected ways. It must also be tested to ensure that it meets users' needs. The creators of a piece of software might observe how people use it. Or they might ask users to provide feedback on certain features and test the software again.

3 Identify This source code contains an error. Infer where the error is located. What does this code "tell" the computer to do? Write your answers below.

_____

_____

_____

```
13
14  # Scores are not tied, so check
15  # which player wins the round
16 ▾ if player1_score > player2_score:
17      print ("Player 1 wins!")
18 ▾ else:
19      prnt ("Player 2 wins!")
20


! Syntax error, line 19
```

Test running a program is important for finding and fixing errors in the code.

Play it Safe

How should I work with computers?

It is easy to lose track of time when you're sitting in front of a computer or game console. It's also easy to forget that things you say or do online can be seen and shared by many different people. Here are some tips for using computers safely and responsibly.

✓ Maintain good posture

Time can pass by quickly when you are working on a computer or another device. Balance computer time with other activities, including plenty of physical activity. When you are sitting at a computer, sit upright with your shoulders relaxed. Your eyes should be level with the top of the monitor and your feet should be flat on the ground.

✓ Observe electrical safety

Building your own electronics projects can be fun, but it's important to have an understanding of circuits and electrical safety first. Otherwise, you could damage your components or hurt yourself. The potential for an electrical shock is real when you open up a computer, work with frayed cords or, use ungrounded plugs or attempt to replace parts without understanding how to do so safely. Ask an adult for help before starting any projects. Also, avoid using a connected computer during thunderstorms.

head and neck in a straight, neutral position

shoulders are relaxed

wrists are straight ↓

feet are flat on the ground

Good posture will help you avoid the aches and injuries related to sitting in front of a computer for a long time.

✓ Handle and maintain computers properly

Be cautious when handling and transporting electronic devices. Dropping them or spilling liquids on them could cause serious damage. Keep computers away from dirt, dust, liquids, and moisture. Never use wet cleaning products unless they are specifically designed for use on electronics. Microfiber cloths can be used to clear smudges from device screens. Spilled liquids can cause circuits to short out and hardware to corrode. If a liquid spills on a device, unplug it and switch it off immediately, remove the battery and wipe up as much of the liquid inside the device as possible. Don't switch the device back on until it is completely dry.

✓ Do not post private information online

Talk to your family about rules for Internet use. Do not use the Internet to share private information such as photographs, your phone number, or your address. Do not respond to requests for personal details from people you do not know.

✓ Treat yourself and others with respect

It is important to treat others with respect when on the Internet. Don't send or post messages online that you wouldn't say to someone in person. Unfortunately, not everyone acts respectfully while online. Some people may say hurtful things to you or send you unwanted messages. Do not reply to unwanted messages. Alert a trusted adult to any forms of contact, such as messages or photos, that make you feel uncomfortable.

4 Apply Fill in the chart below with a suitable response to each scenario.

SCENARIO	YOUR RESPONSE
You receive a text message from an online store asking for your home address.	
You've been lying down in front of a laptop, and you notice that your neck is feeling a little sore.	
You need to take a laptop computer with you on your walk to school.	
You want to try assembling a robotics kit with a friend.	
Someone posts unfriendly comments directed at you.	

Career in Computing:
Game Programmer

What do video game programmers do?
Creating your own universe with its own set of rules is fun. Just ask a programmer who works on video games!

What skills are needed in game programming?
A programmer should know how to write code, but there are other important skills a programmer needs as well. An understanding of physics and math is important for calculating how objects move and interact in a game. Game programmers usually work on a team with other people, such as artists, designers, writers, and musicians. They must be able to communicate effectively, and ideally, the programmer should understand the other team members' roles.

How can I get started with game development?
You don't need a big budget or years of experience to try it out. There are books, videos, and websites that can help you get started. When you're first experimenting with game development, start small. Try making a very simple game like Tic-Tac-Toe. Once you've mastered that, you can try something more complex.

5 Brainstorm Why would working on a team be important to the game development process?

_____

_____

_____

Look It Up!

References

Mineral Properties

Here are five steps to take in mineral identification:

1 Determine the color of the mineral. Is it light-colored, dark-colored, or a specific color?

2 Determine the luster of the mineral. Is it metallic or non-metallic?

3 Determine the color of any powder left by its streak.

4 Determine the hardness of your mineral. Is it soft, hard, or very hard? Using a glass plate, see if the mineral scratches it.

5 Determine whether your sample has cleavage or any special properties.

TERMS TO KNOW	DEFINITION
adamantine	a non-metallic luster like that of a diamond
cleavage	how a mineral breaks when subject to stress on a particular plane
luster	the state or quality of shining by reflecting light
streak	the color of a mineral when it is powdered
submetallic	between metallic and nonmetallic in luster
vitreous	glass-like type of luster

Silicate Minerals					
Mineral	**Color**	**Luster**	**Streak**	**Hardness**	**Cleavage and Special Properties**
Beryl	deep green, pink, white, bluish green, or yellow	vitreous	white	7.5–8	1 cleavage direction; some varieties fluoresce in ultraviolet light
Chlorite	green	vitreous to pearly	pale green	2–2.5	1 cleavage direction
Garnet	green, red, brown, black	vitreous	white	6.5–7.5	no cleavage
Hornblende	dark green, brown, or black	vitreous	none	5–6	2 cleavage directions
Muscovite	colorless, silvery white, or brown	vitreous or pearly	white	2–2.5	1 cleavage direction
Olivine	olive green, yellow	vitreous	white or none	6.5–7	no cleavage
Orthoclase	colorless, white, pink, or other colors	vitreous	white or none	6	2 cleavage directions
Plagioclase	colorless, white, yellow, pink, green	vitreous	white	6	2 cleavage directions
Quartz	colorless or white; any color when not pure	vitreous or waxy	white or none	7	no cleavage

Nonsilicate Minerals					
Mineral	**Color**	**Luster**	**Streak**	**Hardness**	**Cleavage and Special Properties**
Native Elements					
Copper	copper-red	metallic	copper-red	2.5–3	no cleavage
Diamond	pale yellow or colorless	adamantine	none	10	4 cleavage directions
Graphite	black to gray	submetallic	black	1–2	1 cleavage direction
Carbonates					
Aragonite	colorless, white, or pale yellow	vitreous	white	3.5–4	2 cleavage directions; reacts with hydrochloric acid
Calcite	colorless or white to tan	vitreous	white	3	3 cleavage directions; reacts with weak acid; double refraction
Halides					
Fluorite	light green, yellow, purple, bluish green, or other colors	vitreous	none	4	4 cleavage directions; some varieties fluoresce
Halite	white	vitreous	white	2.0–2.5	3 cleavage directions
Oxides					
Hematite	reddish brown to black	metallic to earthy	dark red to red-brown	5.6–6.5	no cleavage; magnetic when heated
Magnetite	iron-black	metallic	black	5.5–6.5	no cleavage; magnetic
Sulfates					
Anhydrite	colorless, bluish, or violet	vitreous to pearly	white	3–3.5	3 cleavage directions
Gypsum	white, pink, gray, or colorless	vitreous, pearly, or silky	white	2.0	3 cleavage directions
Sulfides					
Galena	lead-gray	metallic	lead-gray to black	2.5–2.8	3 cleavage directions
Pyrite	brassy yellow	metallic	greenish, brownish, or black	6–6.5	no cleavage

References

Geologic Time Scale

Geologists developed the geologic time scale to represent the 4.6 billion years of Earth's history that have passed since Earth formed. This scale divides Earth's history into blocks of time. The boundaries between these time intervals (shown in millions of years ago or mya in the table below), represent major changes in Earth's history. Some boundaries are defined by mass extinctions, major changes in Earth's surface, and/or major changes in Earth's climate.

The four major divisions that encompass the history of life on Earth are Precambrian time, the Paleozoic era, the Mesozoic era, and the Cenozoic era. The largest divisions are eons. **Precambrian time** is made up of the first three eons, over 4 billion years of Earth's history.

The **Paleozoic era** lasted from 542 mya to 251 mya. All major plant groups, except flowering plants, appeared during this era. By the end of the era, reptiles, winged insects, and fishes had also appeared. The largest known mass extinction occurred at the end of this era.

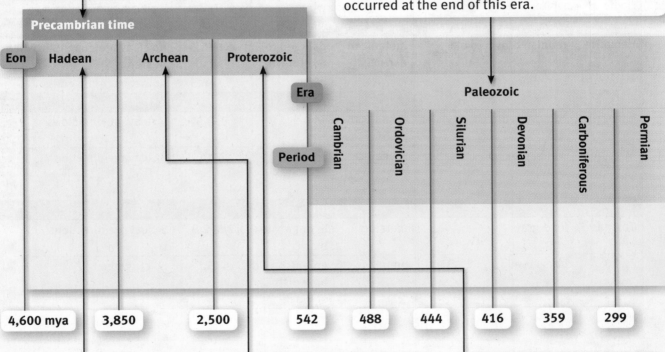

The **Hadean eon** lasted from about 4.6 billion years ago (bya) to 3.85 bya. It is described based on evidence from meterorites and rocks from the moon.

The **Archean eon** lasted from 3.85 bya to 2.5 bya. The earliest rocks from Earth that have been found and dated formed at the start of this eon.

The **Proterozoic eon** lasted from 2.5 bya to 542 mya. The first organisms, which were single-celled organisms, appeared during this eon. These organisms produced so much oxygen that they changed Earth's oceans and Earth's atmosphere.

Divisions of Time

The divisions of time shown here represent major changes in Earth's surface and when life developed and changed significantly on Earth. As new evidence is found, the boundaries of these divisions may shift. The Phanerozoic eon is divided into three eras. The beginning of each of these eras represents a change in the types of organisms that dominated Earth. And, each era is commonly characterized by the types of organisms that dominated the era. These eras are divided into periods, and periods are divided into epochs.

The **Mesozoic era** lasted from 251 mya to 65.5 mya. During this era, many kinds of dinosaurs dominated land, and giant lizards swam in the ocean. The first birds, mammals, and flowering plants also appeared during this time. About two-thirds of all land species went extinct at the end of this era.

The **Phanerozoic eon** began 542 mya. We live in this eon.

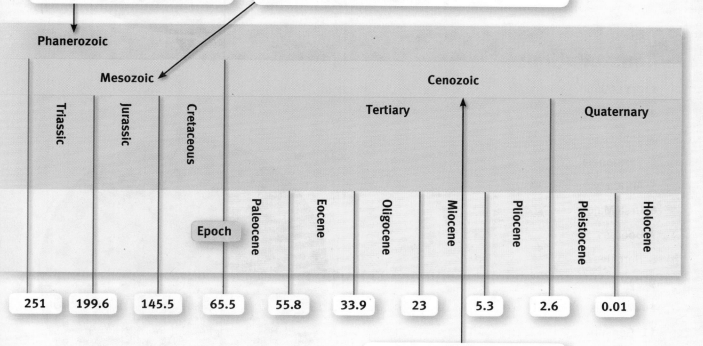

The **Cenozoic era** began 65.5 mya and continues today. Mammals dominate this era. During the Mesozoic era, mammals were small in size but grew much larger during the Cenozoic era. Primates, including humans, appeared during this era.

Star Charts for the Northern Hemisphere

A star chart is a map of the stars in the night sky. It shows the names and positions of constellations and major stars. Star charts can be used to identify constellations and even to orient yourself using Polaris, the North Star.

Because Earth moves through space, different constellations are visible at different times of the year. The star charts on these pages show the constellations visible during each season in the Northern Hemisphere.

Spring

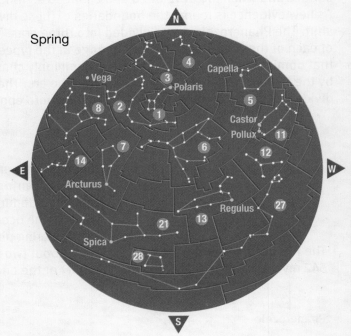

Summer

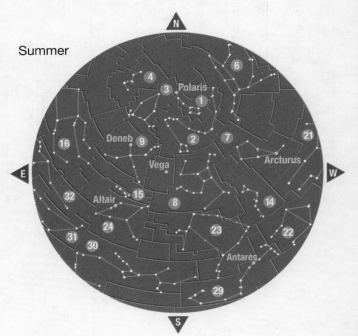

Constellations

1 Ursa Minor

2 Draco

3 Cepheus

4 Cassiopeia

5 Auriga

6 Ursa Major

7 Boötes

8 Hercules

9 Cygnus

10 Perseus

11 Gemini

12 Cancer

13 Leo

14 Serpens

15 Sagitta

16 Pegasus

17 Pisces

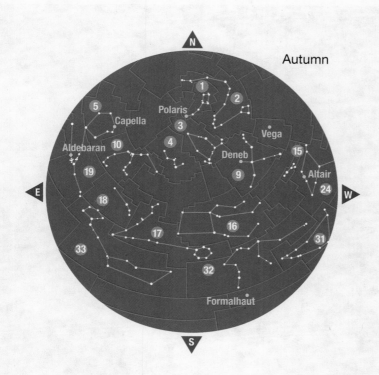

Autumn

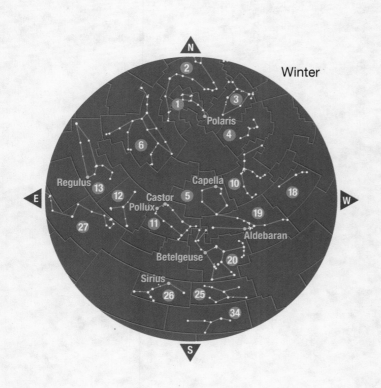

Winter

Constellations

18 Aries

19 Taurus

20 Orion

21 Virgo

22 Libra

23 Ophiuchus

24 Aquila

25 Lepus

26 Canis Major

27 Hydra

28 Corvus

29 Scorpius

30 Sagittarius

31 Capricornus

32 Aquarius

33 Cetus

34 Columba

World Map

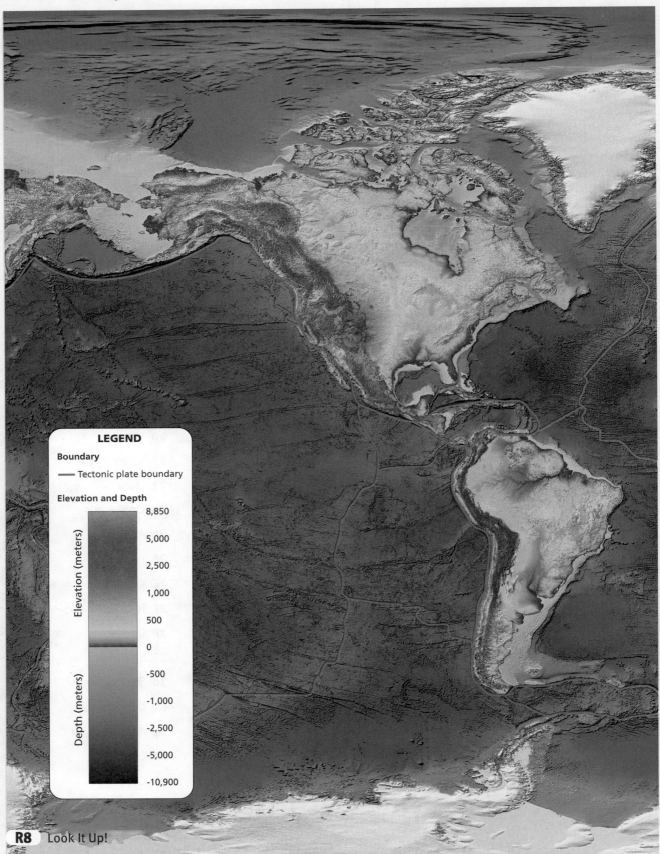

LEGEND

Boundary

—— Tectonic plate boundary

Elevation and Depth

Elevation (meters)

- 8,850
- 5,000
- 2,500
- 1,000
- 500
- 0

Depth (meters)

- -500
- -1,000
- -2,500
- -5,000
- -10,900

References

Classification of Living Things

Domains and Kingdoms

All organisms belong to one of three domains: Domain Archaea, Domain Bacteria, or Domain Eukarya. Some of the groups within these domains are shown below. (Remember that genus names are italicized.)

Domain Archaea

The organisms in this domain are single-celled prokaryotes, many of which live in extreme environments.

Archaea		
Group	**Example**	**Characteristics**
Methanogens	*Methanococcus*	produce methane gas; can't live in oxygen
Thermophiles	*Sulpholobus*	require sulphur; can't live in oxygen
Halophiles	*Halococcus*	live in very salty environments; most can live in oxygen

Domain Bacteria

Organisms in this domain are single-celled prokaryotes and are found in almost every environment on Earth.

Bacteria		
Group	**Example**	**Characteristics**
Bacilli	*Escherichia*	rod shaped; some bacilli fix nitrogen; some cause disease
Cocci	*Streptococcus*	spherical shaped; some cause disease; can form spores
Spirilla	*Treponema*	spiral shaped; cause diseases such as syphilis and Lyme disease

Domain Eukarya

Organisms in this domain are single-celled or multicellular eukaryotes.

Kingdom Protista Many protists resemble fungi, plants, or animals, but are smaller and simpler in structure. Most are single celled.

Protists		
Group	**Example**	**Characteristics**
Sarcodines	*Amoeba*	radiolarians; single-celled consumers
Ciliates	*Paramecium*	single-celled consumers
Flagellates	*Trypanosoma*	single-celled parasites
Sporozoans	*Plasmodium*	single-celled parasites
Euglenas	*Euglena*	single celled; photosynthesize
Diatoms	*Pinnularia*	most are single celled; photosynthesize
Dinoflagellates	*Gymnodinium*	single celled; some photosynthesize
Algae	*Volvox*	single celled or multicellular; photosynthesize
Slime molds	*Physarum*	single celled or multicellular; consumers or decomposers
Water molds	powdery mildew	single celled or multicellular; parasites or decomposers

Kingdom Fungi Most fungi are multicellular. Their cells have thick cell walls. Fungi absorb food from their environment.

Fungi		
Group	**Examples**	**Characteristics**
Threadlike fungi	bread mold	spherical; decomposers
Sac fungi	yeast; morels	saclike; parasites and decomposers
Club fungi	mushrooms; rusts; smuts	club shaped; parasites and decomposers
Lichens	British soldier	a partnership between a fungus and an alga

Kingdom Plantae Plants are multicellular and have cell walls made of cellulose. Plants make their own food through photosynthesis. Plants are classified into divisions instead of phyla.

Plants		
Group	**Examples**	**Characteristics**
Bryophytes	mosses; liverworts	no vascular tissue; reproduce by spores
Club mosses	*Lycopodium;* ground pine	grow in wooded areas; reproduce by spores
Horsetails	rushes	grow in wetland areas; reproduce by spores
Ferns	spleenworts; sensitive fern	large leaves called fronds; reproduce by spores
Conifers	pines; spruces; firs	needlelike leaves; reproduce by seeds made in cones
Cycads	*Zamia*	slow growing; reproduce by seeds made in large cones
Gnetophytes	*Welwitschia*	only three living families; reproduce by seeds
Ginkgoes	*Ginkgo*	only one living species; reproduce by seeds
Angiosperms	all flowering plants	reproduce by seeds made in flowers; fruit

Kingdom Animalia Animals are multicellular. Their cells do not have cell walls. Most animals have specialized tissues and complex organ systems. Animals get food by eating other organisms.

Animals		
Group	**Examples**	**Characteristics**
Sponges	glass sponges	no symmetry or specialized tissues; aquatic
Cnidarians	jellyfish; coral	radial symmetry; aquatic
Flatworms	planaria; tapeworms; flukes	bilateral symmetry; organ systems
Roundworms	*Trichina;* hookworms	bilateral symmetry; organ systems
Annelids	earthworms; leeches	bilateral symmetry; organ systems
Mollusks	snails; octopuses	bilateral symmetry; organ systems
Echinoderms	sea stars; sand dollars	radial symmetry; organ systems
Arthropods	insects; spiders; lobsters	bilateral symmetry; organ systems
Chordates	fish; amphibians; reptiles; birds; mammals	bilateral symmetry; complex organ systems

References

Periodic Table of the Elements

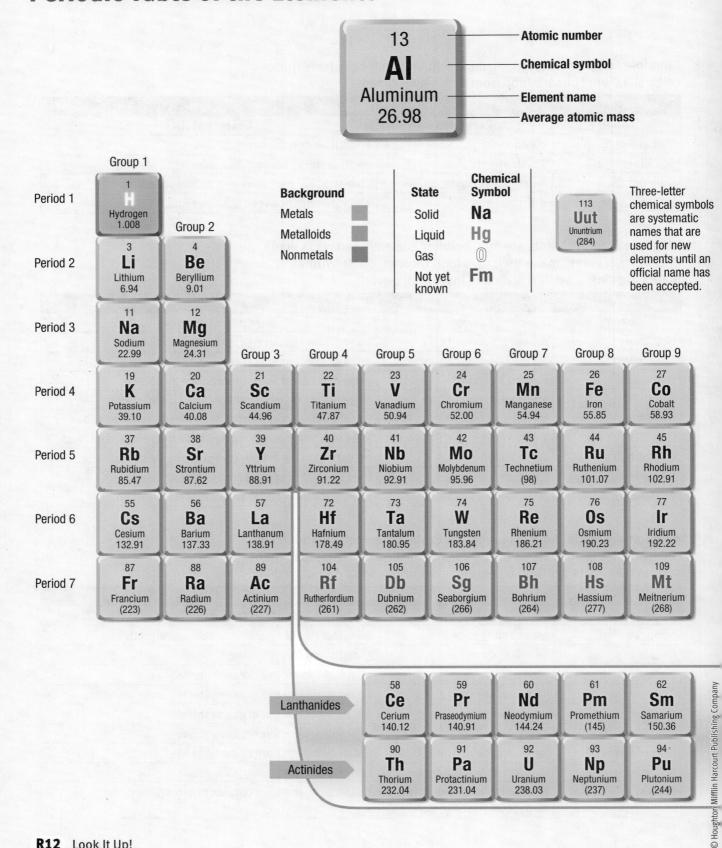

	Atomic number
13	
Al	Chemical symbol
Aluminum	Element name
26.98	Average atomic mass

Background
- Metals
- Metalloids
- Nonmetals

State
- Solid
- Liquid
- Gas
- Not yet known

Chemical Symbol
- **Na**
- Hg
- O
- Fm

Three-letter chemical symbols are systematic names that are used for new elements until an official name has been accepted.

113 **Uut** Ununtrium (284)

	Group 1	Group 2	Group 3	Group 4	Group 5	Group 6	Group 7	Group 8	Group 9
Period 1	1 **H** Hydrogen 1.008								
Period 2	3 **Li** Lithium 6.94	4 **Be** Beryllium 9.01							
Period 3	11 **Na** Sodium 22.99	12 **Mg** Magnesium 24.31							
Period 4	19 **K** Potassium 39.10	20 **Ca** Calcium 40.08	21 **Sc** Scandium 44.96	22 **Ti** Titanium 47.87	23 **V** Vanadium 50.94	24 **Cr** Chromium 52.00	25 **Mn** Manganese 54.94	26 **Fe** Iron 55.85	27 **Co** Cobalt 58.93
Period 5	37 **Rb** Rubidium 85.47	38 **Sr** Strontium 87.62	39 **Y** Yttrium 88.91	40 **Zr** Zirconium 91.22	41 **Nb** Niobium 92.91	42 **Mo** Molybdenum 95.96	43 **Tc** Technetium (98)	44 **Ru** Ruthenium 101.07	45 **Rh** Rhodium 102.91
Period 6	55 **Cs** Cesium 132.91	56 **Ba** Barium 137.33	57 **La** Lanthanum 138.91	72 **Hf** Hafnium 178.49	73 **Ta** Tantalum 180.95	74 **W** Tungsten 183.84	75 **Re** Rhenium 186.21	76 **Os** Osmium 190.23	77 **Ir** Iridium 192.22
Period 7	87 **Fr** Francium (223)	88 **Ra** Radium (226)	89 **Ac** Actinium (227)	104 **Rf** Rutherfordium (261)	105 **Db** Dubnium (262)	106 **Sg** Seaborgium (266)	107 **Bh** Bohrium (264)	108 **Hs** Hassium (277)	109 **Mt** Meitnerium (268)

Lanthanides

58 **Ce** Cerium 140.12	59 **Pr** Praseodymium 140.91	60 **Nd** Neodymium 144.24	61 **Pm** Promethium (145)	62 **Sm** Samarium 150.36

Actinides

90 **Th** Thorium 232.04	91 **Pa** Protactinium 231.04	92 **U** Uranium 238.03	93 **Np** Neptunium (237)	94 **Pu** Plutonium (244)

The International Union of Pure and Applied Chemistry (IUPAC) has determined that, because of isotopic variance, the average atomic mass is best represented by a range of values for each of the following elements: hydrogen, lithium, boron, carbon, nitrogen, oxygen, silicon, sulfur, chlorine, and thallium. However, the values in this table are appropriate for everyday calculations.

Elements with atomic numbers of 95 and above are not known to occur naturally, even in trace amounts. They have only been synthesized in the lab. The physical and chemical properties of elements with atomic numbers 100 and above cannot be predicted with certainty. The states for elements with atomic numbers 100 and above are therefore shown as not yet known.

Group 18
2 **He** Helium 4.003

Group 13	Group 14	Group 15	Group 16	Group 17	
5 **B** Boron 10.81	6 **C** Carbon 12.01	7 **N** Nitrogen 14.01	8 **O** Oxygen 16.00	9 **F** Fluorine 19.00	10 **Ne** Neon 20.18
13 **Al** Aluminum 26.98	14 **Si** Silicon 28.09	15 **P** Phosphorus 30.97	16 **S** Sulfur 32.06	17 **Cl** Chlorine 35.45	18 **Ar** Argon 39.95

Group 10	Group 11	Group 12						
28 **Ni** Nickel 58.69	29 **Cu** Copper 63.55	30 **Zn** Zinc 65.38	31 **Ga** Gallium 69.72	32 **Ge** Germanium 72.63	33 **As** Arsenic 74.92	34 **Se** Selenium 78.96	35 **Br** Bromine 79.90	36 **Kr** Krypton 83.80
46 **Pd** Palladium 106.42	47 **Ag** Silver 107.87	48 **Cd** Cadmium 112.41	49 **In** Indium 114.82	50 **Sn** Tin 118.71	51 **Sb** Antimony 121.76	52 **Te** Tellurium 127.60	53 **I** Iodine 126.90	54 **Xe** Xenon 131.29
78 **Pt** Platinum 195.08	79 **Au** Gold 196.97	80 **Hg** Mercury 200.59	81 **Tl** Thallium 204.38	82 **Pb** Lead 207.2	83 **Bi** Bismuth 208.98	84 **Po** Polonium (209)	85 **At** Astatine (210)	86 **Rn** Radon (222)
110 **Ds** Darmstadtium (271)	111 **Rg** Roentgenium (272)	112 **Cn** Copernicium (285)	113 **Uut** Ununtrium (284)	114 **Fl** Flerovium (289)	115 **Uup** Ununpentium (288)	116 **Lv** Livermorium (293)	117 **Uus** Ununseptium (294)	118 **Uuo** Ununoctium (294)

63 **Eu** Europium 151.96	64 **Gd** Gadolinium 157.25	65 **Tb** Terbium 158.93	66 **Dy** Dysprosium 162.50	67 **Ho** Holmium 164.93	68 **Er** Erbium 167.26	69 **Tm** Thulium 168.93	70 **Yb** Ytterbium 173.05	71 **Lu** Lutetium 174.97
95 **Am** Americium (243)	96 **Cm** Curium (247)	97 **Bk** Berkelium (247)	98 **Cf** Californium (251)	99 **Es** Einsteinium (252)	100 **Fm** Fermium (257)	101 **Md** Mendelevium (258)	102 **No** Nobelium (259)	103 **Lr** Lawrencium (262)

© Houghton Mifflin Harcourt Publishing Company

References

Physical Science Refresher

Atoms and Elements

Every object in the universe is made of matter. **Matter** is anything that takes up space and has mass. All matter is made of atoms. An **atom** is the smallest particle into which an element can be divided and still be the same element. An **element**, in turn, is a substance that cannot be broken down into simpler substances by chemical means. Each element consists of only one kind of atom. An element may be made of many atoms, but they are all the same kind of atom.

Atomic Structure

Atoms are made of smaller particles called **electrons**, **protons**, and **neutrons**. Electrons have a negative electric charge, protons have a positive charge, and neutrons have no electric charge. Together, protons and neutrons form the **nucleus**, or small dense center, of an atom. Because protons are positively charged and neutrons are neutral, the nucleus has a positive charge. Electrons move within an area around the nucleus called the **electron cloud**. Electrons move so quickly that scientists cannot determine their exact speeds and positions at the same time.

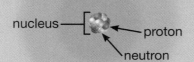

electron cloud

nucleus — proton

neutron

Atomic Number

To help distinguish one element from another, scientists use the atomic numbers of atoms. The **atomic number** is the number of protons in the nucleus of an atom. The atoms of a certain element always have the same number of protons.

When atoms have an equal number of protons and electrons, they are uncharged, or electrically neutral. The atomic number equals the number of electrons in an uncharged atom. The number of neutrons, however, can vary for a given element. Atoms of the same element that have different numbers of neutrons are called **isotopes**.

Periodic Table of the Elements

In the periodic table, each element in the table is in a separate box. And the elements are arranged from left to right in order of increasing atomic number. That is, an uncharged atom of each element has one more electron and one more proton than an uncharged atom of the element to its left. Each horizontal row of the table is called a **period**. Changes in chemical properties of elements across a period correspond to changes in the electron arrangements of their atoms.

Each vertical column of the table is known as a **group.** A group lists elements with similar physical and chemical properties. For this reason, a group is also sometimes called a family. The elements in a group have similar properties because their atoms have the same number of electrons in their outer energy level. For example, the elements helium, neon, argon, krypton, xenon, and radon all have similar properties and are known as the noble gases.

Molecules and Compounds

When two or more elements join chemically, they form a **compound**. A compound is a new substance with properties different from those of the elements that compose it. For example, water, H_2O, is a compound formed when hydrogen (H) and oxygen (O) combine. The smallest complete unit of a compound that has the properties of that compound is called a **molecule**. A chemical formula indicates the elements in a compound. It also indicates the relative number of atoms of each element in the compound. The chemical formula for water is H_2O. So, each water molecule consists of two atoms of hydrogen and one atom of oxygen. The subscript number after the symbol for an element shows how many atoms of that element are in a single molecule of the compound.

Chemical Equations

A chemical reaction occurs when a chemical change takes place. A chemical equation describes a chemical reaction using chemical formulas. The equation indicates the substances that react and the substances that are produced. For example, when carbon and oxygen combine, they can form carbon dioxide, shown in the equation below: $C + O_2 \longrightarrow CO_2$

Acids, Bases, and pH

An **ion** is an atom or group of chemically bonded atoms that has an electric charge because it has lost or gained one or more electrons. When an acid, such as hydrochloric acid, HCl, is mixed with water, it separates into ions. An **acid** is a compound that produces hydrogen ions, H^+, in water. The hydrogen ions then combine with a water molecule to form a hydronium ion, H_3O^+. A **base**, on the other hand, is a substance that produces hydroxide ions, OH^-, in water.

To determine whether a solution is acidic or basic, scientists use pH. The **pH** of a solution is a measure of the hydronium ion concentration in a solution. The pH scale ranges from 0 to 14. Acids have a pH that is less than 7. The lower the number, the more acidic the solution. The middle point, pH = 7, is neutral, neither acidic nor basic. Bases have a pH that is greater than 7. The higher the number is, the more basic the solution.

The pH of Some Common Materials

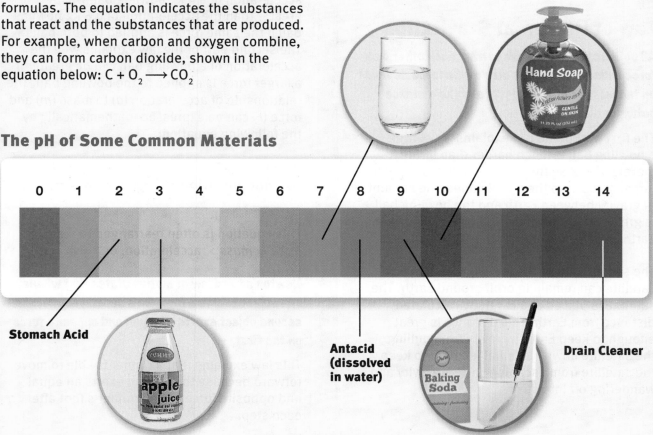

Stomach Acid

Antacid (dissolved in water)

Drain Cleaner

References

Physical Laws and Useful Equations

Law of Conservation of Mass

Mass cannot be created or destroyed during ordinary chemical or physical changes.

The total mass in a closed system is always the same no matter how many physical changes or chemical reactions occur.

Law of Conservation of Energy

Energy can be neither created nor destroyed.

The total amount of energy in a closed system is always the same. Energy can be changed from one form to another, but all of the different forms of energy in a system always add up to the same total amount of energy, no matter how many energy conversions occur.

Law of Universal Gravitation

All objects in the universe attract each other by a force called gravity. The size of the force depends on the masses of the objects and the distance between the objects.

The first part of the law explains why lifting a bowling ball is much harder than lifting a marble. Because the bowling ball has a much larger mass than the marble does, the amount of gravity between Earth and the bowling ball is greater than the amount of gravity between Earth and the marble.

The second part of the law explains why a satellite can remain in orbit around Earth. The satellite is placed at a carefully calculated distance from Earth. This distance is great enough to keep Earth's gravity from pulling the satellite down, yet small enough to keep the satellite from escaping Earth's gravity and wandering off into space.

Newton's Laws of Motion

Newton's first law of motion states that an object at rest remains at rest, and an object in motion remains in motion at constant speed and in a straight line unless acted on by an unbalanced force.

The first part of the law explains why a football will remain on a tee until it is kicked off or until a gust of wind blows it off. The second part of the law explains why a bike rider will continue moving forward after the bike comes to an abrupt stop. Gravity and the friction of the sidewalk will eventually stop the rider.

Newton's second law of motion states that the acceleration of an object depends on the mass of the object and the amount of force applied.

The first part of the law explains why the acceleration of a 4 kg bowling ball will be greater than the acceleration of a 6 kg bowling ball if the same force is applied to both balls. The second part of the law explains why the acceleration of a bowling ball will be greater if a larger force is applied to the bowling ball. The relationship of acceleration (a) to mass (m) and force (F) can be expressed mathematically by the following equation:

$$acceleration = \frac{force}{mass}, \ or \ a = \frac{F}{m}$$

This equation is often rearranged to read *force = mass × acceleration*, or $F = m \times a$

Newton's third law of motion states that whenever one object exerts a force on a second object, the second object exerts an equal and opposite force on the first.

This law explains that a runner is able to move forward because the ground exerts an equal and opposite force on the runner's foot after each step.

Average speed

$$\text{average speed} = \frac{\text{total distance}}{\text{total time}}$$

Example:
A bicycle messenger traveled a distance of 136 km in 8 h. What was the messenger's average speed?

$$\frac{136\ km}{8\ h} = 17\ km/h$$

The messenger's average speed was **17 km/h**.

Average acceleration

$$\text{average acceleration} = \frac{\text{final velocity} - \text{starting velocity}}{\text{time it takes to change velocity}}$$

Example:
Calculate the average acceleration of an Olympic 100 m dash sprinter who reached a velocity of 20 m/s south at the finish line. The race was in a straight line and lasted 10 s.

$$\frac{20\ m/s - 0\ m/s}{10\ s} = 2\ m/s/s$$

The sprinter's average acceleration was **2 m/s/s south**.

Net force
Forces in the Same Direction

When forces are in the same direction, add the forces together to determine the net force.

Example:
Calculate the net force on a stalled car that is being pushed by two people. One person is pushing with a force of 13 N northwest, and the other person is pushing with a force of 8 N in the same direction.

$$13\ N + 8\ N = 21\ N$$

The net force is **21 N northwest**.

Forces in Opposite Directions

When forces are in opposite directions, subtract the smaller force from the larger force to determine the net force. The net force will be in the direction of the larger force.

Example:
Calculate the net force on a rope that is being pulled on each end. One person is pulling on one end of the rope with a force of 12 N south. Another person is pulling on the opposite end of the rope with a force of 7 N north.

$$12\ N - 7\ N = 5\ N$$

The net force is **5 N south**.

Pressure

Pressure is the force exerted over a given area. The SI unit for pressure is the pascal. Its symbol is Pa.

$$\text{pressure} = \frac{\text{force}}{\text{area}}$$

Example:
Calculate the pressure of the air in a soccer ball if the air exerts a force of 10 N over an area of 0.5 m².

$$\text{pressure} = \frac{10N}{0.5\ m^2} = \frac{20N}{m^2} = 20\ Pa$$

The pressure of the air inside the soccer ball is **20 Pa**.

Reading and Study Skills

A How-To Manual for Active Reading

This book belongs to you, and you are invited to write in it. In fact, the book won't be complete until you do. Sometimes you'll answer a question or follow directions to mark up the text. Other times you'll write down your own thoughts. And when you're done reading and writing in the book, the book will be ready to help you review what you learned and prepare for tests.

Active Reading Annotations

Before you read, you'll often come upon an Active Reading prompt that asks you to underline certain words or number the steps in a process. Here's an example.

Active Reading

12 Identify In this paragraph, number the sequence of sentences that describe replication.

Marking the text this way is called **annotating,** and your marks are called **annotations.** Annotating the text can help you identify important concepts while you read.

There are other ways that you can annotate the text. You can draw an asterisk (*) by vocabulary terms, mark unfamiliar or confusing terms and information with a question mark (?), and mark main ideas with a double underline. And you can even invent your own marks to annotate the text!

Other Annotating Opportunities

Keep your pencil, pen, or highlighter nearby as you read, so you can make a note or highlight an important point at any time. Here are a few ideas to get you started.

- Notice the headings in red and blue. The blue headings are questions that point to the main idea of what you're reading. The red headings are answers to the questions in the blue ones. Together these headings outline the content of the lesson. After reading a lesson, you could write your own answers to the questions.

- Notice the bold-faced words that are highlighted in yellow. They are highlighted so that you can easily find them again on the page where they are defined. As you read or as you review, challenge yourself to write your own sentence using the bold-faced term.

- Make a note in the margin at any time. You might
  - Ask a "What if" question
  - Comment on what you read
  - Make a connection to something you read elsewhere
  - Make a logical conclusion from the text

Use your own language and abbreviations. Invent a code, such as using circles and boxes around words to remind you of their importance or relation to each other. Your annotations will help you remember your questions for class discussions, and when you go back to the lesson later, you may be able to fill in what you didn't understand the first time you read it. Like a scientist in the field or in a lab, you will be recording your questions and observations for analysis later.

Active Reading Questions

After you read, you'll often come upon Active Reading questions that ask you to think about what you've just read. You'll write your answer underneath the question. Here's an example.

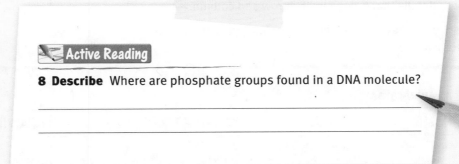

Active Reading

8 Describe Where are phosphate groups found in a DNA molecule?

_____

_____

This type of question helps you sum up what you've just read and pull out the most important ideas from the passage. In this case the question asks you to **describe** the structure of a DNA molecule that you have just read about. Other times you may be asked to do such things as **apply** a concept, **compare** two concepts, **summarize** a process, or **identify a cause-and-effect** relationship. You'll be strengthening those critical thinking skills that you'll use often in learning about science.

Reading and Study Skills

Using Graphic Organizers to Take Notes

Graphic organizers help you remember information as you read it for the first time and as you study it later. There are dozens of graphic organizers to choose from, so the first trick is to choose the one that's best suited to your purpose. Following are some graphic organizers to use for different purposes.

To remember lots of information	To relate a central idea to subordinate details	To describe a process	To make a comparison
• Arrange data in a Content Frame • Use Combination Notes to describe a concept in words and pictures	• Show relationships with a Mind Map or a Main Idea Web • Sum up relationships among many things with a Concept Map	• Use a Process Diagram to explain a procedure • Show a chain of events and results in a Cause-and-Effect Chart	• Compare two or more closely related things in a Venn Diagram

Content Frame

1 Make a four-column chart.

2 Fill the first column with categories (e.g., snail, ant, earthworm) and the first row with descriptive information (e.g., group, characteristic, appearance).

3 Fill the chart with details that belong in each row and column.

4 When you finish, you'll have a study aid that helps you compare one category to another.

Invertebrates

NAME	GROUP	CHARACTERISTICS	DRAWING
snail	mollusks	mangle	
ant	arthropods	six legs, exoskeleton	
earthworm	segmented worms	segmented body, circulatory and digestive systems	
heartworm	roundworms	digestive system	
sea star	echinoderms	spiny skin, tube feet	
jellyfish	cnidarians	stinging cells	

Combination Notes

1 Make a two-column chart.

2 Write descriptive words and definitions in the first column.

3 Draw a simple sketch that helps you remember the meaning of the term in the second column.

NOTES

Types of Forces
- contact force
- gravity
- friction

forces on a box being pushed

contact force

gravity

friction

Mind Map

1 Draw an oval, and inside it write a topic to analyze.

2 Draw two or more arms extending from the oval. Each arm represents a main idea about the topic.

3 Draw lines from the arms on which to write details about each of the main ideas.

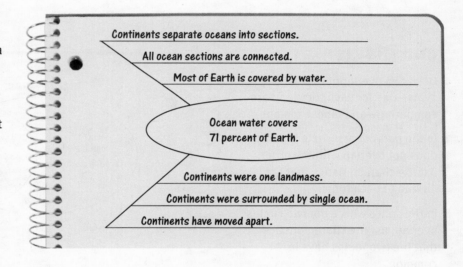

Continents separate oceans into sections.

All ocean sections are connected.

Most of Earth is covered by water.

Ocean water covers 71 percent of Earth.

Continents were one landmass.

Continents were surrounded by single ocean.

Continents have moved apart.

Main Idea Web

1 Make a box and write a concept you want to remember inside it.

2 Draw boxes around the central box, and label each one with a category of information about the concept (e.g., definition, formula, descriptive details).

3 Fill in the boxes with relevant details as you read.

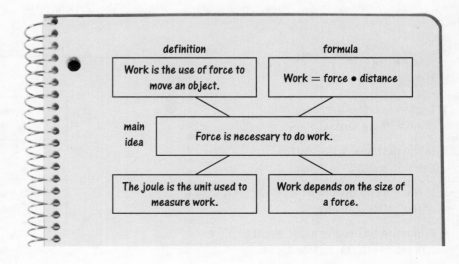

definition

Work is the use of force to move an object.

formula

Work = force • distance

main idea

Force is necessary to do work.

The joule is the unit used to measure work.

Work depends on the size of a force.

Reading and Study Skills

Concept Map

1 Draw a large oval, and inside it write a major concept.

2 Draw an arrow from the concept to a smaller oval, in which you write a related concept.

3 On the arrow, write a verb that connects the two concepts.

4 Continue in this way, adding ovals and arrows in a branching structure, until you have explained as much as you can about the main concept.

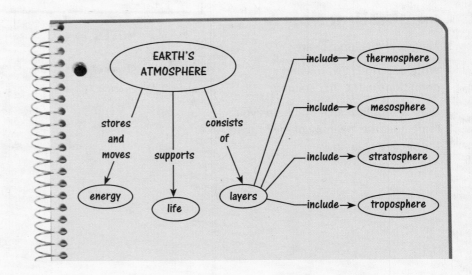

Venn Diagram

1 Draw two overlapping circles or ovals—one for each topic you are comparing—and label each one.

2 In the part of each circle that does not overlap with the other, list the characteristics that are unique to each topic.

3 In the space where the two circles overlap, list the characteristics that the two topics have in common.

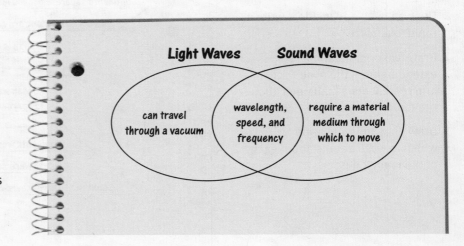

Cause-and-Effect Chart

1 Draw two boxes and connect them with an arrow.

2 In the first box, write the first event in a series (a cause).

3 In the second box, write a result of the cause (the effect).

4 Add more boxes when one event has many effects, or vice versa.

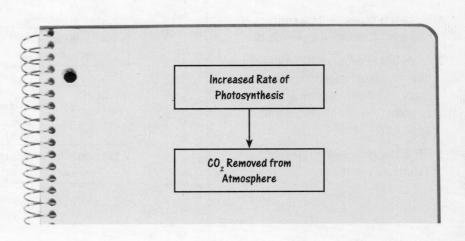

Process Diagram

A process can be a never-ending cycle. As you can see in this technology design process, engineers may backtrack and repeat steps, they may skip steps entirely, or they may repeat the entire process before a useable design is achieved.

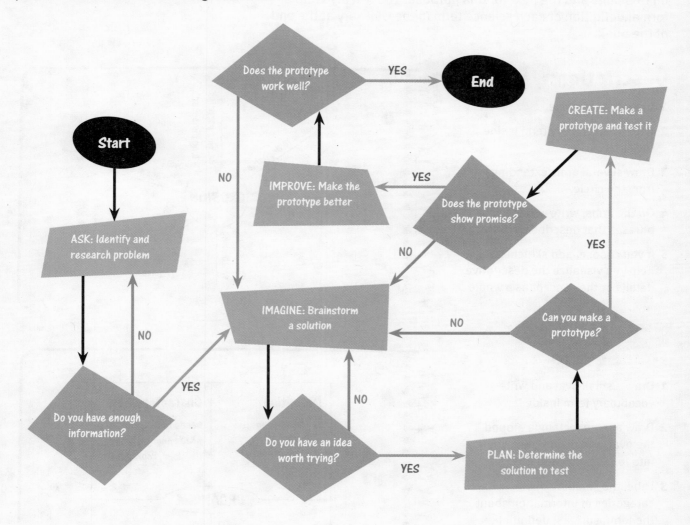

Reading and Study Skills

Using Vocabulary Strategies

Important science terms are highlighted where they are first defined in this book. One way to remember these terms is to take notes and make sketches when you come to them. Use the strategies on this page and the next for this purpose. You will also find a formal definition of each science term in the Glossary at the end of the book.

Description Wheel

1 Draw a small circle.

2 Write a vocabulary term inside the circle.

3 Draw several arms extending from the circle.

4 On the arms, write words and phrases that describe the term.

5 If you choose, add sketches that help you visualize the descriptive details or the concept as a whole.

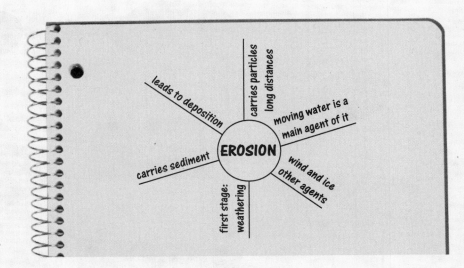

Four Square

1 Draw a small oval and write a vocabulary term inside it.

2 Draw a large rectangle around the oval, and divide the rectangle into four smaller squares.

3 Label the smaller squares with categories of information about the term, such as: definition, characteristics, examples, non-examples, appearance, and root words.

4 Fill the squares with descriptive words and drawings that will help you remember the overall meaning of the term and its essential details.

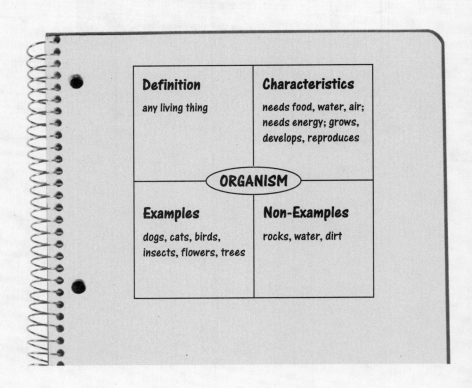

Frame Game

1 Draw a small rectangle, and write a vocabulary term inside it.

2 Draw a larger rectangle around the smaller one. Connect the corners of the larger rectangle to the corners of the smaller one, creating four spaces that frame the word.

3 In each of the four parts of the frame, draw or write details that help define the term. Consider including a definition, essential characteristics, an equation, examples, and a sentence using the term.

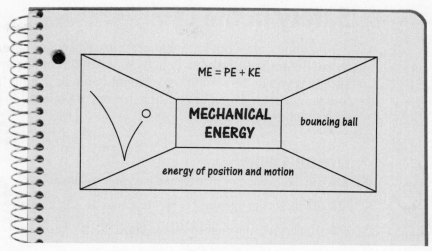

Magnet Word

1 Draw horseshoe magnet, and write a vocabulary term inside it.

2 Add lines that extend from the sides of the magnet.

3 Brainstorm words and phrases that come to mind when you think about the term.

4 On the lines, write the words and phrases that describe something essential about the term.

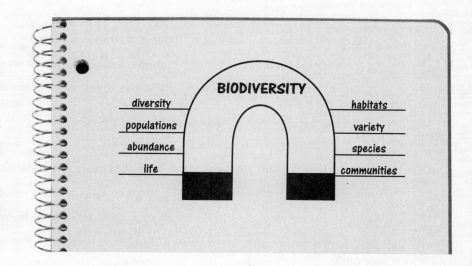

Word Triangle

1 Draw a triangle, and add lines to divide it into three parts.

2 Write a term and its definition in the bottom section of the triangle.

3 In the middle section, write a sentence in which the term is used correctly.

4 In the top section, draw a small picture to illustrate the term.

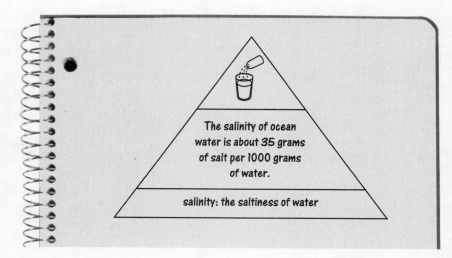

Science Skills

Safety in the Lab

Before you begin work in the laboratory, read these safety rules twice. Before starting a lab activity, read all directions and make sure that you understand them. Do not begin until your teacher has told you to start. If you or another student are injured in any way, tell your teacher immediately.

Dress Code

Eye Protection

- Wear safety goggles at all times in the lab as directed.
- If chemicals get into your eyes, flush your eyes immediately.
- Do not wear contact lenses in the lab.
- Do not look directly at the sun or any intense light source or laser.

Hand Protection

- Do not cut an object while holding the object in your hand.
- Wear appropriate protective gloves as directed.
- Wear an apron or lab coat at all times in the lab as directed.

Clothing Protection

- Tie back long hair, secure loose clothing, and remove loose jewelry.
- Do not wear open-toed shoes, sandals, or canvas shoes in the lab.

Glassware and Sharp Object Safety

Glassware Safety

- Do not use chipped or cracked glassware.
- Use heat-resistant glassware for heating or storing hot materials.
- Notify your teacher immediately if a piece of glass breaks.
- Use extreme care when handling all sharp and pointed instruments.

Sharp Objects Safety

- Cut objects on a suitable surface, always in a direction away from your body.

Chemical Safety

Chemical Safety

- If a chemical gets on your skin, on your clothing, or in your eyes, rinse it immediately (shower, faucet or eyewash fountain) and alert your teacher.
- Do not clean up spilled chemicals unless your teacher directs you to do so.
- Do not inhale any gas or vapor unless directed to do so by your teacher.
- Handle materials that emit vapors or gases in a well-ventilated area.

Electrical Safety

Electrical Safety

- Do not use equipment with frayed electrical cords or loose plugs.

- Do not use electrical equipment near water or when clothing or hands are wet.

- Hold the plug housing when you plug in or unplug equipment.

Heating and Fire Safety

Heating Safety

- Be aware of any source of flames, sparks, or heat (such as flames, heating coils, or hot plates) before working with any flammable substances.

- Know the location of lab fire extinguishers and fire-safety blankets.

- Know your school's fire-evacuation routes.

- If your clothing catches on fire, walk to the lab shower to put out the fire.

- Never leave a hot plate unattended while it is turned on or while it is cooling.

- Use tongs or appropriate insulated holders when handling heated objects.

- Allow all equipment to cool before storing it.

Wafting

Plant and Animal Safety

Plant Safety

Animal Safety

- Do not eat any part of a plant.

- Do not pick any wild plants unless your teacher instructs you to do so.

- Handle animals only as your teacher directs.

- Treat animals carefully and respectfully.

- Wash your hands thoroughly after handling any plant or animal.

Cleanup

Proper Waste Disposal

Hygienic Care

- Clean all work surfaces and protective equipment as directed by your teacher.

- Dispose of hazardous materials or sharp objects only as directed by your teacher.

- Keep your hands away from your face while you are working on any activity.

- Wash your hands thoroughly before you leave the lab or after any activity.

Science Skills

Designing, Conducting, and Reporting an Experiment

An experiment is an organized procedure to study something under specific conditions. Use the following steps of the scientific method when designing or conducting a controlled experiment.

1 Identify a Research Problem

Every day, you make observations by using your senses to gather information. Careful observations lead to good questions, and good questions can lead you to an experiment. Imagine, for example, that you pass a pond every day on your way to school, and you notice green scum beginning to form on top of it. You wonder what it is and why it seems to be growing. You list your questions, and then you do a little research to find out what is already known. A good place to start a research project is at the library. A library catalog lists all of the resources available to you at that library and often those found elsewhere. Begin your search by using:

- keywords or main topics.

- similar words, or synonyms, of your keyword.

The types of resources that will be helpful to you will depend on the kind of information you are interested in. And, some resources are more reliable for a given topic than others. Some different kinds of useful resources are:

- magazines and journals (or periodicals)—articles on a topic.

- encyclopedias—a good overview of a topic.

- books on specific subjects—details about a topic.

- newspapers—useful for current events.

The Internet can also be a great place to find information. Some of your library's reference materials may even be online. When using the Internet, however, it is especially important to make sure you are using appropriate and reliable sources. Websites of universities and government agencies are usually more accurate and reliable than websites created by individuals or businesses. Decide which sources are relevant and reliable for your topic. If in doubt, check with your teacher.

Take notes as you read through the information in these resources. You will probably come up with many questions and ideas for which you can do more research as needed. Once you feel you have enough information, think about the questions you have on the topic. Then, write down the problem that you want to investigate. Your notes might look like these.

Research Questions	Research Problem	Library and Internet Resources
• How do algae grow? • How do people measure algae? • What kind of fertilizer would affect the growth of algae? • Can fertilizer and algae be used safely in a lab? How?	How does fertilizer affect the algae in a pond?	Pond fertilization: initiating an algal bloom – from University of California Davis website. Blue-Green algae in Wisconsin waters-from the Department of Natural Resources of Wisconsin website.

As you gather information from reliable sources, record details about each source, including author name(s), title, date of publication, and/or web address. Make sure to also note the specific information that you use from each source. Staying organized in this way will be important when you write your report and create a bibliography or works cited list. Recording this information and staying organized will help you credit the appropriate author(s) for the information that you have gathered.

Representing someone else's ideas or work as your own, (without giving the original author credit), is known as plagiarism. Plagiarism can be intentional or unintentional. The best way to make sure that you do not commit plagiarism is to always do your own work and to always give credit to others when you use their words or ideas.

Current scientific research is built on scientific research and discoveries that have happened in the past. This means that scientists are constantly learning from each other and combining ideas to learn more about the natural world through investigation. But, a good scientist always credits the ideas and research that they have gathered from other people to those people. There are more details about crediting sources and creating a bibliography under step 9.

2 Make a Prediction

A prediction is a statement of what you expect will happen in your experiment. Before making a prediction, you need to decide in a general way what you will do in your procedure. You may state your prediction in an if-then format.

Prediction

If the amount of fertilizer in the pond water is increased, then the amount of algae will also increase.

Science Skills

3 Form a Hypothesis

Many experiments are designed to test a hypothesis. A hypothesis is a tentative explanation for an expected result. You have predicted that additional fertilizer will cause additional algae growth in pond water; your hypothesis should state the connection between fertilizer and algal growth.

Hypothesis

The addition of fertilizer to pond water will affect the amount of algae in the pond.

4 Identify Variables to Test the Hypothesis

The next step is to design an experiment to test the hypothesis. The experimental results may or may not support the hypothesis. Either way, the information that results from the experiment may be useful for future investigations.

Experimental Group and Control Group

An experiment to determine how two factors are related has a control group and an experimental group. The two groups are the same, except that the investigator changes a single factor in the experimental group and does not change it in the control group.

Experimental Group: two containers of pond water with one drop of fertilizer solution added to each

Control Group: two containers of the same pond water sampled at the same time but with no fertilizer solution added

Variables and Constants

In a controlled experiment, a variable is any factor that can change. Constants are all of the variables that are kept the same in both the experimental group and the control group.

The independent variable is the factor that is manipulated or changed in order to test the effect of the change on another variable. The dependent variable is the factor the investigator measures to gather data about the effect.

Independent Variable	Dependent Variable	Constants
Amount of fertilizer in pond water	Growth of algae in the pond water	• Where and when the pond water is obtained • The type of container used • Light and temperature conditions where the water is stored

5 Write a Procedure

Write each step of your procedure. Start each step with a verb, or action word, and keep the steps short. Your procedure should be clear enough for someone else to use as instructions for repeating your experiment.

Procedure

1. Use the masking tape and the marker to label the containers with your initials, the date, and the identifiers "Jar 1 with Fertilizer," "Jar 2 with Fertilizer," "Jar 1 without Fertilizer," and "Jar 2 without Fertilizer."

2. Put on your gloves. Use the large container to obtain a sample of pond water.

3. Divide the water sample equally among the four smaller containers.

4. Use the eyedropper to add one drop of fertilizer solution to the two containers labeled, "Jar 1 with Fertilizer," and "Jar 2 with Fertilizer".

5. Cover the containers with clear plastic wrap. Use the scissors to punch ten holes in each of the covers.

6. Place all four containers on a window ledge. Make sure that they all receive the same amount of light.

7. Observe the containers every day for one week.

8. Use the ruler to measure the diameter of the largest clump of algae in each container, and record your measurements daily.

Science Skills

6 Experiment and Collect Data

Once you have all of your materials and your procedure has been approved, you can begin to experiment and collect data. Record both quantitative data (measurements) and qualitative data (observations), as shown below.

Algal Growth and Fertilizer

Date and Time	Experimental Group		Control Group		Observations
	Jar 1 with Fertilizer (diameter of algal clump in mm)	Jar 2 with Fertilizer (diameter of algal clump in mm)	Jar 1 without Fertilizer (diameter of algal clump in mm)	Jar 2 without Fertilizer (diameter of algal clump in mm)	
5/3 4:00 p.m.	0	0	0	0	condensation in all containers
5/4 4:00 p.m.	0	3	0	0	tiny green blobs in Jar 2 with fertilizer
5/5 4:15 p.m.	4	5	0	3	green blobs in Jars 1 and 2 with fertilizer and Jar 2 without fertilizer
5/6 4:00 p.m.	5	6	0	4	water light green in Jar 2 with fertilizer
5/7 4:00 p.m.	8	10	0	6	water light green in Jars 1 and 2 with fertilizer and Jar 2 without fertilizer
5/8 3:30 p.m.	10	18	0	6	cover off of Jar 2 with fertilizer
5/9 3:30 p.m.	14	23	0	8	drew sketches of each container

Drawings of Samples Viewed Under Microscope on 5/9 at 100x

Jar 1 with Fertilizer

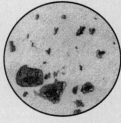
Jar 2 with Fertilizer

Jar 1 without Fertilizer

Jar 2 without Fertilizer

7 Analyze Data

After you complete your experiment, you must analyze all of the data you have gathered. Tables, statistics, and graphs are often used in this step to organize and analyze both the qualitative and quantitative data. Sometimes, your qualitative data are best used to help explain the relationships you see in your quantitative data.

Computer graphing software is useful for creating a graph from data that you have collected. Most graphing software can make line graphs, pie charts, or bar graphs from data that has been organized in a spreadsheet. Graphs are useful for understanding relationships in the data and for communicating the results of your experiment.

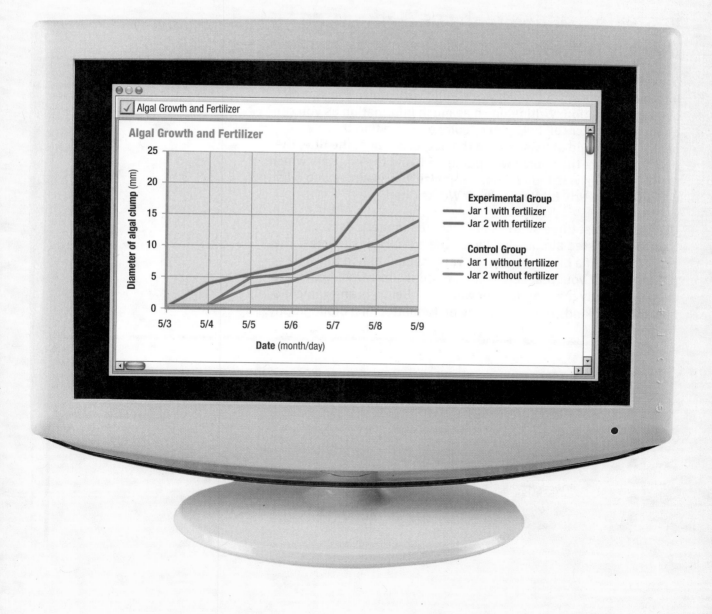

Science Skills

8 Make Conclusions

To draw conclusions from your experiment, first, write your results. Then, compare your results with your hypothesis. Do your results support your hypothesis? What have you learned?

Conclusion

More algae grew in the pond water to which fertilizer had been added than in the pond water to which fertilizer had not been added. My hypothesis was supported. I conclude that it is possible that the growth of algae in ponds can be influenced by the input of fertilizer.

9 Create a Bibliography or Works Cited List

To complete your report, you must also show all of the newspapers, magazines, journals, books, and online sources that you used at every stage of your investigation. Whenever you find useful information about your topic, you should write down the source of that information. Writing down as much information as you can about the subject can help you or someone else find the source again. You should at least record the author's name, the title, the date and where the source was published, and the pages in which the information was found. Then, organize your sources into a list, which you can title Bibliography or Works Cited.

Usually, at least three sources are included in these lists. Sources are listed alphabetically, by the authors' last names. The exact format of a bibliography can vary, depending on the style preferences of your teacher, school, or publisher. Also, books are cited differently than journals or websites. Below is an example of how different kinds of sources may be formatted in a bibliography.

BOOK: Hauschultz, Sara. Freshwater Algae. Brainard, Minnesota: Northwoods Publishing, 2011.

ENCYCLOPEDIA: Lasure, Sedona. "Algae is not all just pond scum." Encyclopedia of Algae. 2009.

JOURNAL: Johnson, Keagan. "Algae as we know it." Sci Journal, vol 64. (September 2010): 201-211.

WEBSITE: Dout, Bill. "Keeping algae scum out of birdbaths." Help Keep Earth Clean. News. January 26, 2011. <www.SaveEarth.org>.

Using a Microscope

Scientists use microscopes to see very small objects that cannot easily be seen with the eye alone. A microscope magnifies the image of an object so that small details may be observed. A microscope that you may use can magnify an object 400 times—the object will appear 400 times larger than its actual size.

Eyepiece Objects are viewed through the eyepiece. The eyepiece contains a lens that commonly magnifies an image ten times.

Body The body separates the lens in the eyepiece from the objective lenses below.

Nosepiece The nosepiece holds the objective lenses above the stage and rotates so that all lenses may be used.

High-Power Objective Lens This is the largest lens on the nosepiece. It magnifies an image approximately 40 times.

Stage The stage supports the object being viewed.

Diaphragm The diaphragm is used to adjust the amount of light passing through the slide and into an objective lens.

Mirror or Light Source Some microscopes use light that is reflected through the stage by a mirror. Other microscopes have their own light sources.

Coarse Adjustment This knob is used to focus the image of an object when it is viewed through the low-power lens.

Fine Adjustment This knob is used to focus the image of an object when it is viewed through the high-power lens.

Low-Power Objective Lens This is the smallest lens on the nosepiece. It magnifies images about 10 times.

Arm The arm supports the body above the stage. Always carry a microscope by the arm and base.

Stage Clip The stage clip holds a slide in place on the stage.

Base The base supports the microscope.

Science Skills

Measuring Accurately

Precision and Accuracy

When you do a scientific investigation, it is important that your methods, observations, and data be both precise and accurate.

Low precision: The darts did not land in a consistent place on the dartboard.

Precision, but not accuracy: The darts landed in a consistent place, but did not hit the bull's eye.

Prescision and accuracy: The darts landed consistently on the bull's eye.

Precision

In science, *precision* is the exactness and consistency of measurements. For example, measurements made with a ruler that has both centimeter and millimeter markings would be more precise than measurements made with a ruler that has only centimeter markings. Another indicator of precision is the care taken to make sure that methods and observations are as exact and consistent as possible. Every time a particular experiment is done, the same procedure should be used. Precision is necessary because experiments are repeated several times and if the procedure changes, the results might change.

Example
Suppose you are measuring temperatures over a two-week period. Your precision will be greater if you measure each temperature at the same place, at the same time of day, and with the same thermometer than if you change any of these factors from one day to the next.

Accuracy

In science, it is possible to be precise but not accurate. *Accuracy* depends on the difference between a measurement and an actual value. The smaller the difference, the more accurate the measurement.

Example
Suppose you look at a stream and estimate that it is about 1 meter wide at a particular place. You decide to check your estimate by measuring the stream with a meter stick, and you determine that the stream is 1.32 meters wide. However, because it is difficult to measure the width of a stream with a meter stick, it turns out that your measurement was not very accurate. The stream is actually 1.14 meters wide. Therefore, even though your estimate of about 1 meter was less precise than your measurement, your estimate was actually more accurate.

Graduated Cylinders

How to Measure the Volume of a Liquid with a Graduated Cylinder

- Be sure that the graduated cylinder is on a flat surface so that your measurement will be accurate.

- When reading the scale on a graduated cylinder, be sure to have your eyes at the level of the surface of the liquid.

- The surface of the liquid will be curved in the graduated cylinder. Read the volume of the liquid at the bottom of the curve, or meniscus (muh-NIHS-kuhs).

- You can use a graduated cylinder to find the volume of a solid object by measuring the increase in a liquid's level after you add the object to the cylinder.

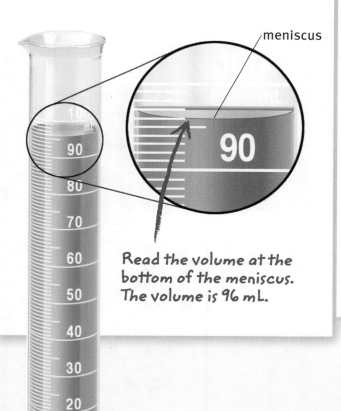

meniscus

Read the volume at the bottom of the meniscus. The volume is 96 mL.

Metric Rulers

How to Measure the Length of a Leaf with a Metric Ruler

1 Lay a ruler flat on top of the leaf so that the 1-centimeter mark lines up with one end. Make sure the ruler and the leaf do not move between the time you line them up and the time you take the measurement.

2 Look straight down on the ruler so that you can see exactly how the marks line up with the other end of the leaf.

3 Estimate the length by which the leaf extends beyond a marking. For example, the leaf below extends about halfway between the 4.2-centimeter and 4.3-centimeter marks, so the apparent measurement is about 4.25 centimeters.

4 Remember to subtract 1 centimeter from your apparent measurement, since you started at the 1-centimeter mark on the ruler and not at the end. The leaf is about 3.25 centimeters long (4.25 cm − 1 cm = 3.25 cm).

Science Skills

Triple Beam Balance

This balance has a pan and three beams with sliding masses, called riders. At one end of the beams is a pointer that indicates whether the mass on the pan is equal to the masses shown on the beams.

How to Measure the Mass of an Object

1 Make sure the balance is zeroed before measuring the mass of an object. The balance is zeroed if the pointer is at zero when nothing is on the pan and the riders are at their zero points. Use the adjustment knob at the base of the balance to zero it.

2 Place the object to be measured on the pan.

3 Move the riders one notch at a time away from the pan. Begin with the largest rider. If moving the largest rider one notch brings the pointer below zero, begin measuring the mass of the object with the next smaller rider.

4 Change the positions of the riders until they balance the mass on the pan and the pointer is at zero. Then add the readings from the three beams to determine the mass of the object.

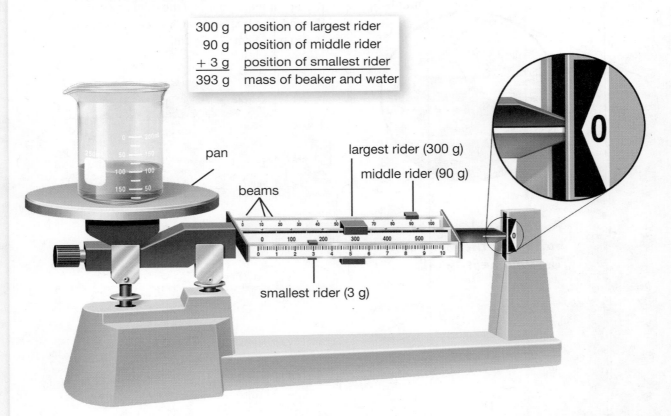

300 g	position of largest rider
90 g	position of middle rider
+ 3 g	position of smallest rider
393 g	mass of beaker and water

pan

beams

largest rider (300 g)

middle rider (90 g)

smallest rider (3 g)

Using the Metric System and SI Units

Scientists use International System (SI) units for measurements of distance, volume, mass, and temperature. The International System is based on powers of ten and the metric system of measurement.

Basic SI Units		
Quantity	**Name**	**Symbol**
length	meter	m
volume	liter	L
mass	gram	g
temperature	kelvin	K

SI Prefixes		
Prefix	**Symbol**	**Power of 10**
kilo-	k	1000
hecto-	h	100
deca-	da	10
deci-	d	0.1 or $\frac{1}{10}$
centi-	c	0.01 or $\frac{1}{100}$
milli-	m	0.001 or $\frac{1}{1000}$

Changing Metric Units

You can change from one unit to another in the metric system by multiplying or dividing by a power of 10.

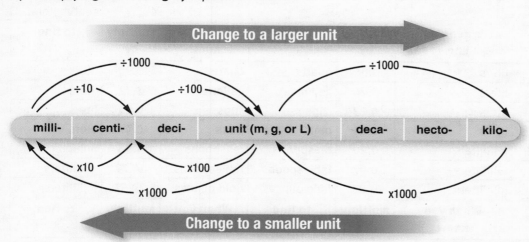

Example

Change 0.64 liters to milliliters.
  1 Decide whether to multiply or divide.
  2 Select the power of 10.

Change to a smaller unit by multiplying

mL ◄——— x 1000 ——— L

0.64 x 1000 = 640.

ANSWER 0.64 L = 640 mL

Example

Change 23.6 grams to kilograms.
  1 Decide whether to multiply or divide.
  2 Select the power of 10.

Change to a larger unit by dividing

g ——— ÷ 1000 ——► kg

26.3 ÷ 1000 = 0.0263

ANSWER 23.6 g = 0.0236 kg

Science Skills

Converting Between SI and U.S. Customary Units

Use the chart below when you need to convert between SI units and U.S. customary units.

SI Unit	From SI to U.S. Customary			From U.S. Customary to SI		
Length	**When you know**	**multiply by**	**to find**	**When you know**	**multiply by**	**to find**
kilometer (km) = 1000 m	kilometers	0.62	miles	miles	1.61	kilometers
meter (m) = 100 cm	meters	3.28	feet	feet	0.3048	meters
centimeter (cm) = 10 mm	centimeters	0.39	inches	inches	2.54	centimeters
millimeter (mm) = 0.1 cm	millimeters	0.04	inches	inches	25.4	millimeters
Area	**When you know**	**multiply by**	**to find**	**When you know**	**multiply by**	**to find**
square kilometer (km²)	square kilometers	0.39	square miles	square miles	2.59	square kilometers
square meter (m²)	square meters	1.2	square yards	square yards	0.84	square meters
square centimeter (cm²)	square centimeters	0.155	square inches	square inches	6.45	square centimeters
Volume	**When you know**	**multiply by**	**to find**	**When you know**	**multiply by**	**to find**
liter (L) = 1000 mL	liters	1.06	quarts	quarts	0.95	liters
	liters	0.26	gallons	gallons	3.79	liters
	liters	4.23	cups	cups	0.24	liters
	liters	2.12	pints	pints	0.47	liters
milliliter (mL) = 0.001 L	milliliters	0.20	teaspoons	teaspoons	4.93	milliliters
	milliliters	0.07	tablespoons	tablespoons	14.79	milliliters
	milliliters	0.03	fluid ounces	fluid ounces	29.57	milliliters
Mass	**When you know**	**multiply by**	**to find**	**When you know**	**multiply by**	**to find**
kilogram (kg) = 1000 g	kilograms	2.2	pounds	pounds	0.45	kilograms
gram (g) = 1000 mg	grams	0.035	ounces	ounces	28.35	grams

Temperature Conversions

Even though the kelvin is the SI base unit of temperature, the degree Celsius will be the unit you use most often in your science studies. The formulas below show the relationships between temperatures in degrees Fahrenheit (°F), degrees Celsius (°C), and kelvins (K).

$$°C = \frac{5}{9}\ (°F - 32) \qquad °F = \frac{9}{5}\ °C + 32 \qquad K = °C + 273$$

Examples of Temperature Conversions		
Condition	**Degrees Celsius**	**Degrees Fahrenheit**
Freezing point of water	0	32
Cool day	10	50
Mild day	20	68
Warm day	30	86
Normal body temperature	37	98.6
Very hot day	40	104
Boiling point of water	100	212

Math Refresher

Performing Calculations

Science requires an understanding of many math concepts. The following pages will help you review some important math skills.

Mean

The mean is the sum of all values in a data set divided by the total number of values in the data set. The mean is also called the *average*.

Example

Find the mean of the following set of numbers: 5, 4, 7, and 8.

Step 1   Find the sum.

5 + 4 + 7 + 8 = 24

Step 2   Divide the sum by the number of numbers in your set. Because there are four numbers in this example, divide the sum by 4.

24 ÷ 4 = 6

Answer The average, or mean, is 6.

Median

The median of a data set is the middle value when the values are written in numerical order. If a data set has an even number of values, the median is the mean of the two middle values.

Example

To find the median of a set of measurements, arrange the values in order from least to greatest. The median is the middle value.

13 mm   14 mm   16 mm   21 mm   23 mm

Answer The median is 16 mm.

Mode

The mode of a data set is the value that occurs most often.

Example

To find the mode of a set of measurements, arrange the values in order from least to greatest and determine the value that occurs most often.

13 mm, 14 mm, 14 mm, 16 mm, 21 mm, 23 mm, 25 mm

Answer The mode is 14 mm.

A data set can have more than one mode or no mode. For example, the following data set has modes of 2 mm and 4 mm:

2 mm   2 mm   3 mm   4 mm   4 mm

The data set below has no mode, because no value occurs more often than any other.

2 mm   3 mm   4 mm   5 mm

Math Refresher

Ratios

A **ratio** is a comparison between numbers, and it is usually written as a fraction.

Example

Find the ratio of thermometers to students if you have 36 thermometers and 48 students in your class.

Step 1   Write the ratio.

$$\frac{36 \text{ thermometers}}{48 \text{ students}}$$

Step 2   Simplify the fraction to its simplest form.

$$\frac{36}{48} = \frac{36 \div 12}{48 \div 12} = \frac{3}{4}$$

The ratio of thermometers to students is 3 to 4 or 3:4.

Proportions

A **proportion** is an equation that states that two ratios are equal.

$$\frac{3}{1} = \frac{12}{4}$$

To solve a proportion, you can use cross-multiplication. If you know three of the quantities in a proportion, you can use cross-multiplication to find the fourth.

Example

Imagine that you are making a scale model of the solar system for your science project. The diameter of Jupiter is 11.2 times the diameter of the Earth. If you are using a plastic-foam ball that has a diameter of 2 cm to represent the Earth, what must the diameter of the ball representing Jupiter be?

$$\frac{11.2}{1} = \frac{x}{2 \text{ cm}}$$

Step 1   Cross-multiply.

$$\frac{11.2}{1} = \frac{x}{2}$$

$$11.2 \times 2 = x \times 1$$

Step 2   Multiply.

$$22.4 = x \times 1$$

$$x = 22.4 \text{ cm}$$

You will need to use a ball that has a diameter of 22.4 cm to represent Jupiter.

Rates

A **rate** is a ratio of two values expressed in different units. A unit rate is a rate with a denominator of 1 unit.

Example

A plant grew 6 centimeters in 2 days. The plant's rate of growth was $\frac{6 \text{ cm}}{2 \text{ days}}$.

To describe the plant's growth in centimeters per day, write a unit rate.

Divide numerator and denominator by 2:

$$\frac{6 \text{ cm}}{2 \text{ days}} = \frac{6 \text{ cm} \div 2}{2 \text{ days} \div 2}$$

Simplify:

$$= \frac{3 \text{ cm}}{1 \text{ day}}$$

Answer   The plant's rate of growth is 3 centimeters per day.

Percent

A **percent** is a ratio of a given number to 100. For example, 85% = 85/100. You can use percent to find part of a whole.

Example
What is 85% of 40?

Step 1 Rewrite the percent as a decimal by moving the decimal point two places to the left.

$$0.85$$

Step 2 Multiply the decimal by the number that you are calculating the percentage of.

$$0.85 \times 40 = 34$$

85% of 40 is 34.

Decimals

To **add** or **subtract decimals**, line up the digits vertically so that the decimal points line up. Then, add or subtract the columns from right to left. Carry or borrow numbers as necessary.

Example
Add the following numbers: 3.1415 and 2.96.

Step 1 Line up the digits vertically so that the decimal points line up.

$$\begin{array}{r} 3.1415 \\ + 2.96 \\ \hline \end{array}$$

Step 2 Add the columns from right to left, and carry when necessary.

$$\begin{array}{r} 3.1415 \\ + 2.96 \\ \hline 6.1015 \end{array}$$

The sum is 6.1015.

Fractions

A **fraction** is a ratio of two nonzero whole numbers.

Example
Your class has 24 plants. Your teacher instructs you to put 5 plants in a shady spot. What fraction of the plants in your class will you put in a shady spot?

Step 1 In the denominator, write the total number of parts in the whole.

$$\frac{?}{24}$$

Step 2 In the numerator, write the number of parts of the whole that are being considered.

$$\frac{5}{24}$$

So, $\frac{5}{24}$ of the plants will be in the shade.

Math Refresher

Simplifying Fractions

It is usually best to express a fraction in its simplest form.
Expressing a fraction in its simplest form is called **simplifying a fraction**.

Example

Simplify the fraction $\frac{30}{45}$ to its simplest form.

Step 1 Find the largest whole number that will divide evenly into both the numerator and denominator. This number is called the greatest common factor (GCF).

Factors of the numerator 30:
1, 2, 3, 5, 6, 10, 15, 30

Factors of the denominator 45:
1, 3, 5, 9, 15, 45

Step 2 Divide both the numerator and the denominator by the GCF, which in this case is 15.

$$\frac{30}{45} = \frac{30 \div 15}{45 \div 15} = \frac{2}{3}$$

Thus, $\frac{30}{45}$ written in its simplest form is $\frac{2}{3}$.

Adding and Subtracting Fractions

To **add** or **subtract fractions** that have the same denominator, simply add or subtract the numerators.

Examples

$\frac{3}{5} + \frac{1}{5} = ?$ and $\frac{3}{4} - \frac{1}{4} = ?$

Step 1 Add or subtract the numerators.
$$\frac{3}{5} + \frac{1}{5} = \frac{4}{} \text{ and } \frac{3}{4} - \frac{1}{4} = \frac{2}{}$$

Step 2 Write in the common denominator, which remains the same.
$$\frac{3}{5} + \frac{1}{5} = \frac{4}{5} \text{ and } \frac{3}{4} - \frac{1}{4} = \frac{2}{4}$$

Step 3 If necessary, write the fraction in its simplest form.
$\frac{4}{5}$ cannot be simplified, and $\frac{2}{4} = \frac{1}{2}$.

To **add** or **subtract** fractions that have **different denominators**, first find the least common denominator (LCD).

Examples

$\frac{1}{2} + \frac{1}{6} = ?$ and $\frac{3}{4} - \frac{2}{3} = ?$

Step 1 Write the equivalent fractions that have a common denominator.
$$\frac{3}{6} + \frac{1}{6} = ? \text{ and } \frac{9}{12} - \frac{8}{12} = ?$$

Step 2 Add or subtract the fractions.
$$\frac{3}{6} + \frac{1}{6} = \frac{4}{6} \text{ and } \frac{9}{12} - \frac{8}{12} = \frac{1}{12}$$

Step 3 If necessary, write the fraction in its simplest form.
$\frac{4}{6} = \frac{2}{3}$, and $\frac{1}{12}$ cannot be simplifed.

Multiplying Fractions

To **multiply fractions**, multiply the numerators and the denominators together, and then simplify the fraction to its simplest form.

Example

$\frac{5}{9} \times \frac{7}{10} = ?$

Step 1 Multiply the numerators and denominators.
$$\frac{5}{9} \times \frac{7}{10} = \frac{5 \times 7}{9 \times 10} = \frac{35}{90}$$

Step 2 Simplify the fraction.
$$\frac{35}{90} = \frac{35 \div 5}{90 \div 5} = \frac{7}{18}$$

Dividing Fractions

To **divide fractions,** first rewrite the divisor (the number you divide by) upside down. This number is called the reciprocal of the divisor. Then multiply and simplify if necessary.

Example

$\frac{5}{8} \div \frac{3}{2} = ?$

Step 1 Rewrite the divisor as its reciprocal.

$$\frac{3}{2} \rightarrow \frac{2}{3}$$

Step 2 Multiply the fractions.

$$\frac{5}{8} \times \frac{2}{3} = \frac{5 \times 2}{8 \times 3} = \frac{10}{24}$$

Step 3 Simplify the fraction.

$$\frac{10}{24} = \frac{10 \div 2}{24 \div 2} = \frac{5}{12}$$

Using Significant Figures

The **significant figures** in a decimal are the digits that are warranted by the accuracy of a measuring device.

When you perform a calculation with measurements, the number of significant figures to include in the result depends in part on the number of significant figures in the measurements. When you multiply or divide measurements, your answer should have only as many significant figures as the measurement with the fewest significant figures.

Examples

Using a balance and a graduated cylinder filled with water, you determined that a marble has a mass of 8.0 grams and a volume of 3.5 cubic centimeters. To calculate the density of the marble, divide the mass by the volume.

Write the formula for density: $\text{Density} = \frac{\text{mass}}{\text{volume}}$

Substitute measurements: $= \frac{8.0\ g}{3.5\ cm^3}$

Use a calculator to divide: $\approx 2.285714286\ g/cm^3$

Answer Because the mass and the volume have two significant figures each, give the density to two significant figures. The marble has a density of 2.3 grams per cubic centimeter.

Using Scientific Notation

Scientific notation is a shorthand way to write very large or very small numbers. For example, 73,500,000,000,000,000,000,000 kg is the mass of the moon. In scientific notation, it is 7.35×10^{22} kg. A value written as a number between 1 and 10, times a power of 10, is in scientific notation.

Examples

You can convert from standard form to scientific notation.

Standard Form	Scientific Notation
720,000	7.2×10^5
5 decimal places left	Exponent is 5.
0.000291	2.91×10^{-4}
4 decimal places right	Exponent is −4.

You can convert from scientific notation to standard form.

Scientific Notation	Standard Form
4.63×10^7	46,300,000
Exponent is 7.	7 decimal places right
1.08×10^{-6}	0.00000108
Exponent is −6.	6 decimal places left

Math Refresher

Making and Interpreting Graphs

Circle Graph

A circle graph, or pie chart, shows how each group of data relates to all of the data. Each part of the circle represents a category of the data. The entire circle represents all of the data. For example, a biologist studying a hardwood forest in Wisconsin found that there were five different types of trees. The data table at right summarizes the biologist's findings.

Wisconsin Hardwood Trees	
Type of tree	**Number found**
Oak	600
Maple	750
Beech	300
Birch	1,200
Hickory	150
Total	3,000

How to Make a Circle Graph

1 To make a circle graph of these data, first find the percentage of each type of tree. Divide the number of trees of each type by the total number of trees, and multiply by 100%.

$$\frac{600 \text{ oak}}{3,000 \text{ trees}} \times 100\% = 20\%$$

$$\frac{750 \text{ maple}}{3,000 \text{ trees}} \times 100\% = 25\%$$

$$\frac{300 \text{ beech}}{3,000 \text{ trees}} \times 100\% = 10\%$$

$$\frac{1,200 \text{ birch}}{3,000 \text{ trees}} \times 100\% = 40\%$$

$$\frac{150 \text{ hickory}}{3,000 \text{ trees}} \times 100\% = 5\%$$

2 Now, determine the size of the wedges that make up the graph. Multiply each percentage by 360°. Remember that a circle contains 360°.

$20\% \times 360° = 72°$ $25\% \times 360° = 90°$

$10\% \times 360° = 36°$ $40\% \times 360° = 144°$

$5\% \times 360° = 18°$

3 Check that the sum of the percentages is 100 and the sum of the degrees is 360.

$20\% + 25\% + 10\% + 40\% + 5\% = 100\%$

$72° + 90° + 36° + 144° + 18° = 360°$

4 Use a compass to draw a circle and mark the center of the circle.

5 Then, use a protractor to draw angles of 72°, 90°, 36°, 144°, and 18° in the circle.

6 Finally, label each part of the graph, and choose an appropriate title.

A Community of Wisconsin Hardwood Trees

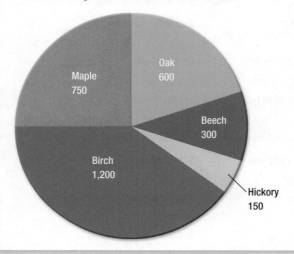

Line Graphs

Line graphs are most often used to demonstrate continuous change. For example, Mr. Smith's students analyzed the population records for their hometown, Appleton, between 1910 and 2010. Examine the data at right.

Because the year and the population change, they are the variables. The population is determined by, or dependent on, the year. Therefore, the population is called the **dependent variable,** and the year is called the **independent variable**. Each year and its population make a **data pair**. To prepare a line graph, you must first organize data pairs into a table like the one at right.

Population of Appleton, 1910–2010	
Year	**Population**
1910	1,800
1930	2,500
1950	3,200
1970	3,900
1990	4,600
2010	5,300

How to Make a Line Graph

1 Place the independent variable along the horizontal (x) axis. Place the dependent variable along the vertical (y) axis.

2 Label the x-axis "Year" and the y-axis "Population." Look at your greatest and least values for the population. For the y-axis, determine a scale that will provide enough space to show these values. You must use the same scale for the entire length of the axis. Next, find an appropriate scale for the x-axis.

3 Choose reasonable starting points for each axis.

4 Plot the data pairs as accurately as possible.

5 Choose a title that accurately represents the data.

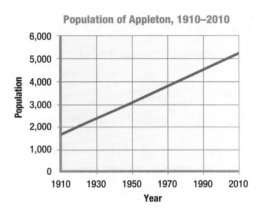

Population of Appleton, 1910–2010

How to Determine Slope

Slope is the ratio of the change in the y-value to the change in the x-value, or "rise over run."

1 Choose two points on the line graph. For example, the population of Appleton in 2010 was 5,300 people. Therefore, you can define point A as (2010, 5,300). In 1910, the population was 1,800 people. You can define point B as (1910, 1,800).

2 Find the change in the y-value. (y at point A) − (y at point B) = 5,300 people − 1,800 people = 3,500 people

3 Find the change in the x-value. (x at point A) − (x at point B) = 2010 − 1910 = 100 years

4 Calculate the slope of the graph by dividing the change in y by the change in x.

$$slope = \frac{change\ in\ y}{change\ in\ x}$$

$$slope = \frac{3,500\ people}{100\ years}$$

$$slope = 35\ people\ per\ year$$

In this example, the population in Appleton increased by a fixed amount each year. The graph of these data is a straight line. Therefore, the relationship is **linear**. When the graph of a set of data is not a straight line, the relationship is **nonlinear**.

Math Refresher

Bar Graphs

Bar graphs can be used to demonstrate change that is not continuous. These graphs can be used to indicate trends when the data cover a long period of time. A meteorologist gathered the precipitation data shown here for Summerville for April 1–15 and used a bar graph to represent the data.

Precipitation in Summerville, April 1–15			
Date	Precipitation (cm)	Date	Precipitation (cm)
April 1	0.5	April 9	0.25
April 2	1.25	April 10	0.0
April 3	0.0	April 11	1.0
April 4	0.0	April 12	0.0
April 5	0.0	April 13	0.25
April 6	0.0	April 14	0.0
April 7	0.0	April 15	6.50
April 8	1.75		

How to Make a Bar Graph

1 Use an appropriate scale and a reasonable starting point for each axis.

2 Label the axes, and plot the data.

3 Choose a title that accurately represents the data.

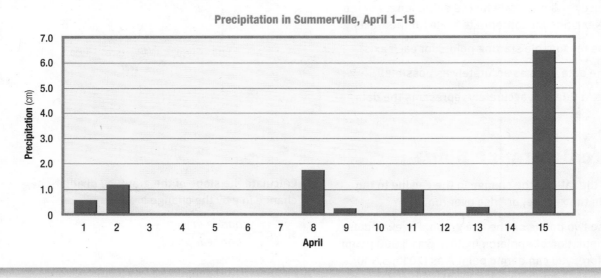

Precipitation in Summerville, April 1–15

Glossary

Pronunciation Key							
Sound	**Symbol**	**Example**	**Respelling**	**Sound**	**Symbol**	**Example**	**Respelling**
ă	a	pat	PAT	ŏ	ah	bottle	BAHT'l
ā	ay	pay	PAY	ō	oh	toe	TOH
âr	air	care	KAIR	ô	aw	caught	KAWT
ä	ah	father	FAH•ther	ôr	ohr	roar	ROHR
är	ar	argue	AR•gyoo	oi	oy	noisy	NOYZ•ee
ch	ch	chase	CHAYS	ŏŏ	u	book	BUK
ĕ	e	pet	PET	ōō	oo	boot	BOOT
ĕ (at end of a syllable)	eh	settee lessee	seh•TEE leh•SEE	ou	ow	pound	POWND
ĕr	ehr	merry	MEHR•ee	s	s	center	SEN•ter
ē	ee	beach	BEECH	sh	sh	cache	CASH
g	g	gas	GAS	ŭ	uh	flood	FLUHD
ĭ	i	pit	PIT	ûr	er	bird	BERD
ĭ (at end of a syllable)	ih	guitar	gih•TAR	z	z	xylophone	ZY•luh•fohn
ī	y eye (only for a complete syllable)	pie island	PY EYE•luhnd	z	z	bags	BAGZ
				zh	zh	decision	dih•SIZH•uhn
îr	ir	hear	HIR	ə	uh	around broken focus	uh•ROWND BROH•kuhn FOH•kuhs
j	j	germ	JERM	ər	er	winner	WIN•er
k	k	kick	KIK	th	th	thin they	THIN THAY
ng	ng	thing	THING	w	w	one	WUHN
ngk	ngk	bank	BANGK	wh	hw	whether	HWETH•er

absolute magnitude (AB·suh·loot MAG·nih·tood) a measure of how bright a star would be if it were seen from a standard distance (21)

   magnitud absoluta una medida del brillo que tendría una estrella vista desde una distancia estándar

aphelion (uh·FEE·lee·uhn) in the orbit of a planet or other body in the solar system, the point that is farthest from the sun (63)

   afelio en la órbita de un planeta u otros cuerpos en el sistema solar, el punto que está más lejos del Sol

apparent magnitude (uh·PAIR·uhnt MAG·nih·tood) the brightness of a star as seen from Earth (20)

   magnitud aparente el brillo de una estrella como se percibe desde la Tierra

artificial satellite (ar·tuh·FISH·uhl SAT·l·yt) any human-made object placed in orbit around a body in space (208)

   satélite artificial cualquier objeto hecho por los seres humanos y colocado en órbita alrededor de un cuerpo en el espacio

asteroid (AS·tuh·royd) a small, rocky object that orbits the sun; most asteroids are located in a band between the orbits of Mars and Jupiter (122)

   asteroide un objeto pequeño y rocoso que se encuentra en órbita alrededor del Sol; la mayoría de los asteroides se ubican en una banda entre las órbitas de Marte y Júpiter

astronomical unit (as·truh·NAHM·ih·kuhl YOO·nit) the average distance between Earth and the sun; approximately 150 million kilometers (symbol, AU) (88)

   unidad astronómica la distancia promedio entre la Tierra y el Sol; aproximadamente 150 millones de kilómetros (símbolo: UA)

centripetal force (sen·TRIP·ih·tl FOHRS) the inward force required to keep a particle or an object moving in a circular path (66)

   fuerza centrípeta la fuerza hacia adentro que se requiere para mantener en movimiento una partícula o un objeto en un camino circular

comet (KAHM·it) a small body that gives off gas and dust as it passes close to the sun; a typical comet moves in an elliptical orbit around the sun and is made of dust and frozen gases (120)

   cometa un cuerpo pequeño que libera gas y polvo al pasar cerca del Sol; un cometa típico está formado por polvo y gases congelados y sigue una órbita elíptica alrededor del Sol

day (DAY) the time required for Earth to rotate once on its axis (142)

   día el tiempo que se requiere para que la Tierra rote una vez sobre su eje

dwarf planet (DWOHRF PLAN·it) a celestial body that orbits the sun, is round because of its own gravity, but has not cleared its orbital path (117)

   planeta enano un cuerpo celeste que orbita alrededor del Sol, es redondo debido a su propia fuerza de gravedad, pero no ha despejado los alrededores de su trayectoria orbital

eclipse (ih·KLIPS) an event in which the shadow of one celestial body falls on another (158)

   eclipse un suceso en el que la sombra de un cuerpo celeste cubre otro cuerpo celeste

electromagnetic spectrum (ee·lek·troh·mag·NET·ik SPEK·truhm) all of the frequencies or wavelengths of electromagnetic radiation (188)

   espectro electromagnético todas las frecuencias o longitudes de onda de la radiación electromagnética

equinox (EE·kwuh·nahks) the moment when the sun appears to cross the celestial equator (146)

   equinoccio el momento en que el Sol parece cruzar el ecuador celeste

galaxy (GAL·uhk·see) a collection of stars, dust, and gas bound together by gravity (8)

   galaxia un conjunto de estrellas, polvo y gas unidos por la gravedad

gas giant (GAS JY·uhnt) a planet that has a deep, massive atmosphere, such as Jupiter, Saturn, Uranus, or Neptune (104)

   gigante gaseoso un planeta con una atmósfera masiva y profunda, como por ejemplo, Júpiter, Saturno, Urano o Neptuno

geocentric (jee·oh·SEN·trik) describes something that uses Earth as the reference point (50)

   geocéntrico término que describe algo que usa a la Tierra como punto de referencia

gravity (GRAV·ih·tee) a force of attraction between objects that is due to their masses (62, 154)

   gravedad una fuerza de atracción entre dos objetos debido a sus masas

H-R diagram (aych·AR DY·uh·gram) Hertzsprung-Russell diagram, a graph that shows the relationship between a star's surface temperature and absolute magnitude (34)
diagrama H-R diagrama de Hertzsprung-Russell; una gráfica que muestra la relación entre la temperatura de la superficie de una estrella y su magnitud absoluta

heliocentric (hee·lee·oh·SEN·trik) sun-centered (50)
heliocéntrico centrado en el Sol

Kuiper Belt (KY·per BELT) a region of the solar system that starts just beyond the orbit of Neptune and that contains dwarf planets and other small bodies made mostly of ice (118)
cinturón de Kuiper una región del Sistema Solar que comienza justo después de la órbita de Neptuno y que contiene planetas enanos y otros cuerpos pequeños formados principalmente de hielo

Kuiper Belt object (KY·per BELT AHB·jekt) one of the hundreds or thousands of small bodies that orbit the sun in a flat belt beyond Neptune's orbit; also includes dwarf planets located in the Kuiper Belt (118)
objeto del cinturón de Kuiper uno de los cientos o miles de cuerpos pequeños que orbitan alrededor del Sol en un cinturón plano, más allá de la órbita de Neptuno; también incluye los planetas enanos ubicados en el cinturón de Kuiper

L

lander (LAN·der) an automated, uncrewed vehicle that is designed to touch down safely on an extraterrestrial body; often carries equipment for exploration of that body (207)
módulo de aterrizaje un vehículo automatizado, no tripulado, diseñado para aterrizar sin peligro en un cuerpo extraterrestre; con frecuencia lleva equipos para explorar ese cuerpo

light-year (LYT·yir) the distance that light travels in one year; about 9.46 trillion kilometers (10)
año luz la distancia que viaja la luz en un año; aproximadamente 9.46 trillones de kilómetros

luminosity (loo·muh·NAHS·ih·tee) the actual brightness of an object such as a star (21)
luminosidad el brillo real de un objeto, como por ejemplo, una estrella

lunar phases (LOO·ner FAYZ·iz) the different appearances of the moon from Earth throughout the month (156)
fases lunares la diferente apariencia que tiene la Luna cuando se ve desde la Tierra a lo largo del mes

main sequence (MAYN SEE·kwuhns) the location on the H-R diagram where most stars lie; it has a diagonal pattern from the lower right (low temperature and luminosity) to the upper left (high temperature and luminosity) (35)
secuencia principal la ubicación en el diagrama H-R donde se encuentran la mayoría de las estrellas; tiene un patrón diagonal de la parte inferior derecha (baja temperatura y luminosidad) a la parte superior izquierda (alta temperatura y luminosidad)

meteor (MEE·tee·er) a bright streak of light that results when a meteoroid burns up in Earth's atmosphere (124)
meteoro un rayo de luz brillante que se produce cuando un meteoroide se quema en la atmósfera de la Tierra

meteorite (MEE·tee·uh·ryt) a meteoroid that reaches Earth's surface without burning up completely (124)
meteorito un meteoroide que llega a la superficie de la Tierra sin quemarse por completo

meteoroid (MEE·tee·uh·royd) a relatively small, rocky body that travels through space (124)
meteoroide un cuerpo rocoso relativamente pequeño que viaja en el espacio

NASA (NAS·uh) the National Aeronautics and Space Administration (220)
NASA la Administración Nacional de Aeronáutica y del Espacio

neap tide (NEEP TYD) a tide of minimum range that occurs during the first and third quarters of the moon (171)
marea muerta una marea que tiene un rango mínimo, la cual ocurre durante el primer y el tercer cuartos de la Luna

nebula (NEB·yuh·luh) a large cloud of gas and dust in interstellar space; a region in space where stars are born (28)
nebulosa una nube grande de gas y polvo en el espacio interestelar; una región en el espacio donde las estrellas nacen

neutron star (NOO·trahn STAR) a star that has collapsed under gravity to the point that the electrons and protons have smashed together to form neutrons (33)
estrella de neutrones una estrella que se ha colapsado debido a la gravedad hasta el punto en que los electrones y protones han chocado unos contra otros para formar neutrones

nuclear fusion (NOO·klee·er FYOO·zhuhn) the process by which nuclei of small atoms combine to form a new, more massive nucleus; the process releases energy (78)
fusión nuclear el proceso por medio del cual los núcleos de átomos pequeños se combinan y forman un núcleo nuevo con mayor masa; el proceso libera energía

© Houghton Mifflin Harcourt Publishing Company

Oort cloud (OHRT KLOWD) a spherical region that surrounds the solar system, that extends from the Kuiper Belt to almost halfway to the nearest star, and that contains billions of comets (121)
nube de Oort una región esférica que rodea al Sistema Solar, que se extiende desde el cinturón de Kuiper hasta la mitad del camino hacia la estrella más cercana y contiene miles de millones de cometas

orbit (OHR·bit) the path that a body follows as it travels around another body in space (62)
órbita la trayectoria que sigue un cuerpo al desplazarse alrededor de otro cuerpo en el espacio

orbiter (OHR·bih·ter) a spacecraft that is designed to orbit a planet, moon, or other body without landing on the body's surface (207)
orbitador una nave espacial diseñada para orbitar alrededor de un planeta, luna u otro cuerpo sin aterrizar sobre la superficie de dicho cuerpo

parallax (PAIR·uh·laks) an apparent shift in the position of an object when viewed from different locations (50)
paralaje un cambio aparente en la posición de un objeto cuando se ve desde lugares distintos

penumbra (pih·NUHM·bruh) the outer part of a shadow such as the shadow cast by Earth or the moon in which sunlight is only partially blocked (158)
penumbra la parte exterior de la sombra (como la sombra producida por la Tierra o la Luna) en la que la luz solar solamente se encuentra bloqueada parcialmente

perihelion (pehr·ih·HEE·lee·uhn) in the orbit of a planet or other body in the solar system, the point that is closest to the sun (63)
perihelio en la órbita de un planeta u otros cuerpos en el sistema solar, el punto que está más cerca del Sol

planet (PLAN·it) a relatively large spherical body that orbits a star (7)
planeta un cuerpo esférico relativamente grande que orbita alrededor de una estrella

planetary ring (PLAN·ih·tehr·ee RING) a disk of matter that encircles a planet that consists of numerous particles in orbit, which range in size from dust grains up to objects tens of meters across (106)
anillo planetario un disco de materia que rodea un planeta y está compuesto por numerosas partículas en órbita que pueden ser desde motas de polvo hasta objetos de decenas de metros

planetesimal (plan·ih·TES·uh·muhl) a small body from which a planet originated in the early stages of development of the solar system (69)
planetesimal un cuerpo pequeño a partir del cual se originó un planeta en las primeras etapas de desarrollo del Sistema Solar

probe (PROHB) an uncrewed vehicle that carries scientific instruments into space to collect scientific data (206)
sonda espacial en astronomía [O "en exploración espacial"], un vehículo sin tripulación que transporta instrumentos científicos al espacio para recopilar información científica

prominence (PRAHM·uh·nuhns) a loop of relatively cool, incandescent gas that extends above the photosphere and above the sun's edge as seen from Earth (83)
protuberancia una espiral de gas incandescente y relativamente frío que, vista desde la Tierra, se extiende por encima de la fotosfera y la superficie del Sol

revolution (rev·uh·LOO·shuhn) the motion of a body that travels around another body in space; one complete trip along an orbit (143)
revolución el movimiento de un cuerpo que viaja alrededor de otro cuerpo en el espacio; un viaje completo a lo largo de una órbita

rotation (roh·TAY·shuhn) the spin of a body on its axis (142)
rotación el giro de un cuerpo alrededor de su eje

rover (ROH·ver) a vehicle that is used to explore the surface of an extraterrestrial body (207)
rover un vehículo que se usa para explorar la superficie de un cuerpo extraterrestre

satellite (SAT·l·yt) a natural or artificial body that revolves around a celestial body that is greater in mass (154)
satélite un cuerpo natural o artificial que gira alrededor de un cuerpo celeste que tiene mayor masa

season (SEE·zuhn) a division of the year that is characterized by recurring weather conditions and determined by both Earth's tilt relative to the sun and Earth's position in its orbit around the sun (146)
estación una de las partes en que se divide el año que se caracteriza por condiciones climáticas recurrentes y que está determinada tanto por la inclinación de la Tierra con relación al Sol como por la posición que ocupa en su órbita alrededor del Sol

solar flare (SOH·ler FLAIR) an explosive release of energy that comes from the sun and that is associated with magnetic disturbances on the sun's surface (83)
erupción solar una liberación explosiva de energía que proviene del Sol y que se asocia con disturbios magnéticos en la superficie solar

solar nebula (SOH·ler NEB·yuh·luh) a rotating cloud of gas and dust from which the sun and planets formed (67)
nebulosa solar una nube de gas y polvo en rotación a partir de la cual se formaron el Sol y los planetas

solar system (SOH·ler SIS·tuhm) the sun and all of the planets and other bodies that travel around it (7, 50)
Sistema Solar el Sol y todos los planetas y otros cuerpos que se desplazan alrededor de él

solstice (SOHL·stis) the point at which the sun is as far north or as far south of the equator as possible (146)
solsticio el punto en el que el Sol está tan lejos del ecuador como es posible, ya sea hacia el norte o hacia el sur

space shuttle (SPAYS SHUHT·l) a reusable space vehicle that takes off like a rocket and lands like an airplane (204)
transbordador espacial un vehículo espacial reutilizable que despega como un cohete y aterriza como un avión

spectrum (SPEK·truhm) a range of electromagnetic radiation that is ordered by wavelength or frequency, such as the band of colors that is produced when white light passes through a prism (188)
espectro una gama de radiación electromagnética ordenada por longitud de onda o frecuencia, como la banda de colores que se produce cuando la luz blanca pasa a través de un prisma

spring tide (SPRING TYD) a tide of increased range that occurs two times a month, at the new and full moons (170)
marea viva una marea de mayor rango que ocurre dos veces al mes, durante la luna nueva y la luna llena

star (STAR) a large celestial body that is composed of gas and that emits light; the sun is a typical star (8, 18)
estrella un cuerpo celeste grande que está compuesto de gas y emite luz; el Sol es una estrella típica

sunspot (SUHN·spaht) a dark area of the photosphere of the sun that is cooler than the surrounding areas and that has a strong magnetic field (82)
mancha solar un área oscura en la fotosfera del Sol que es más fría que las áreas que la rodean y que tiene un campo magnético fuerte

supernova (soo·per·NOH·vuh) a gigantic explosion in which a massive star collapses and throws its outer layers into space (32)
supernova una explosión gigantesca en la que una estrella masiva se colapsa y lanza sus capas externas hacia el espacio

terrestrial planet (tuh·RES·tree·uhl PLAN·it) one of the highly dense planets nearest to the sun; Mercury, Venus, Mars, and Earth (88)
planeta terrestre uno de los planetas muy densos que se encuentran más cerca del Sol; Mercurio, Venus, Marte y la Tierra

tidal range (TYD·l RAYNJ) the difference in levels of ocean water at high tide and low tide (170)
rango de marea la diferencia en los niveles del agua del océano entre la marea alta y la marea baja

tide (TYD) the periodic rise and fall of the water level in the oceans and other large bodies of water (168)
marea el ascenso y descenso periódico del nivel del agua en los océanos y otras masas grandes de agua

umbra (UHM·bruh) a shadow that blocks sunlight, such as the conical section in the shadow of Earth or the moon (158)
umbra una sombra que bloquea la luz solar, como por ejemplo, la sección cónica en la sombra de la Tierra o la Luna

universe (YOO·nuh·vers) space and all the matter and energy in it (11)
universo el espacio y toda la materia y energía que hay dentro de él

wavelength (WAYV·lengkth) the distance from any point on a wave to the corresponding point on the next wave (188)
longitud de onda la distancia entre cualquier punto de una onda y el punto correspondiente de la siguiente onda

white dwarf (WYT DWOHRF) a small, hot, dim star that is the leftover center of an old sunlike star (31)
enana blanca una estrella pequeña, caliente y tenue que es el centro sobrante de una estrella vieja parecida al Sol

year (YIR) the time required for Earth to orbit once around the sun (143)
año el tiempo que se requiere para que la Tierra le dé la vuelta al Sol una vez

Index

Page numbers for definitions are printed in **boldface** type.
Page numbers for illustrations, maps, and charts are printed in *italics*.

M

N

O

P

© Houghton Mifflin Harcourt Publishing Company

© Houghton Mifflin Harcourt Publishing Company